Sales – What A Concept!

A Guidebook for Sales Process Performance Improvement

Sales – What A Concept!

A Guidebook for Sales Process Performance Improvement

Henry C. (Sandy) Waters III

ISBN 978-1-105-24654-8

SW Consulting
2373 Lazy River Drive
Raleigh, NC
Phone 919-231-8384
sandy@sandywaters.com

Dedication

This book is dedicated to the memories of both my mother and my father who passed away within six months of each other. Each instilled in me a number of points related to the art and science of selling. My mother sold Encyclopedia Britannica for years, at a time when women were not viewed favorably as sales people. She was a pioneer in the field of sales, and produced outstanding results. My father was the product of the General Electric management training program for World War II veterans, and he went on to masterfully sell power plants in many third world countries. Both of them were dedicated to the practice of selling, at a point in time where the profession of sales was a seemingly kinder and gentler era. To both of them, I am thankful that they taught me continuous relationship development required an investment in developing an understanding of the other person's needs, and the ability to visualize the nature of the solution that would be most meaningful to them. I miss them both, and especially the opportunity to share with them conversations related to helping others to sell more effectively.

Henry C. (Sandy) Waters III

Acknowledgements

Behind every good man is a great woman, or so the description goes. My situation is no different, and I gratefully acknowledge, the effort expended by my wife to allow me to complete this project amidst great person turmoil, and the loss of both of my parents within the last year. Her sacrifices made my pursuit of this long, and drawn out project, cannot be covered merely by words. It was truly love that guided her patience and support, and I appreciate it no end.

Posthumously, I would also like to acknowledge both of my parents who provided the initial kick in the pants to get this project going. Without that parental motivation, that familial special sauce, I might have shelved the project for completion someday.

Henry C. (Sandy) Waters III
Raleigh, North Carolina
November 2011

PREFACE

"If we do not change direction, we are likely to end up where we are headed." - Chinese Proverb

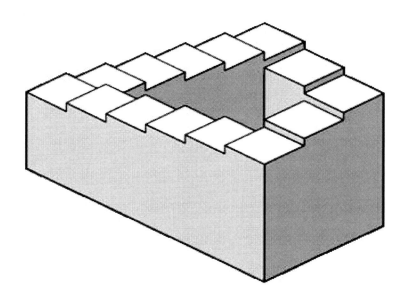

PREFACE

"Setting an example is not the main means of influencing others; it is the only means."
Albert Einstein, Genius

"Strategy without tactics is the slowest route to victory. Tactics without strategy is the noise before defeat." *Sun Tzu, Chinese General, Circa 500 B.C.E...*

"Strategy requires thought, tactics require observation." *Max Euwe, Dutch Chess Grandmaster*

Firstly, the reader should be advised that this book is less about "selling" and more about the "sales process." There are plenty of books about how to sell from beginner to expert. However, this book is about the intricacies of the selling process itself, and the machinery each company has in place, related to their system of engaging, evaluating, and the assessing the efforts and contributions of those in the company who play specific roles as a part of that sales system. Every company has a sales system of sort, but few take the time to examine it carefully and approach it as a system that can be improved.

Secondly, individuals who sell vary in their skills, experience level, and abilities. This book is less about them and more about the corporate mechanisms that support the efforts of the people who are charged with sales and how they approach utilizing corporate assets to achieve sales results.

As an experienced observer and business consultant to companies of all sizes, I witness a lot of methods, approaches, structures, processes and styles that contribute to the success of how businesses sell. I also witness all too frequently the impact of poor process and execution of failures in others over time. Survival is of course, an overarching goal.

Why are some small and medium enterprise companies just more effective and successful than others? Is it the uniqueness of their products or services, their sales channels, or is it more likely to be due to luck?

Thirdly, this publication strives to explore these questions and others as we examine together what differentiates businesses in their selling operations. It is also to develop a level of understanding to highlight where and how improvements to the system can be made.

Today, even more so than in the past, a great many more products and service choices are available there are more options for types of solutions than ever before. Information about the technologies, the advice on how to use them, and great amounts of easy to find examples are all available to both enlighten and have the potential to confuse potential buyers.

The level of complexity of a sale, beyond just a commodity purchase, continues to increase with each passing year. To smaller enterprises that means more experienced sales professionals are required to join the sales ranks of the businesses, to assist them with attaining success. Keep in mind the thought that it is not only raw sales talent that generates business alone, but also the processes and structure need to be there to support them in their efforts.

Have you had an experience where a small company won your business for any particular reason? What were those reasons? How did you as the buyer make the buying decisions to select one company over another when buying? Did they actively try to sell you in some special way or did they play some other role in helping you to choose a solution?

Think for a moment that if we as buyers could all buy from small businesses using only the Internet we might never need to interact with a sales person again. Life without face-to-face decision-making would become easier, but we might entirely miss the interactive experience of working with a seller to get the best product, service or value for us, and the opportunity to create a business relationship without the necessary interactions. Those companies that excel with face-to-face transactions, service, and support, have greater results with regard to customer satisfaction, sales growth and repeat business and referrals.

The bottom line for companies of any size with a sales force is that by putting in place processes and methodologies to improve consistency does directly impact results. Process is not just a term that should conjure up thoughts of bureaucracy or complexity. In fact, just the opposite should be true. Process empowers companies and forces them to be better at what they do. If left unchecked however, the processes that are not good or allowed to be overridden for no good reason will result in increasing the chaos. Not a good thing is a company with limited resources, and it is likely an indicator that their future may not be as bright as planned.

At an early stage of my career path, I was starting out as a research scientist developing new technologies and techniques I learned that process could be my best friend. Not only did it simplify things, but also it provided the means for my results to be quantitative, reproducible, and producing higher yields than if I just let things get out of control.

It is said by innovators themselves for example that the Edisonian approach to innovation consists of 99% perspiration and 1% inspiration and it was a more likely indicator that the introduction of process into whatever is being attempted could improve results significantly.

Please understand this basic point. Edison was exceptionally methodical in his approach to creativity, but not in executing business performance according to any documented business plan. Those breakthrough and inspirational products designed by the inventor still needed to be sold for any benefit to accrue to his company and investors. After a great many missteps, the Edison companies developed and applied processes to selling and deal making that led to greater and greater successes over time as their sales system became clearer.

Look at the process of baking a cake as another analogy for illustrating a set of steps in sequences that are repeatable. Follow the recipe, the process, or set of process steps with precision that eliminated variables resulted in and a more satisfying outcome. Deviate outside the defined parameters of the recipe and the outcomes would be questionable and the results less than satisfying.

Although analogies abound for selling it not been routinely thought of as a process or a methodology or seen as a concrete art form. There is also science to consider when selling from the point of view of developing and adhering to processes and management that lead to outcomes that are more successful.

Selling as either a science or an art form has proven that innovation is achieved by controlling processes time and time again within many industries and by applying processes that result in a sales system resulting in higher levels of performance through improving consistency and minimizing uncertainties.

My path to sales came about by transitioning from a scientist to sales person and it was an interesting transformation. I went from being a practitioner and adherent of consistency to a practitioner of fomenting change. I learned science and the scientific methods first, and then I learned how to adapt and apply qualitative and quantitative measures in selling to delivery better results.

One example of a methodology I gained early exposure to is from the Miller Heiman Corporation. Miller Heiman had created through observations of what companies did to achieve sales success an approach. That approach constituted understanding what contributed to successful and repeatable selling.

They then set about documenting the approach culminating with the release of the Strategic Selling book and courseware developed by Bob Miller and Steve Heiman in 1985. They succinctly described what differentiated highly effective sales organizations was a set of processes that when methodically followed formed a sales system.

The results of their observations of successful companies clearly showed it was those who consistently implemented and practiced a repeatable process were better able to achieve consistent win-win results with clients.

I was exposed of the essential elements of strategic selling around 1986 as a senior sales team member of an elite group put together to try to position a bleeding edge technology and sell to early adopters. We were selling to small reseller businesses and I in turn learned how they sold to their clients. We were wildly successful.

We did not fully understand why we were so successful at the time. This was my first exposure to the concept of what I would learn later was a more successful model of selling and using a defined sales system and adhering to processes that helped us achieve the goals.

Prior to that, I had learned and practiced the early form of consultative and communicative selling known as the XEROX Professional Sales Skills approach. Communications and controlling the conversation to try to uncover need, develop it in the mind of a prospect, and then go for the close was the basis for the approach. In some instances, this novel approach worked but usually in the simplest of sales involving only one main decision maker.

For my over twenty years of sales involvement and business management I have been a practitioner of helping companies internally and externally to be more effective, productive, forward thinking and for the last eight years worked as a business consultant to uncover, diagnose and solve problems interfering with their success.

In all my years of selling or being sold to, I did not uncovered any magical techniques nor any silver bullets or special sauce to guarantee the acquisition of clients buy nor any mass hypnosis methods that would alter the outcome of a sale. What I have discovered about the various aspects of the buying and selling processes, how when they are synchronized, results in a great deal more business being transacted, and how that works is shared in this book. What I have learned from those experiences has been refined for use by the small and medium enterprise companies to impact their sales performance.

The reader will find that this book differs somewhat from most other books relating to company process transformation, or in the approach to the understanding of basic dynamic processes found in any company. The difference is that the reader has been provided with working templates, workshops, checklists and other graphics that are enlarged for the purposes of being used to conduct in-house activities.

The users of the stated approach in this book will not expressly have to buy any other materials. I share this material with the buyers of the book in hopes that in some small way they contribute to your sales performance enhancement and a better understanding of the sales system concepts. Although all of the material in the book is copyrighted and contain intellectual property, please feel free to copy the pages of exercises and templates as you see fit to conduct the exercises. I grant the use hopeful you will let me know if together we accomplish the stated objectives for the book as described.

I am your guide for this journey and I will help you where I can to explore your company's sales system. Nevertheless, the heavy lifting it is up to you to take up the serious challenges of finding better ways to change your organization and to achieve and exceed your sales goals. I encourage you, as the reader, to read a little and to think a little more on the thoughts discussed to put it all together with your own experiences for the maximum impact on your business operation.

Henry C. (Sandy) Waters III

November 2011

Table of Contents

Table of Figures

SECTION (1)

Introduction

SECTION (1)

Sales – What A Concept!

Continuous Progress Model

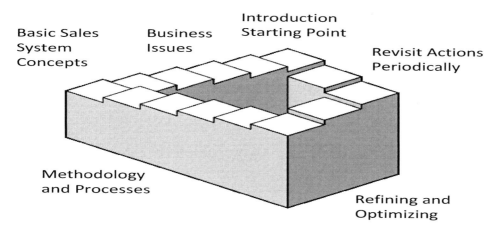

Introduction
Starting Point

Basic Sales
System
Concepts

Business
Issues

Revisit Actions
Periodically

Methodology
and Processes

Refining and
Optimizing

Introduction

"The definition of insanity is doing the same thing over and over again and expecting different results." Albert Einstein.

Sales. What a concept! Ever thought about what makes sales work? Work really well? Why is it that some companies have fewer problems with their sales and a greater return on their investment in the sales effort? It could be that for each of them the concept of sales and selling differs greatly, hence the wide divergence in performance across the spectrum of companies. For a great many people what they identify as selling is a simple transactional sales process. It might be described by some as simple as just following a cookbook approach of A, B, C.

    A) Call a lot of people and sell the product, service, or solution
    B) Sign the contracts and receive the money
    C) Repeat A

Early on in our path to discovering some aspects of sales as a process, it is important to acknowledge that our own management is prone to follow the simple model stated whether true or not. Management generally acknowledges that sales outcomes are among the most difficult business processes to predict and manage. This simplest process stated example could be the sum total of how they use their current sales system and the processes in support of it. To others, those who have to work from a somewhat more methodically and productive viewpoint, they know sales are harder to achieve to make their company successful, or to just merely survive.

They routinely encounter situations where the end-to-end selling process is a bit more complex. In fact, the organization that has a sales system and embraces processes will know the overall approach may contain a number of selected repeatable sub-processes, and operate from a list of tasks from a playbook that must be performed to increase the probability of a successful sale.

If you compare side by side the characteristics of two companies, both selling the identical product, service or solution, one may have considerably more success with their sales efforts than the other may. Why is that? In order to compare and contrast the two we need to dig a little deeper into the actual selling processes each company employs to understand better why one outperforms the other. The most common difference between companies is in how their sales system and the selling process connect with prospective clients.

Those who are most successful know that if they miss performing any of the detailed activities and sub-processes, or they fail to communicate accurately what the situation is surrounding the prospective sale then you set yourself up for more instances of failure. If your company is experiencing more of the complex types of selling situations then the approach taken by this book is for you. Let me be clear though, that no one size sales system fits with every company. The cookbook approach to selling is not always the best as there are too many situations, circumstances, and variables lurking nearby ready to impede a successful outcome to the sales efforts.

Success is achieved through analysis, thoughtful insight into your business and the implementation of new processes or refinements to older ones. It is a model of truly dynamic situations. Think about for a moment your internal discussions regarding sales. Is there a process for discussing sales opportunities or progress in the sales area against plans? Do you use a tracking methodology for sales activities, revenue, bookings, or a managed funnel of opportunities? Who gets a seat at the table and who drives the discussion regarding where those sales opportunities? Where did the opportunities come from, how they will be evaluated for investments of time and effort, and how are they supported? Do your sales and marketing efforts appear to be aligned? What does a prospective client look like? Who makes the decisions regarding the criteria for deciding to vigorously pursue an opportunity or not? You should have answers.

As we explore appropriately how your organization conducts the sales process and works to align with the client buying process these types of questions need to be answered by all participants in that process. After all, is not the "name of the game," results? Therefore, nothing in your organization that contributes to the sale or impedes the sales in any way is off limits as you think of how your organization responds to creating, managing, and winning opportunities.

If you want to optimize your sales, you need to be ever vigilant with understanding the internal and external forces that are at work, and how your organization reacts to those forces. Selling is about getting people to see the need to change, and about the constant need to respond to change as it occurs within both your customer's organization, and in your organization.

Objectives for the Book

"Never tell people how to do things. Tell them what to do and they will surprise you with their ingenuity." General George S. Patton Jr., Famous WWII General and tactician.

This book was written with several objectives in mind and designed to help enterprise businesses of all sizes obtain a significant improvement in their sales performance. It is not intended to be a tutorial in the art and science of selling per se. Where appropriate, a number of elemental concepts that contribute to forming a better understanding of a sales system are addressed, the mainstream of the information presented pertains to the concept of a sales system. My intention is to provide some guidance and share with you a deterministic outcomes methodology that will help businesses to analyze, evaluate, and identify where they can make improvements in their sales system, and in the processes that support that sales system.

There are five core sections to the book. They arranged around topics that provide a way to approach your own company selling processes. Each section serves a purpose and is designed to provide useful insight to get you started with the fulfillment of the earlier objectives stated for the book itself.

1. The first section covers introductory thoughts about basic business issues and topics to get you thinking about how they can relate to processes. You will be exposed to some off the beaten pathways approaches to examining you own internal organization and its processes. This will prepare you for the deeper dive into some of the new concepts and establish a common perspective. Then in the second section, we will build upon the thoughts as we dive deeper into the sales system, and the processes that are used to sell to customers.

2. In the second section, we will approach and explore some of the business issues that contribute to the sales process. The intent is ground the reader in some aspects of the dynamics that impact how your systems and processes respond to the general conduct of the selling process.

3. The third section describes the basic concepts around what is defined as a sales system. Many of the thoughts and concepts you might have encountered already in your own experience, but with a more analytical and methodical manner they can be used to guide you through the important elements for dissecting, and improving your understanding of your system. We think about more the processes and the ways to approach improving them. Exploring your concepts knowledge allows you to begin to strategize and select best actions for changing the system.

4. The fourth section will provide you with a basic methodology. It is an approach with guidance and advice on discovering, and mapping, what you currently have to get a clearer view of what you need to change in your sales system. It provides a range of templates, activities and workshops that cover how to measure the short and long-term impact upon results, as well as pointing out the most common pitfalls encountered and offer suggestions on how to avoid them.

5. The fifth section will give you some additional ideas, such as alignment of sales and marketing, business plans and sales, price versus value and ways to assess your competitors like never before to win more business, along with what is needed to refine and optimize your sales system and processes and offer suggestions on how to keep them from becoming unproductive or obsolete over time. If you make the investment in understanding the sales system and supporting processes additional guidance is offered for tuning and transforming them will produce continuous improvements in sales performance results.

After reading this book, you and your executive management team will better understand a number of the key elements that make up best sales practices for your company. I hope that you will take the principles to heart and make them a part of your operational norms. As a lifelong explorer of process and an analyst of how things work, I hope that some of the things that I have observed, learned, and passed to many of my clients will be of value to your company and in some way contribute to your continued sustainable success.

As with any book that you read where you invest your time, your expectation is of gaining ideas and insights, a new perspective, or to develop a genuine desire to be better at what you do. Then my hope is you come away from reading this book with some new ideas to assist with achieving the following goals. Payback comes from taking and using the information gained, and then applied to your specific situation.

The goals and takeaways are:

- Achieve incremental improvements in top line sales performance for your company.

- Develop a deeper understanding of the buying and selling, and purchasing decision making processes that will motivate you to explore and implement improvements.

- Gain exposure to a methodology that if used and embraced by your company will put in place a solid foundation to accommodate the expansion of your business.

- Gain a new perception of why a sales system and supporting processes can help your company to plan for and attain a greater results trajectory.

- Gain improvements in your overall strategic and operational planning approach and execution.

- Greater internal communications between all who are involved in sales using a common set of concepts and terms.

- Understand what is required of your company to enhance your position with regard to competition, and to focus on strengthening your differentiation.

- Attain a closer alignment of your sale and marketing efforts to get a greater returns on investments in both sales and marketing.

When studying management science, we learn the value of analysis. We see how dynamic and ad hoc assessments can aid us with planning, understanding problems, and in developing a course of action to timely resolve problems. Management science also teaches us the importance and value of having metrics throughout our company to monitor and manage operations more effectively.

Management science however, does not generally provide us with a sound understanding of the various methods and approaches to the practice of the art and science of selling because that is too broad, and vague. Decision-making, as it relates strictly to sales performance, is left wanting because what we need to do is to determine appropriate actions first, then respond. Experienced sales leaders are however, clear on the notion that selling is both an art and a science when practicing it. They know how to engage in the practice of sales activities, in methodical and systematic ways.

Some salespeople are better artists than they are scientists when it comes to selling. What others need to appreciate is there at there are many factors that go into selecting salespeople who can be successful at selling our product, service, or solution. The new salesperson that takes the approach of reading a book called "closing a sale in one minute" will not generally be the salesperson that understands enough of how the buying, selling, and decision-making processes interact.

For reference, there are scores of skills based programs available to train sales people, but for the most part, they teach generic skills. Few programs are about the thoughtfully prepared and systematic approach that contributes more to sales success. Fewer still programs work with the core management team to understand better the processes and structure that make a functional environment for successful sales operations. An understanding and acceptance of the importance of strategy and tactics is also a more productive skill set in sales people and support management and worth finding or developing in people working to drive or support sales efforts.

This book will provide you with a solid orientation of how to examine your current sales methods and its practice, and how those processes that contribute to successful selling are a part of your sales system. No two companies will be alike in terms of the findings after completing the assessment analysis strategy and action determination portions of what is covered in this book. What we strive for is to help you distill and enhance that which is your special sales sauce as it relates to your product, service, or solutions in such a manner that you are able to position it in front of prospective customers in a way that connects directly with their need for results.

So the best initial advice I can give the reader of this book will be follow along as closely as you can and determine which subjects are most meaningful and productive for your own corporate operational selling situations. Although indications are that business, and the conduct of business, is far more complex than it was decades ago it is important to point out that we should also have learned from management science that we could make improvements through analysis, strategizing and seeking ways to achieve simplification. Therefore, no "one size fits all" will always be far more apparent when it comes to more precise selling methods.

The greatest disservice that the management key team can inflict upon their own company is to ignore the simple truth that things can be made to operate more productively, and to impact results by considering ways that might not have been thought of or adequately discussed and explored. In my meetings both individually and together as a group with a key management team members I strive to take into account their background knowledge and that which they have learned in past experiences.

Putting the experiences and observations I have accumulated I will also identify areas where I believe that they can make improvements and enhancements over what they know and have experienced in the past, but also emphasize how important it is to try to apply new techniques and methods to improve upon that which they may already know.

Speaking to you the reader I will consider it a major accomplishment if in the course of reading this book but the reader is able to learn something new that proves to be very useful to them and accommodates their present circumstances and situation in such a way as they can impact and improve outcomes.

The best test of any organization I have found is in their ability to assimilate new knowledge and apply it in ways that do in fact improve their results. As companies grow and mature in their experiences they generally develop a solid understanding of what success looks like, and what areas that should be avoided or overcome to ensure that failure is not part of their future reality.

Sales -- What a Concept!

"Everyone lives by selling something." Robert Lewis Stevenson, Author.

Sales – What a Concept! We start with the premise that selling is a necessary fact of business. Sales is the fuel for all industries not matter how large or small. To assume sales will always be present is a mistake. Some organizations are better at achieving sales, others not. No discussion of sales activities should be without some examples of less than optimum results as lessons from the past with future value to those planning for not following in their footsteps.

There are times when I hear the members of the management team describe selling and sales processes and some of their customers in un-flattering terms. For a great many years, I have witnessed companies of all sizes that have wandered off a potential path to success only to rapidly accelerate their demise and achieve failure by failing to understand the importance of a sales process and to calibrate what they needed to change to remedy their self-imposed situation.

Example (1) – One such example is a company that was known as Bunker–Ramo, a spinoff from Thompson-Ramo-Wooldridge (TRW), a highly respected in its day purveyor of translating technology into practical solutions. Bunker-Ramo was the creator of the modern stock information trading systems that have evolved from the late 1920s after the ticker tape model to be the foundation for the electronic financial industry systems of today.

Bunker-Ramo in its day was very successful, with cutting edge ideas, satisfied customers in ways that other companies could only look upon with envy because their ideas dominated the industry. However, Bunker Ramo, like many great and pioneering companies fell into complacency and stopped listening to customers. Some could fault a lack of innovation as the cause of their demise but they clearly forgot both the "why" and the "what" customers bought from them in the past.

Therefore, this is an example of a company where they pioneered in created an industry but they were forced into the failure and were acquired by another company that essentially could not understand how to bring the former loyal customers into the modern world with better product services and solutions. What happened? The sales organization grew complacent until it was too late.

Example (2) - Another example still fresh in my mind is that I worked for Digital Equipment Corporation in the 1980s and early 1990s at a time when the company was making major breakthroughs in mini-computer and distributed and desktop computing technologies but chose to believe that they knew better what customers wanted without listening to their customers.

The results for Digital Equipment Corporation were that it failed in the market after having led in creating new markets for many computers after twenty plus years of success. No amount of sales or marketing per se would have helped the outcome. The bottom line was they lost track of what their customers truly wanted them to produce and a continuation of the reasons why they bought from DEC anyway. Therefore, logically, they went to other companies that did offer what they were looking after. What happened? Selling was usurped by focusing on products, not need.

These are examples similar to the term of art known as the "Titanic Effect" where the premise is that if you ignore information that indicates something is not right and needs to be corrected sooner rather than later and that you choose to ignore it or you do not think the unthinkable, then you simply go out of existence. We will explore more examples later in other sections.

Perhaps optimism, or at least the belief that your company has created something in the way of a product, service, or solution that prospective clients must have, still leaves a gap in reality between a customer and the customer buying your product, service, or solution. In the instance of relying upon some single feature, function, or specification a rapid decline in customer loyalty and continued business may be observed.

Example (3) – A small company develops from a concept they have a product, service or solution viewed as the greatest thing since sliced bread and in search of a market and customers. In this example concept, knowledge is great, but there is a distinct lack of market and customer knowledge.

The basic assumption here is described as "just build it and they will come". Ever heard that statement before? How about "the greatest thing since sliced bread"? Alternatively, have you heard the lament of the "better mousetrap" solution?

Of course, you have. And you can relate to companies you know or have worked for that have taken such an approach to market as to develop the product, service or solution in a veritable vacuum with little or misguided knowledge of the environment where they will attempt to sell their new widget.

The starting point for many companies is their core idea. Does that core idea translate in to connecting with prospective customers in some identifiable and accessible market segment? Having realistic business, sales, marketing, and support plans is all well and good but do not forget about the metrics, implementation, and execution.

There are those in the industries and in the companies cited above who believe that the failure of those companies was due to a series of actions that set in motion the ultimate demise of each of the companies. In the first example the action was a failure to plan and to accommodate and understand what it is that the customers wanted to buy and why.

In the second example, the action was that the company failed to differentiate their product, services, and solutions from those of their competitors. Alternatively, it was done in ways that the value that was in the product, service, or solution was lost to the prospective customer because there was no clarity around how, or why, the products could solve the customer's problems better than the competitors could.

Further, in the second example the action was that internally the company had evolved a management structure that relied heavily upon this management model to move things forward and to make decisions.

In the third example, the actions are common in companies where the founder is the inventor of the idea and has somehow justified the existence of the product or service and their company based on the premise the world needs their solution. The translation of the idea into a commercially viable and sustainable revenue generator is lacking. This same small company may have on paper a great business plan and excellent product development plan but is missing the mark with regard to connecting the dots between product, service or solution and a prospective customer who is willing to buy it.

Can you imagine if every company has to make decisions based on consensus management for extremely long-term commitments? The players the people involved in the decision-making process would have entered and left the company in their roles would have changed so the view of what the proper solution was would also have changed over time. Lastly, the failure of the management to be both disciplined in its planning and flexible in its implementing the plans contributed to the demise of those companies.

What does your Sales Trend Look Like?

For most companies there is some daily ritual to examine the progress of their sales. It could be orders, bookings, contracts, revenue stream measures, or some other set of metrics. However, in the grand scheme of things what does the overall trend picture look like?

Does your trend look like any of the three sales scenarios shown in Figure (1)? Alternatively, does it look like a roller coaster ride that is to say cyclical and very hard to project? Understandably, there is an explanation of what is happening with your sales trends. Consider though that underlying the information are the processes that drive the cadence of sales for your company. To understand in far greater detail how those processes impact your sales efforts, and how to potentially realize your greatest strengths to improve the return on sales investments of time, effort and funds.

Figure (1) Growth vs. Time Indicated State

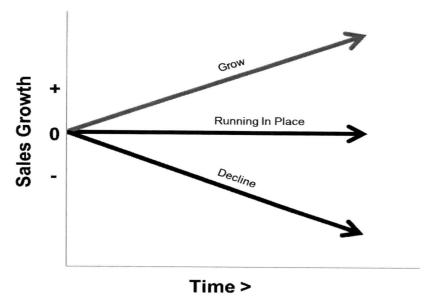

Time >

Source: SW Consulting, 2011

Why Processes Are Important

One thing all businesses have in common whether small or large is the recognized universal and fundamental need to sell something. How this is accomplished is by the involvement of one or more people and processes? Regardless of the size of the enterprise, they all share the same conceptual need to match a selling process to a buying process and generate revenue. Some situations are simple and transactional in their approach, while others require far more methodical planning, strategy development, and measured execution to align the two processes for maximum impact on results.

Although few think about the clear distinction that there are two clearly separate and distinct universal processes of buying and selling fewer still think of the need for them to be aligned and synchronized in order for a transaction to be a more probable direct result. By synchronized we mean that the seller (your company) recognizes where they are in the overall process and then responds to the buyers (a number of participants in the decision making process supporting the buying process) appropriately. In some instances, the alignment will initiate the buying later after more time has elapsed.

This timing aspect can be described according the visual image of a funnel, and where, in the funnel, the opportunity is at any given moment. Potential opportunities for sellers are above the funnel and are not yet at the stage in the process where a buyer is making commitments but moving in that direction from the information at hand. Those in the body of the funnel are moving because the seller and buyer are coming closer together on arriving at the solution to the buyers need for a product or a service and the buyer is more comfortable what the seller is proposing.

This portion of the process moves faster or slower at times, taking in to consideration such factors as the need for urgency, or the source of funds available to make a purchase.

Alignment progresses as answers remove questions and the buyer visualizes the solution as being the one they want to buy or not. Success comes when all issues are resolved to the point where the buyer agrees that seller has matched the proposed solution to the best fit in the buyers mind.

A great many businesses start the selling process with the creation of opportunities through calling prospective buyers that have been identified as possibly interested in what the business is selling. Marketing might do this or sales might be charged with performing the activity.

Marketing plays a role admittedly with the intent to stimulating interest and trying to increase awareness of the product, service, or solution or increase awareness to the name of the company where they try branding with mixed sales results. Often how the prospective customer is engaged is by either a direct call or where marketing brings the process of aligning buying and selling together early.

Occasionally, but with increasing frequency today, newer modes of how clients uncover prospective providers or how the providers themselves uncover clients are continuously evolving. Witness the rise of social and professional networking and word of mouth as powerful tools for establishing visibility and connectivity between the two buying and selling processes. These new forms of electronic linkages infuse added communications capabilities to those who align their sales and marketing practices for maximum impact.

For transactional face-to-face businesses with walk-in prospective customers, such as a bakery or merchant shop, the shop surroundings will stimulate the initial discussions about why the prospective customer is there. The proverbial "can I help you" approach of the sales person could trigger the opportunity creation. Sometimes prospective customers truly are "just looking" or collecting information for possible reference and use later on. They will remember the store, the items, and the salesperson, all of which can be factored in to later decisions to initiate the buying process.

One small merchant I witnessed who had a walk-in artistic garden and pottery shop would either collect some info from the prospect or ask them fill out a card for future sales during the first minutes of the conversation.

They also, because of a conversation however brief on a particular subject, would offer up a discount coupon for the prospect to purchase that day or at a future time. Depending upon the products and services being sold this approach obviously works for some retail businesses. For sales that are more complex it has less impact where "tire kicking" is not regarded as an option.

Consider the software company that has developed a suite that improves personal productivity of businesses professionals. It is easy to use, requires a little self-study to get maximum use, and the cost is reasonable enough given the promise of improving time management, personal information organization and the like.

There is the perception of value as recognized by the prospective buyer. However, when the software company is trying to sell in the broad marketplace finding a specific prospective customer according to professional title, or role, it becomes more difficult because they are attempting to sell direct to the unknown but possibly interested parties.

At the highest level, the selling and buying processes can be described as partitioned into areas according to the stage of the development of an opportunity or an account. The three core areas are:

- Developing opportunities (understanding and developing opportunities from the earliest point through the development of some form of relationship)

- Managing the appropriate selected opportunities (building a strategy designed to cover all the requisite questions to win the business, consistently

- Longer term management of relationships (when a select preferred account with potential for multiple opportunities is targeted for further investments)

These core areas overlap, and are interconnected in some way determined by the course of action taken by you, and your customer, over some period of time. Small companies have a distinct advantage over larger ones in that they have very little critical mass to change direction if need be. As long as the people involved in the selling process are willing to adopt some discipline the practice of successful sales, the ones that are more predictable and repeatable, will occur with more frequency than without the use of process.

The typical sales organization, if there is such a thing in a small company, is not layers deep or isolated from the leadership. Quite often, the leadership is the sales force and the team consists mainly of the Me, Myself, and I team. To the organizations that are methodical, organized and understand the value of planning and implementing strategies go the spoils and the profits.

A case in point is a small manufacturer of technical tools for the government and civilian first responder and law enforcement markets. The company has no formal sales force other than its founding president who is also the technical force behind the solution.

In the small company we often find that the president also functions in the roles of the chief engineer, the financial officer, public relations, and marketing manager and helps with the manufacturing processes. In small businesses, one person wears many hats, sometimes all at once. Not always with the desired results, and especially when we try to develop shortcuts that frequently produce less than desirable results.

Using this as a backdrop let us look at the topic of time allotment as a problem facing any company to gauge the importance of what the use of process and a systematic approach can do to save time and increase productivity. Every small company needs to invest time in the understanding of the who, what, when and where the prospective customers are in their buying process. Without the investment in sufficient time, a lack of awareness almost invariably negatively impacts a potential sale. Marketing impact to some extent may be also negated, or the time spent reaching out to the mass of un-identified prospective buyers will keep, the sales funnel relatively empty.

Time must be allocated to research prospect opportunities and determine just who is involved, where in the buying process, they are and what the opportunity might look like, and finally what form the solution will take as necessary to win the business.

Next, the multi-talented small business owner will need to engage in face time and in answering questions once they have figured out which ones to ask. This can be a lengthy process and we counsel businesses to invest time in understanding the questions that are critical to the prospects needs and vision for the solution, in other words his concept of what the ideal solution might look like. Uncovering what the prospect has as a concept of the product, service, or solution has proven to be a valuable differentiator when comparing companies in the mind of the prospect. It allows your company to begin the synchronization of buying and selling processes.

As a professional sales consultant, I repeatedly hear that companies like how I sell to them. Why? Perhaps it is because I am methodical in my approach to problem solving. They recognize and appreciate how very well prepared I come to understand their business, and from experience I know what questions will gain the greatest insight when pursing them as a client. We walk the talk together as it were. If together we uncover in their prospective clients the development of an opportunity, the selection and managing of the selected opportunity, and for their existing customers with strategic growth potential, we can demonstrate better management of selected key or strategic account relationships and aligning them to appropriate resources using the methods in this book.

In addition, I learned as a sales leader and manager of sales professionals, the value of investing in time to improve our understanding, as much as possible, about the prospective customers and their situation, in a notable way to ascertain who best fits our chosen selection criteria, will directly impact the end product results.

Let us turn our attention to understanding the notion and impact on our approach arising from a complex sale for a moment. First, a complex sale is one where there are many people involved in the decision making process. Not the degree of difficulty associated with your product, service, or solution.

If your sale only has one person to satisfy then choose the path to keep it simple and satisfy that prospective buyer by following the general processes described in this book.

If on the other hand, your product, service or solution requires the involvement of a number of people who are involved in the buying process then it becomes far more critical you understand the nature of their role, contribution to the decision, their personal attitude and receptivity to the changes your solution will bring about to make the successful sale.

Your task, as the management of the resources, is to reduce the uncertainties by following a process that results in achievement of the goal, to sell to the specific needs of the client. In order to reduce the uncertainties and to improve the odds of winning your organization needs to support the notion that by assimilating and using processes your outcomes will be more predictable and productive.

Customer? Who is the Customer?

Although this book is not about how to sell per se, we need to address a couple of points to make the linkage to the sales process more meaningful.

Look at Figure (2). A good starting point is to know who we believe constitutes a company that may or may not be interested in our product, service, or solutions. At first we identify those companies who through current or past experience or some specific market research identifies that they appear to fit a profile we construct indicates it is possible to develop an opportunity to sell our product, service, or solution. They are at this point "suspects" and become prospects when and if we can more succinctly identify and qualify them as a true prospective customer.

Some companies will rely heavily upon marketing to match the descriptions of what you have to sell with the companies that would be targeted for additional investments in time and energy to determine if they are in fact prospects. In other companies sales performs the targeting of their own initiative. The universe of potential customers is quite large.

Where do you find your customers? What defines them as "good" or potentially "bad" customers based on the collective wisdom and experience of the entire company?

When you say "need", what is your basis for describing and defining that need? Are you clear on all of the people who are involved in the decision making process when it comes to the purchasing any a product, service or solution?

As simple as these questions appear to be, a great many organizations approach finding the answers in a "fuzzy" fashion. They are also unclear on the value of having the information or know how to obtain and use it to assist them in making better connections with the prospective clients.

Always in sales, what matters most is selling something that matches what the prospective client views as the concept of the solution they select to help them solve their business problems, whatever those problems are. How can you do that without gaining the appropriate knowledge or without developing an in-depth assessment of how best to help them?

Figure (2) How do you identify prospective customers, opportunities.

In the Universe of prospective opportunities you should know the characteristics that define your targeted Best Customer Profile and why.

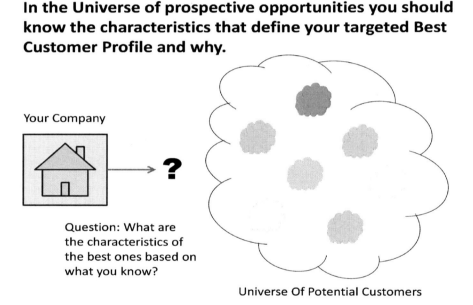

Your Company

Question: What are the characteristics of the best ones based on what you know?

Universe Of Potential Customers

Source: SW Consulting, 2011

Simple vs. Complex Selling

Nearly every industry has evolved with ever-increasing levels of complexity associated with its products, services, and solutions. There are sufficient options and choices available to confuse and confound any prospective buyer. A simple sale is one in which our product, service, or solution, does not require a lot of involvement of different decision-makers and in fact the decision-making process is quite simple in its approach.

The best illustration of this can be where there is a purchasing department and a purchaser is faced with the task of getting quotes from as many vendors as they can, and decides on the basis of conformance to specifications, along with the price and delivery timeframe. Internal to the company the user of whatever product, service, or solution, that is being acquired will do a simple comparison and the number of people involved is very small for this simple type of purchase. Typically, these purchases are undifferentiated from each with small discernible differences if any.

You may have heard that selling is analogous to a team sport in a highly competitive situation. The more appropriate description is that the team concept is not competitive at all and it is in fact more collaborative team and joint venture partnering in its approach in the most successful sales situations.

A more complex selling situation, regardless of the complexity of late product, service, or solution, being sold, the process involves a great many more people influencing buying who participate in the decision-making process. They look for clear differentiation.

The astute salesperson will recognize the difference between simple and complex selling situations, and will understand the need to prepare appropriate plans and act accordingly to engage the prospective client in the proper approach to selling their product, service, or solution, into the account. For further reading into complex selling approaches, I recommend the book *The New Strategic Selling by Robert (Bob) Miller and Steve Heiman*, published by Business Plus, Hachette Book Group, New York.

It bears reinforcing that to have the maximum impact upon the purchasing decision making process within your prospective client you need to engage early, be well prepared, make the invest the time to learn all that you can about the people influencing buying concept of the best fit solution before proposing your solution. If you have worked together with each of the people influencing buying from the very early stages when there concept is being refined you greatly improve your chances of winning the opportunity and differentiating your solution from all others.

Your sales system, the methods and process you use to generate sales, will need to be able to accommodate both simple and complex selling if the breadth and depth of your products services and solutions requires that. As you are examining your current sales system and planning the processes that you already have or do not have in place consider that a process roadmap will always help guide you when you have to decide between choosing one selling approach over another or at least developing and maintaining a playbook of alternatives.

Customer Centricity -- What Does That Mean?

Your company is competing with other companies for almost every sale. How your company views the customer, how you treat the customer during the selling process and how you help them to make better buying decisions will impact how they feel about your company and your solution.

Today, various aspects of customer satisfaction are routinely measured by surveys and follow-up questionnaires and in some cases by outreach phone calls to assess how well that person was treated during the selling process. The questions that are often asked do not get at whether, or not, the solution that a customer purchased was in fact an optimal solution for their company. Did it help achieve the goals for purchasing the products, or the resource solution? In general, the pressing question is, was the company able to realize the promised benefits, and value, from that particular purchase.

If it feels like from their perspective that they bought a poor fit solution then the proverbial buyer's remorse will have to be dealt with by the selling company sooner rather than later. It will be an uncomfortable exercise for all and can potentially be avoided with better strategy and planning.

Customer centricity would be always viewed from the perspective of the customer. Not from us looking at how we treated the customer per se, but did we answer all of their questions, in a way that the information was useful to help guide them to make a decision, and for them to achieve the best possible outcome.

In a customer centric company is not the customer satisfaction aspect of being customer centric as much as it is providing the necessary support to the sales person and reinforcing that the salesperson must help guide the customer towards making the best possible solution choice for their needs.

It must also be recognized that in some cases what your company sells as a product, service, or solution, may not be the best fit with what the customer actually needs. Therefore, the message is make sure that you do not sell the customer something that both parties will ultimately regret.

Look at Figure (3). In the traditional sales approach, we put our own interests ahead of those of the customer beginning with the planning process. Traditionally, companies plan for revenue and base assumptions and metrics upon the overarching goal of achieving the revenue. Quotas are assigned and resources planned on the basis of the revenue.

In a sales system approach the analysis of the market, the situational landscape is assessed the same way as with the traditional approach but then deviates to spend time strategizing on what patterns indicate prospective clients can be identified based on understanding the prospective client pain points and reasons for buying. The sales system captures the needs of the prospective clients and assists with understanding the actions and processes needed to win the business.

Traditional selling focuses a lot of internal energy on creating a revenue number and then trying to allocate resources and expenses to achieve that overall number and then divided among the sale people. Forecasting and tracking the prospective opportunities then involves an exceptional amount of time and management cycles to determine if progress is being made towards the forecast. Rarely do the two align for more than a brief moment.

In the sales system customer centric approach, planning seeks to identify and plan for the actions required to sell the desired amount of business. It examines and compares the impact of applying resources effectively to achieve desired sales. In the sales system model, the internal resources align in support of the efforts to engage prospective clients and they are aligned in all departments contributing to support the sales efforts. Marketing is aligned with sales, sales is aligned with production and planning, and management is aligned with the execution of the goals and objectives supporting the sales plans.

For most companies this concept of customer-centric translates in to how they handle either sales or support but generally not both. The traditional model compartmentalizes the responsibilities while the sales system approach places a heavier emphasis on using a holistic use of all resources, knowledge and experience, and understands far better the need to have the sales system accommodate every aspect of the selling and buying processes including the post sales ongoing relationship management with the customers.

Figure (3) Comparing Traditional with the Sales System Approach.

Traditional Sales Versus Sales System Approach

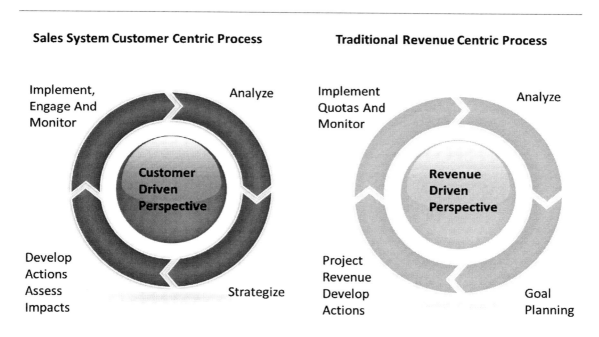

Source: SW Consulting, 2011

Myths, Fads, Reality

If you were to go to the Amazon website and enter a search for books about sales, you will find hundreds of entries related to ways to make your sales faster, better, cheaper or some other aspect. The simple truth is in sales, as in many other pursuits, there are no silver bullets, magic incantations, or get–rich-quick schemes that apply to the process of selling. Perhaps fewer than a dozen of those titles you will find on the Amazon website will actually provide you meaningful understanding or insight into the subtleties of the selling process, or raise your hopes of gaining a better understanding so that you and your management team can better facilitate, manage, and impact your results. Attempts to use shortcut approaches to better sales are a quick pathway to sales decline and most certainly to be avoided.

One noteworthy example when discussing the concepts behind improving sales performance is that by better understanding your sales system, and the processes that are associated with it, you have more control and impact over your sales efforts. If you want to view other examples of less than optimum, in fact humorous approaches, then go to YouTube and entering search references to the video entitled "selling magic." I know the person who created the video had good intentions, but it seems that those intentions had more to do with selling you some new training videos, specialized wall charts, and other paraphernalia that claims to make your approach to selling and the results that you should expect greatly simplified. Again, there are no simple solutions to selling when you have complex or long-term sales opportunities to pursue.

I want to reassure you however, that a sale does in fact come about as the result of investing appropriately in time and effort to achieve the desired revenues. As such, it is our intention through this book to provide you with a sound understanding of your own sales system and the processes that contribute to your sales results in such a way that you can improve and enhance them to deliver better results.

Today's selling reality is there are no magical techniques, silver bullets, or special incantations or potions that will impact your sales. The simplest truth is the more you understand about the buying, and the selling process, the more likely you will be to achieve results, consistently and with more manageability than before you studied the processes.

There have been a number of waves of change associated with selling over the years. A de-facto term of art to describe selling is Sales 1.0. It is a more traditional view of the ABCs of sales methods and processes.

Throughout history, selling first focused on conversations heavily centered on the product feature and functional aspects of what was being sold. That evolved in to relationship building and ways of asking questions of the prospective clients that could be used to frame a solution to address concerns and highlight the areas that fit with the client needs.

Sales 2.0 is more succinctly defined in the manner in which organizations develop capabilities to take advantage of the evolving client's needs and with transforming the selling processes to align with the buying processes. This includes using technology and tools to facilitate aligning marketing, developing strategies and working through heavy utilization of the internet's capabilities to assist from initial client connecting with the product, service, or solution, through tracking sales and the delivery of those solutions along the way.

It is the highly interactive approach to selling using such tools as CRM and ties with social media networking used to get closer to and engage prospective clients through linking with their interests. This approach continues to evolve, and it should figure prominently in any company's plans to engage prospective clients.

Sales 3.0 has yet to emerge as any concrete approach, but social selling is a part of it, and so is the internet. For a great many followers, it seems that it might entail using the internet to precisely select the solution from the overload of information using some yet undeveloped toolkit to make selections more methodically, analytically. This means implicitly conducted with reduced relationship development. In other words, it is potentially a sterile environment devoid of sales people, as we know them today.

You might put it in the same category as science fiction selling. You as a buyer query the web to find an answer to your specific problem and narrow the selection as more criteria are methodically addressed. You then sift the sources, find the best fit from your analysis and seek to reach out to the prospective providers in much the same way as RFIs and RFPs are handled with requests for quotes and parameter verification that the provider can meet the specifications.

All of this takes place without talking with a salesperson even though a chat window is likely to pop up to connect you with some script trained lower level person to ask you more questions. In this model, there is a heavy reliance on the ability of systems to pinpoint and correctly assess what you are looking to accomplish.

The point here is not so much some science fiction approach to aligning the buying, and the selling processes in new ways. It about finding new ways to sufficiently differentiate your company and its products, services, and solutions, and to make selection more accurate in the eyes of the client by matching their concept of the what the best solution looks like with the highest precision, and a clear picture of the least amount of risk. A complex scenario at best, where you need all the advantage you can develop. If you can do it, the probability you will sell more effectively increases dramatically.

Your sales system will become the great equalizer that helps you build that differentiation and tighten the relationship and increase credibility between your company and any prospective client. It is not totally about trust, its trust, plus making sure in some quantifiable and qualifiable ways that the solution you offer is the best-fit and least risky one in the client's mind.

Characteristics of Top Sales Performers

Before we talk more about the use of sales system and your particular version of one consider that to succeed any system has to be both supportive of the people in the front lines in contact with prospective clients as well as tightly integrated with the fabric of the entire company in support of sales.

What constitutes a great sales system is one that works well for all sales people regardless of their abilities when it comes to satisfying those prospective clients. Sales are, largely, an internal social network of support, knowledge, and collaboration and found in the most successful companies.

Companies of all sizes have a mix of performers when it comes to sales. In any sales organization, the distribution of performers ranges from lowest to highest with the bulk of the performers somewhere in the middle. The challenge of sales management and management in general are to move the bulk of the curve where the average performers are, to a higher level of sales performance.

What is interesting about this activity it is difficult to move the average people to a higher level of performance unless those people are thoroughly familiar with the processes involved in the sales system. Small and medium enterprises in all industries know how critical the contribution to winning a sale is that every person in the organization can make. Consider how different the sales performance is if your company has all exceptional performers versus the company with a range of average or below-average contributors to sales.

Although the message here is make sure you select people into your company who have the capacity for exceptional sales performance, we realize that many small companies nearly everyone sells or contributes to the sale in some way, and that they may not be well suited for selling activities. People whose main job is not directly selling do not necessarily grasp the importance of the buying and selling processes, or even the decision-making processes, that are crucial to winning a sale.

The implementation and use of an effective sales system, aids with managing the way everyone in the company focuses their support contribution. This ensures that the resources are used effectively, and can help the sales individual to be exceptional.

For every sales person in your company the question needs to be asked, how are they being supported and what other processes that will contribute to their success and the success of winning more actionable and profitable business. Actionable means that you are not biting off more than you can handle my investing scarce resources to heavily in unproductive leads or underperforming customers. Each situation requires a process to find the best potential accounts that will be beneficial to the company, and to decide on the strategies and resources that are necessary to pursue them while managing through the entire buying and selling in decision-making processes to achieve a win for all.

The ever-present challenge for the leadership team is to move the vast bulk of the midrange performers towards a continuous level of higher output and to focus on what is required change and assist them achieve better results. Change can be good and the results are rarely static.

What Is A Sales System?

Every company has a sales system. We define a sales system is a set of elements that when set in motion comprise a process. The collection of those processes will address every aspect of sales from the perspective of defining, and creating, opportunities: heightening the focus on the most productive prospects; proper utilization of resources to win the business; developing an understanding in much greater detail of the needs of the prospect; and consistent ways to align the selling and buying processes. The typical sales system also encompasses these additional aspects of selling that include:

- How we manage our opportunities and improve our probability of winning a piece of business from a plan, execute and assess results viewpoint

- How we manage our account and channel relationships, and what do we do to grow and retain those clients over time

- How we manage and support our people internally, and how we engage our client and extra resources such as suppliers can impact the overall sales process

- Management's commitment and involvement are important and lend credibility to the sales system when allocating resources

- Creating the corporate environment that stresses reinforcement of processes and methods and provides support such as CRM systems, and coaching.

So What Is The Bottom Line For Having A Sales System?

The answer, with regard to having a sales system, has been studied by a great many sources. One such source is CSO Insights (www.CSOinsights.com). CSO Insights is a sales and marketing research firm that benchmarks the challenges faced by today's sales and marketing organizations. They track trends in the use of people, process, technology, and knowledge to improve sales effectiveness.

What CSO Insights finds each year, is valuable to those who are not yet fully aware of the benefits of having a sales system and with building and follow processes that can positively and significantly impact results. The Figure (4) reflects what CSO Insights found for example, 86.1% of all companies with a sales system experienced a positive impact. That breaks down into 27.9% as significant, 58.2% as a modest impact on sales performance using a sales system. They had clearly identified a set of sales processes and put a structure in place to support those processes. Yet overall, only 43.5% of all companies surveyed use a formalized or documented dynamic sales process and 56.5 % did not. So ask yourself the following question, "what sales processes, leading to a sales system, does your company have, or need to have?"

Figure (4) Sales Process Impact on Sales Performance.

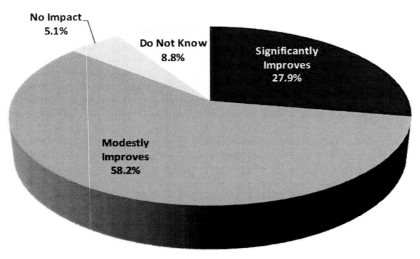

Sales Process Impact on Sales Performance

No Impact 5.1%

Do Not Know 8.8%

Significantly Improves 27.9%

Modestly Improves 58.2%

Miller Heiman, the sales performance company, also annually conducts surveys of several thousand companies to determine the best sales practices, and what constitutes a world-class sales company. They survey companies from one or more sales people to show how the company infrastructure and internal processes work most effectively. The findings may surprise you that small companies perform quite well in some others but not all when it comes to having repeatable processes.

Small companies that are highly effective have a formal sales process in place. They are nimble, responsive, and they have tight lines of communication from top management with involvement across functional lines for responsive, streamlined decision-making.

Larger companies have a longer chain and layers of command and that alters the internal decision making process or adds some degree of complexity that can work effectively when selling and buying processes are synchronized to overall selling cycles.

Smaller companies also enjoy a more innovative approach to their requirements for marketing and other support involvement that is highly tailored to the prospective clients. Their most serious drawback is the amount of available resources to cope with large demanding clients.

Look at Figure (5). Each company whether small or large, experiences the evolution of their business, their processes, their product and services, and the markets and customers they serve. This evolution for some is like a wild roller-coaster ride while for others it follows a progressive cadence linked by cause and effect and competitive pressures.

Figure (5) Business Evolution and Multiple Process Lifecycles.

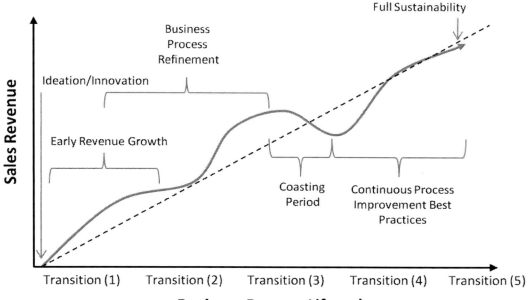

Source: SW Consulting, 2011

New product, or service introductions, have the effect of introducing some destabilizing elements that alter the sales forecasting accuracy. From the prospective customer's point of view, the solution is embodied by whatever product, or service, or combination, will look like that has what it takes to meet their needs. The solution must show it reduces their risks, and at least project the possibility of an improvement somewhere in their organization, or they would not even consider it.

Tied together with the roller coaster, are the sales processes that interact with the prospective clients. Some may be helpful and beneficial, while others interfere with, or negatively impact, the selling, and the buying processes, in ways that change the expected outcomes.

This business evolution affects the outcomes of both the selling and buying companies. The selling company makes its revenue, and responds to market and client needs. The buying company, benefits in some way from the product, or service acquisition, but their bottom line is likely impacted resulting from the purchase decisions, and they must cope with the changes introduced by the solution.

Longer term, over time, the goal of the company is to achieve stability, sustainability in the markets it serves, and to continue to chart the course to uncover additional markets by developing new products, services, and solutions, for those yet unidentified opportunities. At each transition, the playing field changes, both internally and externally.

At each transition, new modifications to existing practices must occur, and some new practices developed, implemented, and continuously monitored.

The measure of the success of the business plan is to examine it for ways to plan for and to ease the transition from one portion of the evolution to another without generating chaos for all areas of the company. A well planned and executed sales system and the processes that work well and continue to evolve position the company for longer lasting success even against fluctuations in the market or emerging disruptions caused by competitors or technologies.

Takeaways

The takeaways discussed in this section are the following:

- The concept of selling means many things to different people. But whether involved in sales directly, or in sales support activities, or ancillary processes, all need to understand how the selling connects to the intended audience for the successful sale of their products, services, or solutions. Your sales system is yours to refine for optimum results.

- Those companies that examine, develop, and implement, and utilize a systematic approach (a process or set of processes) to all aspects of their sales efforts, differentiate themselves from other selling organizations in several ways. The most recognizable way is to note an increase in the return on the sales investment from the combined efforts of all areas of the company that perform, or support, the sales process in any way.

- As your business, markets, or customers evolve, those processes related to selling will increase directly in proportion to the complexity of the sale, as more people are involved in the overall set activities required to complete a sale successfully.

- Sales is a concept that gets reduced to practice through observation and understanding of those processes of what must be done and how to do it effectively to win customers, in a consistent and relatively controlled manner.

- Examining, analyzing, understanding, and modifying processes as required over time directly impact results. Allowing the status quo in sales can reduce performance.

- The bottom line for having a sales system and supporting sales processes is 86.1% of the companies having, and utilizing the approach, show an improvement in sales, yet only 43.5% of all companies surveyed have such a system and processes.

- The reason to pay attention to the evolution of any business is during various transition phases as the company evolves, having in place a sales system and the supporting processes provides continuity, consistency, and improves the flexibility with which each transition occurs as the company flexes to meet the necessary changes,

SECTION (2)

Business Issues

SECTION (2)

Business Issues

"The way a team plays as a whole determines its success. You may have the greatest bunch of individual stars in the world, but if they don't play together, the club won't be worth a dime." Attributed to Babe Ruth.

First Business Issue Question: Where the heck are we?

Today you probably read about some trend or business result that may have an impact directly upon your business. In order to make decisions, we like to call them informed decisions, where you need to triangulate your position by identifying your decisions that led to where you, your company, and your prospective clients are located relative to the opportunities you are pursuing and the decisions that must be made for a sale to take place.

Determining our position includes first understanding why our position is important to us, and second why it is important as well as to our prospective clients, so that the amount of actions and effort required to close the gap between where we are and need to be can be determined. More often than not, to win more business we will be the one who needs to change our position to accommodate the needs of the prospective clients.

The importance of needing to know our position is because our prospective clients may assess our position in ways that are either favorable or unfavorable for them, and they will take it in account when making buying decisions through whatever internal process they use.

The triangulation I am referring to is the reality of where you are in the marketplace relative to any competitor, or any other situational dynamic that is influencing or changing the marketplace as viewed by you and your competitor and your prospective client. Locating your position is multi-dimensional and it is the "difference" between you and the other contenders up for consideration because otherwise you would all look the same to the prospective client.

In sales and marketing, this difference is our differentiation. It is our way to get noticed, and to drive home our advantages relative to the client's view of what is needed. Knowing this we will need to develop that differentiation and leverage it for each opportunity to improve our chances of winning the sale.

A part of what we need to do is to discover and focused on your own sales processes. Nothing impacts the triangulation more than how sales and marketing align and work together to win the sale. Knowledge of the sales processes helps you to understand better why positioning and differentiation of your products, services, and solutions is relative to what the prospective client thinks and becomes a critical success factor when they consider your solution offering.

One thing will be to determine your position, and the other will be what do you need to change, improve, transform, or evolve to be in better alignment with those prospective clients and their needs. Figure (6) illustrates some vital questions to ask about what your company does.

We realize of course, that as an enterprise at any one point in time you are probably heavily involved in multitasking. Multitasking includes the management of your product, or service, or solution, and the manufacturing, or delivery and installation of it. By the end of this book, you will have discovered what role your sales system plays in the success of your business and what can and should be done to improve overall sales.

Figure (6) Ask the questions shown to understand your company's positioning.

How Well Positioned Are You?

Question (1): Does Your Solution Fit With Customer's Image Of What They Believe Will Produce The Desired Results?

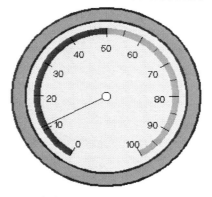

Question (2): How Well Does Your Solution Match And What Evidence Do You Have To Show You Are The "Best Fit" Supplier?

Source: SW Consulting, 2011

Second Business Issue Question: What keeps you up at night?

First, we acknowledge and accept that every business has recognized operational, financial and resource planning issues. Although one of the outcomes of understanding and improving your sales system and approach will likely be better top line sales productivity, the impact on costs may vary considerably. Often we observe from any market research that was conducted about our chosen market that we started out with a limited understanding of the potential buyers in that market, their issues and concerns, and why they will buy or not and who they buy from. The response to how our company addresses issues facing every small company we compete with or those just developing will define and expand our knowledge of the market. There are with any situation a number of business plan specific issues. First will be some unrealistic descriptions of the opportunities. Then, the assessment of the time to market, and time to generate revenue timelines are usually highly optimistic and will clash with the resource requirements to accomplish them.

Some companies will fund their development of their product, service, or solution, but then wait until the Nth hour to begin sales and marketing efforts. Sometimes, companies create a challenging list of specific goals that are beyond the ability of the organization to achieve. Then they wonder why they wind up staring at the end of their runway before they even get off the ground to hit their proverbial stride instead of hitting the wall they tried to avoid in their business plans.

There are and always will be capitalization issues, cash flow, and funding event-timing issues during the early stages of growth in a small company. Those are not the issues or focus of this book. Getting sales results from your sales system are. We also point to the fact that pricing and value monetization issues recur because initially companies are not sure what the value of their product or service is and therefore have difficulty stating the pricing for the specific customer audiences. Quite often, the marketing strategy is at odds with the development schedule for the products services or solutions and consequently the go to market strategies are not along with the efforts that sales must put forth when a new product is launched. Trying to do too much with limited resources is a common complaint of virtually every small company.

Perhaps one of the largest issues experienced by small and medium enterprises is the lack of understanding between the selling, buying, and decision-making processes that must occur for transaction to result in a sale.

The top 5 Small and Medium Enterprise (SME) issues, according to *www.helium.com* are:

    (1) Poor sales (missing the forecasted objectives)

    (2) Not understanding how to generate sales (not following processes that work)

    (3) Poor forecasting accuracy (not measuring the right metrics)

    (4) Hiring, retention and quality issues with the types of employee needed and selected (employing sub-optimal people with improper skill or experience selection criteria)

(5) Failing to build and maintaining relationships with potential client's suppliers and channel partners (not understanding what partners want and need from the relationship to be successful)

We all know the description that is common regarding the definition of insanity. Insanity is doing the same thing over, and over again and expecting different results. That description might describe your current sales system and processes.

Many years ago Robin Williams the great standup comic coined a phrase that became accepted by a number of people who are strategic planners for businesses, the phrase that you hear most often is "reality, what a concept". For those of you under thirty Google "Mork and Mindy" and watch a few minutes on YouTube to gain an alien perspective and commentary on society.

We will be using a discovery method to examine your processes in detail and what we hope to learn is how to make them more productive. Why the discovery approach? The answer lies with uncovering information that can help us connect the dots between the business plan, the sales, and marketing plans, and how they make the connection with the prospective client. The connection of these plans is often an area left unstructured and consequently results in poor performance. Ask yourself the question, how do prospective clients view you? How do your plans for your product or service or solution connect with how your clients view you?

While consulting to small businesses I frequently find that there is a misunderstanding between the selling process and the buying process. It is not a great leap of faith to realize that effective selling occurs when both of these processes, the selling process, and the buying process, are aligned to complete a transaction. In the selling process we are most familiar with various aspects that selling and marketing are supposed to do, which is to generating leads and targeting prospects and to a need for determining how to qualify those leads to become prospective clients. Refer to Figure (7) to illustrate the components of the buying and selling processes.

We need to know what we need to do to close a piece of business within that identified and qualified client, and how to prepare a proposal that will resonate with our clients so that they will understand how our solution can solve their particular problems. Then we enter into the negotiations and closing operations that must occur to complete the transaction, followed by the fulfillment of the obligation created by the transaction, and then the long-term up sell and cross sell activities that we engage in to continue to build a relationship with the client.

On the client or buying side of the set of actions, most clients start with being in a state of status quo, meaning that they are not compelled to buy anything unless and until there is a particular reason for them to act. This notion of a "trigger event" is needed to force them to begin the process of considering how to solve their problem and make a purchase of something to solve that defined problem. The problem itself could be to increase their productivity, or to help them avoid future problems clearly resulting from an internal or external change.

Whatever the nature of the problem, fixing it will cause a change in their organization to accommodate the solution. Change is both, the catalyst and the result, cause and impact, and at some point, it drives the sense of urgency that companies feel. The sense of urgency then drives the pace and time line of purchases for a great many organizations.

Although this concept of a trigger is not new, once the trigger event occurs and change is recognized or the need to change is recognized, then starts an internal process of defining the problem in ways that solutions can be found to address the problem.

Along the way as a part of the buying process, those people who are actively (not as bystanders) involved in the decision-making process must evaluate the options that are available to them and the trade-offs that come with making a purchasing decision.

Also as a part of the buying process, the people directly involved in the decision-making must ultimately select from the best of the options and choices that they have. They own responsibility to figure out the amount of change in their organization and the impact of what the solution will have on their organization, and then develop a plan to implement and to absorb the change into their operations.

At some point early in the process discussions take place about the products or research solution that a client is deciding to buy it and assessments of the value must be made relative to each those buyers involved in the decision making. In some cases, the justification is a return on investments, notable impact on productivity, reduction in costs, and conformance to specifications, terms and conditions, or some other metrics that reinforce why purchasing the products or investing resources in the proposed solution caused by the trigger event will improve the situation somehow within that company with what intended outcomes and results.

Figure (7) Buying and Selling processes must be aligned and synchronized.

Optimizing Selling Time – Using The Funnel Model

Traditional Approach	Sales System Approach
Universe	Universe
Prospects/Leads	Best Customer Profile
Appointments	Qualified by Questions
Presentations	Strategize What A Win Looks Like
Proposals	Solutions Matching Concept
Negotiate/Close	Negotiate/Close
Delivery	Delivery
Win/Loss Analysis or Ratio	Win/Loss Analysis or Ratio
	Relationship Management Stage

Source: SW Consulting, 2011

Third Business Issue Question: What Makes the Exceptional Sale

See if you can remember when your company landed a really great deal where the team pulled together internally, met, and exceeded, the requirements of an exacting client in such ways as to delight them. It was a WIN-WIN for you and for them by everyone's admission and the relationship is expected to grow over time.

When you have this perfect storm of a sale, you want to document everything that contributed to the event by collecting information from all participants involved including all internal comments, and viewpoints from the client's perspective as well. This becomes the shining example of what happened to win the sale. It also serves to identify the elements of the selling activities and circumstances that contributed to make such a memorable sale take place.

Over time, the corporate tribal knowledge will tend to modify the highlights surrounding the transaction outcome by adding additional speculation and thoughts post-sale that may contradict the views of those who participated. Try to keep the folklore apart from the actual fiction behind the events leading to the winning of the sale.

If you have more than one huge success, that everyone feels good about then even better. Document it as well at the most detailed level. In fact, document all of the wins and the monumental colossal failures too. This information helps to identify what makes an exceptional sale exceptional in the first place and serves to keep alive the memories of what works and what does not work. Some companies convert those stories of glory and defeat into a playbook for future reference.

The mark of truly exceptional and consistently successful companies is they waste nothing in terms of knowledge and learn from each and every sale or failure to complete the sale. That information improves the return on sales investments and helps to illustrate clearly how the process works for their market.

The Exceptional Customer

As with the exceptional sale, we gauge the measure of the client as to how well they fit with what we have to sell. In fact, it turns out less to be about what we have to sell, more about the actual fit with the client's view of what is needed, and what they stand to gain from selecting your particular product, service, or solution. If they see the fit and our fit is better than that of the completion then we are more likely to get the business and the client is more likely to be satisfied with selecting our solution offering. In order for use both to be successful in the buying and selling process alignment healthy regard for the client's needs and how well the solutions fits those needs at every step in the buying and selling process.

Exceptional customers are relatively rare in the instances of where a complex solution is involved. Think of the complexity of the Space Shuttle when it was conceived and when it was improved over its product life. The possibilities of things going wrong are quite astounding yet with proper process and procedures in place everything is possible.

So too is the process outcome of a selling situation. Once the million and one things that can go awry have been taken in to consideration, addressed or eliminated, then things can progress to the next level, closer to the actual completion of the sale.

Exceptional customers also tend to exhibit a more progressive approach wherein they learn as the buying and selling processes progress. At one point in my career while in government, my business unit of the agency implemented a suite of services for other agencies the ability to prototype and pilot a technology, process, or idea to gain knowledge of the parameters and possible solutions or workarounds when that type of response was required.

By piloting a technology or solution before scaling it and developing the final solution image that the potential buyers, who paid for the pilot by the way, were able to touch and feel the good and bad points of the concept they were attempting to implement. Such exploration usually identified the flaws or weak points that if unknown would have negated the benefits of implementation of the new system. Exceptional customers are willing to take calculated risks to reduce potential overall risks of choosing one solution over another.

Fourth Business Issue: The Biggest Business Issue = Results

Research by a few leading market research companies into small and medium enterprises has shown that they benefit from implementing a solid sales process foundation upon which they can build and enhance their sales operational practices. The straightforward belief is that having a solid foundation increases the manageability of sales.

The sales process itself encompasses from end to end how the company creates and manages any opportunities to sell their product, service, or solution, and how they establish and manage the relationships with prospective client's accounts and their chosen channel partners. Research into sales process by companies focused on quantifying and qualifying performance such as Miller Heiman and CSO Insights show that by having a consistent and repeatable set of sales processes we readily see improvements in top line revenues.

Also having a clear focus on the resources to actually generate the greatest return on sales efforts, and provide both metrics and ways to assess the company as it grows how the sales system can evolve to accommodate what is needed. Refer to Figure (8).

The results of your efforts running your business to increase sales or to open new markets needs to be assessed against carefully considered metrics and tracked over time to show whether you are achieving your stated business plan goals. Moreover, if your efforts are underperforming what contingency plans will you bring to bear to correct sub-performing activities. If your sales system is performing above the expected levels then you also want to continuously assess and analyze what specifically contributed to the optimizing of results.

Figure (8) Optimizing Results. Where do you fall?

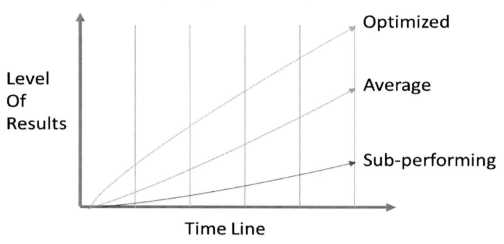

Ensure Timely Responses To Optimize Results

Level Of Results

Optimized

Average

Sub-performing

Time Line

Source: SW Consulting, 2011

The collection of processes and diagnostics that make up a sales system can be managed far more effectively if you identify them, understand their interactions across your operations in terms of resources and results, implement ways to manage them, and then commit to improving them as needed. What every selling organization must do is to understand fundamental core requirements of having a scalable structured methodology for analyzing, strategizing, and developing actionable plans that have a measureable impact on the sales results. Having robust sales processes leads to more productivity and yields more predictable results than that of the older more traditional selling methods where only the revenue figures are the major metric.

Charting any course of action requires that to increase your probability of success we must answer some basic questions such as:

- Do we have the information about our current position regarding the opportunity?
- Do we have a clear understanding of our objective/destination?
- How long will our journey take and what are the progress indicators we expect?
- Do we know the potential competitors, or our client's alternatives to our solution?
- What possible red flags are we likely to encounter? Do we know them?
- What are the indications that give us the necessary conviction to proceed?

When you are proceeding on a path, a wrong turn, or a bad decision, can greatly impact you. In some instances, choosing a wrong path may mean you need to backtrack and chose the alternative pathway. In sales, once the wrong path was committed, the opportunity outcome was most probably not going to be favorable without having time sufficient to backtrack and start over. There are few "do-overs" in selling.

From the sales perspective, a more productive approach is to develop a better understanding of our own corporate direction, and to question the chosen course, and the factors that will have the greatest impact on the direction along the journey.

Depending upon the age and maturity of your business, we know that business lifecycle phases greatly impact results and most certainly require planning. When you are in the early stages of developing sales and revenue for your products services or solutions, you need to understand how to get out of the startup mode and cross that chasm over to growth mode. Once you understand what is required of your processes and the operation of the organization to get you from one point to the next you can put in place proper metrics and you will be able to develop and refine your opportunities with more precision.

As your product, service or solution reaches maturity in the marketplace you will find you need to have plans for what to do next. Good product lifecycle management (PLM) is required which implies that from the beginning of the creation of the new product, service, or solution, that we are already thinking about what happens next, and how we transition or convert an encompass new products and services as we wish to release them. When we are talking about results as a part of our routine operational management of day-to-day activities for marketing and sales we need to plan for and ensure timely responses so that we may optimize the results.

If we find that we have an average performing product, service, or solution, we need to be prepared and understand how to optimize the sales results.

Likewise, if the product, service, or solution, in our portfolio is underperforming we need to understand why it is underperforming and what we must do to take corrective action. In a traditional sales approach a lot of times there is a situation identified as tribal knowledge that helps the salesperson to navigate the internal structure of their own company but does little to help them understand their customer and how to be more effective in selling to the customer.

The traditional sales planning model focuses strictly on driving revenue, and how to implement and monitor quotas for each contribution that I sales representative will make. When you have a functional sales system in place there are some important gets little differences between the traditional model and the sales system all. In the sales system model almost everything we do, think about, or implement, is driven by the customers' perspective and perceptions as to what our product, service, or solution, will do for them to improve their results.

Operationally the difference is that we spend more time focused on understanding our customer, strategizing on ways to assist the customer in to position our product, service, or solution, to match how the customer thinks the solution needs to appear. Also different is that it instead of focusing on quota and monitoring aspects we develop actions and assess the impacts for our actions to help us better understand both the buying and selling processes. When implemented a sales system provides a better platform for engaging customers and for monitoring results than the traditional model.

A process example -- planning for most companies regardless of size plan. The company plans however, may be focused on controlling costs and engineering and production rather than on the aspects of selling it out to be more effective in generating sales.

Frequently I find that the company business, sales, and marketing plans do not even provide feedback mechanisms to accommodate changes as problems are encountered with their sales efforts. Plans also generally identify and help us qualify opportunities selected for pursuit and capture. For example, do we know enough about what our best customer profile looks like? For us to invest time and effort in prospecting and sales time in trying to qualify prospective clients we need to make sure that we understand what the best customer profile looks like. We may use that as a filtering mechanism to help us be more productive.

At the most detailed level of planning process will generate more questions that require answers in these answers once obtained from internal and prospective client sources will shape how we position and propose our solution to fit with the client's view of what the solution will do for him or her and how it can impact their company goals.

Do all companies have a formal sales process? If so, what is the impact of those sales processes? In companies that have best sales practices, we find that they may have a tribal knowledge random process for generating sales. Some number of companies will have an informal process that is also brought about by using the tribal knowledge to assist in various stages of in the sale with moving along.

But in high-performance best practices sales companies nearly half of the companies have a structured informal process allows for some dynamic process to occur in those companies have a higher success rate and shorter sales effort cycle than do those in leave it to a random or informal process.

The message here is that we need to be thinking about how these processes internally drive behavior and how they interact with our prospective clients.

Sales Performance in the Aggregate

Examine the distribution curve shown below in Figure (9). If we plot the results of each sales person and then grade their performance, this generalized pattern emerges. We have some stellar performers on the right and laggards on the left with the majority distributed about the average.

High performance sales organizations have a skewed result with more performers to the right of the average range. Although few companies have that situation for long due to advancement and turnover in the sales force, all companies need to have plans to deal with the bottom half of their performers in the distribution. Sales training might not help if the organization has internal process or sales system problems. This point should be kept in mind when evaluating the entire sales team and all who assist them.

Figure (9) Typical Distribution of Sales Performers.

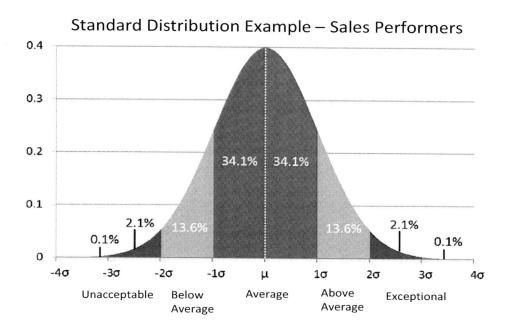

Source: SW Consulting, 2011

Companies of any size know just how critical are the contributions to sales by every sales one working in sales. Consider how different the sales performance is if your company has all exceptional performers versus the company with average or below average contributors.

Although the message here is to make sure you select people who have the capacity for exceptional sales performance, realize that in all companies, nearly every employee sells or contributes to the selling process in some way. Managing the way everyone supports sales efforts, contributes, and uses the resources effectively can help their sales individuals to be exceptional.

For every sales person in your company the question needs to be asked how are they supported and what are the processes that will contribute to the successful winning of actionable business.

Actionable means you are not biting off more than you handle or investing scarce resources too heavily in poor leads or underperforming customers. Each situation requires a process to find the accounts that will be beneficial, decide on the strategies and resources necessary to pursue them and then manage them through the buying/selling process.

The challenge for the leadership team is to move the midpoint for all performers in the distribution towards the much higher performance side of the curve. The more people who are above average for productivity the greater will be the impact on the return on sales efforts and a better top line for sales revenues.

The point to stress when considering this information is what can be done to improve the performance of the whole group. The answer will likely be found in analysis of your sales system and the supporting processes. Understanding how to make those processes more efficient and effective for all contributes to the overall contribution to sales performance improvement.

The following is a brief list of tongue-in-cheek methods often suggested for analyzing, assessing, and forecasting are routinely used in organizations that do not have a sales system in place and where most often their response to an opportunity or a competitive situation compels them to try to use these methods first with unpredictable results.

- SWAG -- Scientific Wildly Assumptive Guess (politically corrected)
- STAB -- Suppose, Think, Assume, Believe (meaning you just don't know)
- SWOT -- Strengths, Weaknesses, Opportunities, Threats (by the time you get your act together around this one and unless the opportunities are very long range you may have missed out on the opportunity due to timing issues)
- SOS -- Some Other Solution (where your customer choses something else)
- ABC -- A Better Course (those who try to accept only elusive perfection)

Change -- The Nitty-Gritty Reality Business Engine

Mentioning change in the context of a causative agent or trigger, and at the output of the product, service or solution implementation illustrates that change is a powerful word whose meanings have increased and broadened since its first common use beginning in the thirteenth century. Webster's Dictionary states "Change" is:

- to make different in some particular (alter)
- to make radically different (transform)
- to give a different position, course, or direction to (impact)
- to replace with another (exchange)
- to make a shift from one to another (switch)
- to exchange for an equivalent sum or comparable item (currency)
- to undergo a modification, transformation, transition or substitution (impact)
- SYN: alter, vary, modify, break, transform

As you can see from the diverse dictionary definitions, the concept of change has many facets. Each one of us may react differently when facing the need to change in our personal and professional lives. We refer back to the earlier discussion of the trigger event as the action that got the ball rolling on a buying decision making path.

Change - The Good Trigger vs. the Bad Trigger

Fundamentally, the world is composed of three types of people with regard to their perspective on change. The mere mention of the word "change" increases the discomfort and heart rate increase in people everywhere.

Some will be the type to openly embrace change as a necessary challenge of their personal and professional life. Others will resist the nature of the change and grudgingly try to find ways to avoid the implications of the change facing them. Still others are likely to be the no-decision types who will put off any decision making perhaps because they feel uncertain of the course of action or because they are fearful of the results and have not adequately thought through the possible outcomes. They may truly be paralyzed by analysis.

All sales people are change agents of the first type mentioned after a fashion. They ply their craft seeking to point out the reasons for making a change and then work with clients to explore the impact of the product, service or solutions being proposed to address their situation. Some are better at this aspect of selling than others. Those sales people who are early on in the discussions with prospective customers are setting the stage for evaluating and understanding the impact of the changes that will result from a sale of their proposed product, service, or solution. They ask very precise questions to understand the "why" motivation behind what is driving their clients.

It is important that we invest the time in developing an understanding of the selling and the buying processes in greater detail to assess adequately the role that change has or contributes to the dynamics of a sale.

From the prospective customer's buying point of view, something causes them to consider entering in to a buying process. We have identified that as a probable trigger event. On the selling side of the equation, a seller has processes that must be fulfilled to respond to the buyers needs and to reach agreement on a particular product, service, or solution sale.

The act of change has an impact on the buying, selling, corporate, and personal decision-making processes. When assessing change in the business situational sense as the concept of a change trigger event that forces the customer to deviate from the status quo and gets them thinking about the need to consider searching for solutions to help them evaluate the most appropriate response to the change trigger event.

To prevent the processes from being too chaotic to use or to manage, we have a sales system. If it is working well for our company, we should be able to uncover, identify, and address those factors that will cause that prospective customer to begin thinking about their need for a solution consisting of some collective image of products, or services that comprise a solution. In other words, the presence of our sales system will guide us to help the prospective client through their trigger event and to deal with the need to change. Understanding the trigger event and greatly improves our ability to formulate a successful solution to solve the client's situation.

Therefore, change is what we as salespeople do. We make things happen for our company and our prospective clients. We are recognized as change agents but perhaps that is why a lot of companies do not like to see salespeople on any regular basis because their reaction is our presence is an indication we are going to have to change something and ask, "I am not sure what the outcomes will be." Change also implies risk, risk implies uncertainty, and uncertainty encourages behavior and prospective buyers that is quite often difficult for the salesperson to manage.

Today when we sell our products, services or solution that carries with it is some degree of change and impact or risk on our prospective customer. It is our job as the salesperson to make sure that we address those changes and potential impacts together with our line. You will have heard several times about people using the term consultative selling. Consultative selling is all about helping your customer or prospective customer through a decision-making process where they assess the risks and rewards of a particular solution. I hope that yours is a solution that addresses their needs, reduces the potential for risk and failure, and results in a win for all parties involved.

As agents of change salespeople always need to do a better job from a consulting point of view, to equip their prospective customers with information and understanding of that will help them make better decisions.

Unfortunately, traditional sales approaches have been to go in with the show up and throw up approach or thousands of pages of marketing and sales literature, or to come in and discuss features and benefits in ways that really do not help the client choose the optimum solution, in fact they will serve to confuse a possible solution. Therefore, the impact of change has to be taken into account when we are selling. How does your company help a client through their decision-making process, both corporate decision-making process and individual decision-making process, to arrive at the best possible solution for their particular needs?

So that takeaway from this topic point is how to be best prepared to recognize, assess and understand, and to respond to the forces of change to help our customers is a differentiator that can make our company the best one to buy from.

The Titanic Effect Explained -- Planning for the Unthinkable

In 1974, a professor of zoology at the University of California Davis campus with the name of Kenneth E. Watt published a book titled *The Titanic effect -- planning for the unthinkable*. At the time, the book was controversial because it spent a considerable amount of time talking about the impending energy crisis and the impact it would have on the world stage of commercial activity. What was interesting about the book was that in the 70s there was considerable turmoil in the energy industry and shortages were resolved of poor planning and having no energy policies or the mechanisms to adequately monitor and control energy consumption. At the center of Dr. Watt's thesis was the notion that ties to the ecology and environmental issues of everything is related to everything else.

Life goes on to state that we consistently demonstrate that a failure to plan effectively, especially our misallocation resources, not only harms the environment and the quality of life but it impacts the economy. He further goes on to point out that companies, just like societies, tend to ignore information until the impact has had serious negative effect. That is the essence of the connection to the Titanic, the most modern and unsinkable ship of the time.

Tied to our sales system model and the processes that are associated with our sales system, we need to be fully aware and start thinking about what happens if we fail to plan for how our sales efforts will work and if they will work effectively. I believe Dr. Watt's book was an early warning indicator of the failure of businesses to plan precise enough to be able to control the destiny. His visionary view of the complex intricacies of and interworking of the economy and both the short and long results when applied to business planning can help avoid falling in to the same traps as others before us.

In the situations of today, we find several examples are referring back to historical events and contributors to thought. To sum up the Titanic effect would be to state the magnitude of disasters decreases to the extent that people believe that they are possible, and that they plan to prevent them, or to minimize their potential impact. Ignoring the warnings regarding the red flags, can lead to the unthinkable and most certainly failure.

More on the Titanic Effect – Unthinkable Consequences = Disaster

As a part of our methodology for helping you build, use, and refining your sales system we introduce the notion of a causal feedback system. We take any idea, or thought that needs to be explored as a part of our analysis and strict strategy development and we assess the pros and the cons and whether or not the idea has any impact that is likely to change the outcome and are expected results.

We do this with a form that is useful for us as a group to sift through the opportunities, options and decisions that we need to make about which processes to use. Before that is included in our workshop and in this book is titled pro/con assessment ratings. The way it works is that we identify the question or the decision that needs to be discussed or an option and we analyze that which we are questioning.

On the left hand side of our form, we list the pros, those things that are in favor of word advantages related to the question we are analyzing. On the right-hand side, we have the cons, or the information that we feel is against the choices and shows the disadvantages of the particular question being analyzed. We have scoring columns on the basis of one being a poor assessment up to 10 being the best assessment as a basis for evaluating each of the pros and cons for and against the question being analyzed. At the bottom, we have a total for the scores from the pros and the cons.

Clearly if a question has considerable negatives and a score that reflects that then we have to decide whether to pursue that particular question decision or option. If we list a great many pros, but they all have a poor assessment in our discussions, then they may also not be among our best choices.

The pro/con assessment ratings are a useful tool to obtain viewpoints from our contributing management leadership team. The purpose of the form is to be a useful tool to help guide us when we are making judgments.

Corporate Zen -- The Six Blind Men and the Elephant Parable

Every company has its own way of thinking that embodies the human value attributes and in some way translates into a code of conduct for the business for everyone to follow. Some companies will state outright that doing the right thing is their goal. Others will simply come up with a branding message that has no relevance to their customers but merely states how they want themselves to be perceived. Corporate Zen in this instance refers to how the beliefs, the code of operation aspects, become internalized as a part of the daily operational norms for the company. It is also looked upon as the collective body of tribal wisdom and knowledge on any particular subject pertaining to our work.

The collective perspective that everyone in a company has with regard to sales, marketing, and the view of customer centricity, can go a long way towards helping everyone understand what communication looks like between the company and the prospective customers. Consider the parable of the six blind men and the elephant. Each blind man was examining a part of the elephant, and drew conclusions about the elephant from past experiences. The folly is that without seeing the entire elephant, and the point here of being blind to the whole elephant, means that without the entire picture they are unable to formulate a response if required to do deal with the elephants.

This is an apt description of the buying process and the selling processes. A similar view can be found from in ancient bit of philosophical wisdom that became known as the Yin and the Yang. In Chinese philosophy, the concept of Yin-Yang often referred to in Western cultures is used to describe how polar or seemingly contrary and antagonistic forces are interconnected and at the same time interdependent in the natural world, and then how they connect with each other in turn. You plan and execute your live knowing how the forces interconnect in every situation.

Both differ as opposing forces but when fused together they show a type of harmony or a Win-Win for both. In selling, a win-win is the best possible outcome from making both parties feel good about the successful solution to the client's problems, and the satisfaction, remuneration, and a good reference for the sales person. Both are satisfied when the "what's in it for me" aspect of a sale comes together with understanding.

The concept of a win-win translates into that perfect alignment of Yin and Yang of both the seller and the buyer. The universe is in harmony and all's right with the business transaction and the relationship.

Decision making related to purchases is a buying process and you must keep that perspective in mind always when pursuing opportunities because your sales people own task of accomplishing the alignment with their selling process. The more involved or complex the solution being decided upon the more involved will be the people who are conducting the evaluation looking at the various aspects of the decision. The selling process can involve marketing, advertising, word of mouth, catalogs, literature and other information contributors to identify prospective customers including just calling out of the blue randomly to people suspected of being involved with a purchase.

Once the contact and connection is established between buyer and seller a lot of other activities must take place for the sale to go in the direction if the completely harmonious Win-Win for both parties. The activities and decision-making milestones along the way need to be aligned for maximum results.

The Diffusion of Innovation Impact on Sales

The diffusion of innovations is a theory of how, why, and at what rate new ideas and technologies spread throughout cultures and business. Much of the modern work was popularized by Everett M. Rogers when in 1962 he released his groundbreaking textbook titled *Diffusion of Innovation*. This theory seeks to explain the spread of new ideas, it continues today to be widely used to illustrate for example with each successive wave of technology companies are forced to make decisions essentially when to adopt or integrate or transform to a new level of innovation. When you assess your clients, do you ask of them what type of adopter of innovation are they? In addition, do you ask or know what factors would trigger their adoption of your solution, especially if it is a new product, service, or solution, that provides or accommodate advances in technology.

Look at Figure (10). There are always innovators when it comes to adopting technologies to assess the risk as being acceptable because they perceive a benefit or gain or improvement to be substantial. Another category of early adopters are ones who spend time analyzing and calculating the risks and perform far more in-depth analyses of the impact of any product, service, or solution, that is new in their particular environment.

Of the large percentage of people who are identified as early majority adopters, they are tolerant of risk because perhaps they have experience that shows them that some risks due to deliver on the promises and therefore their organization is resilient enough to manage the risk. The category of late majority adopters have reduced risk assessment to a routine practice and therefore can make decisions more quickly when it comes to the acceptance of new technology because they have been shown the impact on others and the outcome of the adoption of the product, service, or solution. The last of the group are called laggards because they generally lag behind others in the adoption of new product, service, or solutions, and the assimilation of newer technologies.

What continues to be a question to ask of those companies slow or resistant to embrace change is why they are not taking on the potential risk after a great many other companies have pioneered and shown that the outcome of the adoption of the innovation was successful and where the proven potential rewards can far outweigh any risks.

A great many of them are frequently associated with those companies that have extremely long planning cycles where the introduction of any new or technology for them will carry long-term consequences that must be balanced against short-term implementation.

Figure (10) Source: Bennett Rogers (1962), Diffusion of Innovation

What Type Of Adopters Are Your Clients?
What Factors Would Trigger Their Adoption Of Your Solution?

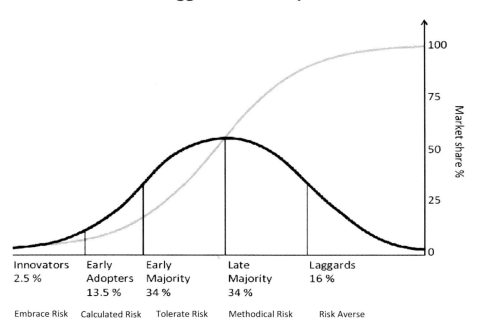

Everett Rogers (1962), Diffusion of Innovations

Take for example utility power generating or water distribution companies that have a 25-year planning cycle for improvements to their infrastructure. Also, consider companies who deliver the support services they require or where other capital-intensive areas must be modernized such as telecommunications. The diagram shows a lighter colored curve that charts the course of the market share penetration of the new product, service, or solution, in the available market. Examples of laggards today are those people who still use daily their old style cathode ray tube television.

It is virtually impossible today to buy certain products among them Would ray tube-based televisions, eight track tape players, VHS video recording players, and soon some other form of technology that is displaced by innovation. The main stream of the market has passed them by and until their system breaks, there is little incentive to upgrade or renew the technology.

Did we mention that laggards are risk averse? These prospective customers truly have a low threshold of acceptance for new ideas. They are therefore, the most difficult targets to penetrate where you wish to sell your particular product, service, or solution.

Crossing the Chasm Impact on Sales

In _Crossing the Chasm_ (1991), Geoffrey A. Moore coined the expression to illustrate what begins with the diffusion of innovations theory based from Everett M. Rogers observations. Moore presents some companies with a chasm between those early adopters of a product identified as the technology enthusiasts, the risk takers and visionaries, and those early majority viewed as the pragmatists having a moderate tolerance risk tolerance, who are sufficiently large in numbers to build up the sustainable business through solid growth. Figure (11) shows the essential elements of the theory.

Moore further stated that in his observations, the visionaries and pragmatists have very different expectations, and were fundamentally differing in their aversion, or openness, to take risks. While Moore explored those differences in his book he suggested techniques to successfully traverse across the "chasm," including, (a) choosing a precise target market, (b) understanding the whole product concept impact, (c) the ways to achieve positioning the product for each type of adopter, (d) the building of a marketing strategy, and (e) choosing the most appropriate distribution channels and pricing associated with the channels.

Crossing the Chasm is closely related to the technology adoption lifecycle where five main segments are recognized: innovators, early adopters, early majority, late majority, and laggards. According to Moore, the more traditional marketers should focus on one group of customers at a time, using each group as a base for marketing to the next group. Today we view the early written work as excluding the necessary linkages between sales and alignment with sales to focus on any prospective audience group where strong indicators are present that those prospective clients would benefit from the innovation and the reasons to change with its adoption.

Sales patterns also have been shown to follow a similar lifecycle related to the adoption of whatever product, service, or solution, a company is selling. The key observation to point out beyond the inherent risk to the adopter is that the selling organization must provide a highly coordinated and methodical selling approach to mitigate many of the fears prospective buyers may have. A number of companies resort to pilot projects, or long-term demonstrations where the outcomes drive the decision to invest in the newer and riskier solution being considered. Real proof points are the norm for the early adopters, versus reference selling later in the maturity of the solution.

The most difficult step is making the transition between visionaries (early adopters) and pragmatists (early majority) requires that a company develop and employ strategies to align the buying and selling decision making processes to achieve the optimum results. This chasm that he refers to requires the selling organization to deeply understand the reasons why a prospective client would take the risks to embrace their solution.

If a successful firm can create a bandwagon effect in which enough momentum builds, then the product becomes a de facto industry standard. This does happens on occasion. The caveat is however, that Moore's theories are only applicable for disruptive or discontinuous innovations. The adoptions of continuous innovations that do not force a significant change of behavior by the customer are still best described by the original technology adoption lifecycle without the presence of a chasm. Confusion between continuous and discontinuous innovation is a leading cause of failure for high tech products.

Figure (11) Technology Adopter Lifecycle Illustration.

Source: SW Consulting, 2011

A Book of Five Rings

The classic guide to strategy was written more than four centuries ago by Miyamoto Musashi, a samurai warrior, who by the age of 30 was one of Japan's most renowned warriors with more than 60 large-scale battles. Satisfied that he was invincible, Musashi then turned his thoughts inward to formulating his philosophy of "the way of the sword", from which he wrote a book called *A Book of Five Rings* , immediately prior to his death. *A Book of Five Rings* contains within it an interlocking philosophy that was influenced by Zen, Shintoism, and Confucianism used them in ways that can be applied to many areas of life other than the martial arts for which it was created.

The philosophy relates the five rings as five elements of battle. The elements are:

- Earth – The disciplined approach to training, leadership and the martial arts.

- Water – Attitude and outlook, flexibility, capabilities, balance, methods, and disciplines.

- Fire – Timing of when to engage, sequencing, assessing situations, preparedness, strategy and tactics.

- Wind – Devotion to understanding your opponent, assessing alternatives.

- Void – That which cannot be seen, the unknown factors, perceptions and interpreting them.

During the 1970s the book was required reading for many Japanese businessmen learning to be entrepreneurial, who used it as a guide, and approach, to business practice, likening the running of sales campaigns to those of military operations, with the same energy that motivated Musashi 400 years earlier. It became highly regarded in Japanese business circles, and then was discovered by the rest of the world.

At the heart of Musashi's philosophy, was a relentless pursuit of an honest ideal, and its truth, emerges from the descriptions in *A Book of Five Rings*. While it is not intended as only a thesis on battle strategy, it is, in Musashi's own words, "a guide for men who want to learn strategy," and, as a guide, always leads, so its contents seem always just beyond the student's immediate understanding.

I point out this book because quite frequently when discussing a sales situation is perceived as a battleground between company representatives and prospective people influencing buying within a company. Unlike the art of warfare, the art of selling deals much more diplomatically with first and foremost, communications. Those communications are blended together with the seller acting as a confidante, consultant, and a guide to provide prospective customers with information to assist them with their decision-making process.

Well thought out communications support the negotiations that are required in the best spirit of the win-win model. This view is consistent with learning what is required to strategize, to best prepare for the communications, and to relentlessly follow the path of the ideal, which for our purposes, is the use of a sales system, and all of its supporting processes that contribute to success.

What we can learn from the military definitions, converted to business use is that as in the art of war, we need to be completely prepared for any engagement. All of the stated elements of Musashi's philosophy apply both to our internal way of doing things, our system, and externally through our preparedness to achieve the best possible outcomes.

Again, the point to stress is, we must have thought through the possibilities, identified what we do know, and what we do not know, and then, based on all our collective knowledge and wisdom, we formulate how best to develop a relationship with our prospective customers. One that convinces them that not only is your salesperson a willing participant and contributor to their success, but that their company benefits, as does the salesperson's company, in tangible and measureable ways. It is this much more refined, and philosophical approach, that when put into actual practice, contributes to significant increases in results.

After following our lead, using a workshop approach presented in later sections to uncover what you know, and do not know, you will gain a better understanding your own sales system, and the role the involved processes play. Your outputs will be a concise action plan, that can be implemented to drive higher sales performance, and provide the necessary guidance at the various stages of the buying, selling, customer, and decision-making processes. You will have much a clearer understanding of what the impact will be of making these changes to your organization.

If Musashi were alive today, and a businessman, he would be a consultant, spreading the five ring concepts of an ideal selling situation as one that embodies his philosophy of preparedness, knowledge and understanding, opportunity-specific strategy and tactical planning, and clear communications.

Takeaways

The takeaways from this section are:

- Change is more than a word. It is what sales people are as change agents and a healthy respect is required to understand the impact on the customer from their perspective and learn to be sensitive to how they are assessing the changes. Some are early adopters and some are laggards when it comes to embracing change and possibly consider your product, service, or solutions.

- Make sure you understand the business issues surrounding your sales processes, and how they relate to the actual process of selling to your customers.

- Understand your own internal tribal ways of doing things and determine what role they play in the process of dealing with customers. Also make sure that everyone is on the same page understanding the subtleties and interactions well enough to address them when faced with changes that can diminish their effectiveness.

- Develop an appreciation for the dynamics of what is driving your customers is a key to being able to plan for and execute on more successful with sales.

- Sales performance must take in to account the internal and external factors related to the selling process. Process awareness and continuous evaluation of what works and what does not work to refine the operational elements of how your company sells is crucial to moving your organization to a higher level of productivity regarding sales.

SECTION (3)
Basic Sales System Concepts

SECTION (3)

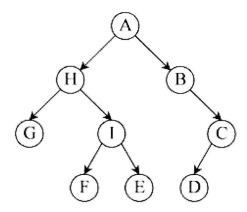

"Being busy does not always mean real work. The object of all work is production or accomplishment and to either of these ends there must be forethought, system, planning, intelligence, and honest purpose, as well as perspiration. Seeming to do is not doing." Thomas A. Edison, Inventor.

Basic Sales System Concepts

What is the premise behind this book? It is based upon the realization that every company needs a set of effective and productive sales processes that yield a foundational sales system that works most effectively for them while preparing them to evolve as they grow.

Basic Sales System Premise -- Developing Better Results

Essentially the premise behind your company having a sales system is to deliver results focused on improvement of topline revenue, improving bottom line profitability and driving customer satisfaction. These results are drivers of internal and external behaviors that impact processes.

By establishing a solid and extensible and foundation for sales activities that position and enable your company to more precisely understand the buying, selling, and decision-making processes of your customers you attain more consistent, measurable and reliable contributions that solve customer problems while delivering improvements to top line revenue improvements and bottom-line cost results.

Small and medium enterprises are the lifeblood of the United States economy and are quite capable of contributing to the growth of an industry. For years, it has been recognized that these contributors generate a substantial number of new jobs, are very entrepreneurial, and are generally regarded as creative in their development of new products, services, or solutions. As robust as this group is, it is important to note that their continued success hinges upon sales. Without sales, they simply exhaust their financial resources and fade away.

Yet sales is an area that most small and medium enterprises need to have a focused, disciplined approach and understand the importance of applying proven processes to make their selling efforts more productive.

Investors in the small and medium enterprises will often ask questions about the composition of the sales leadership, but rarely ask questions about the sales processes the company has adopted, internalized, and demonstrate they have figured out how to focus on the achievement of sales. They assume that the sales management team will figure it out as the course of developing the business unfolds. Many of the most successful investors today have stated their concerns with regard to investing in small and medium companies that the companies must have in place a highly effective sales process that is manageable, and properly utilizes all of the resources available in the small company to impact sales.

Years ago the lead investors would looked primarily at the pedigree of sales leadership and that of the CEO, but often would fail to ask in depth questions about how the sales forecasts would be achieved and through what channels. Was there a workable sales system approach for developing the business, repeatedly and with relatively predictable cost structures behind each of the processes? The ramp up in revenue rarely matched the enthusiasm and optimism expressed in the business plans.

Today however, the conversations are much more rigorous about understanding the sales processes, the channel mix, the nature of the partnerships and alliances related to selling, and if the company has implemented a reliable, repeatable and consistent methods and the sales system to achieve sales performance.

If you were to ask a small or medium sized business what keeps them up at night followed by asking them if they think their sales are where they want them to be relative to their business plans. Do they stay awake specifically thinking about their selling processes? Do they spend time developing strategies for their prospective customers to win their business? Do they invest time in analyzing or brainstorming about the needs of their best choices for target accounts? Usually the answer is no. First, they worry about cash flow and financial commitments, and then they worry about all the rest of their issues. Although that is their reality, they do need to invest some time in understanding the role and the impact process can have on their success.

Working with or in small companies, I encounter a lot of resistance to implementing processes. Why? Because they view process as the antithesis of the reason they got into business in the first place, and they believe avoiding it to be a prime contributor to their success. The fact is that every selling organization who sells product, services, or solutions with any degree of complexity needs to have a methodical, repeatable, and well-ingrained set of processes to ensure they are not wasting time and that they are positioning themselves for success with those accounts they determine they *can win*. I emphasize *can win* because if they approach all prospective opportunities as must win without applying criteria that make sense they leave themselves open to failure.

What has changed over the years is the whole manner of selling. Although we often hear that change and our ability to respond to it is a determining factor to our success small businesses tend not to prepare for the impact on selling to their customers because they do not consider how change is impacting their customers and driving the customer's own internal decision-making processes.

I witness often that companies that get started with great ideas fail to connect the dots between their business plans and product, services or solutions directed at a prospective customer. It seems to be something so obvious yet is not addressed by many.

This book is about businesses of any size attempting to sell to customers of any size, and about what they need to do to increase their success beyond anything they have experienced to date. As a sales performance consultant, I strive to offer sound advice, provide guidance and recommendations to improve sales results for my clients. As a business consultant, I also explore the added dimensions of whether they have the right product and services portfolio for their chosen target markets, or if they have the right selling partners in addition to helping them develop a deeper understanding of their prospective customer's needs and the decision making processes related to buying.

The motivation behind the book is to help small businesses who might not think themselves capable of world-class sales performance. I hope that this book may change that view of small businesses in ways that raise questions about their processes, methods, and approach to driving more results from the limited resources they have at their disposal.

Observations

There is a tendency for companies to force fit the rules upon how they do business with their prospective clients. For the last ten years or so "business rules" and workflow systems were injected in to the corporate infrastructure in ways that lengthened the distance between the prospect and the people in the organization who were most likely to collaborate on the potential sale.

The types of sales systems we are discussing in this book have evolved over time from ad hoc routines in a great many instances. At some point they need serious examination and validation that they contribute to instead of detract from sales performance. Sine many have evolved without the benefit of planning it is strongly advisable to implement a more normalized and routine planning set of activities in your company.

Planning is by itself a continuous process, or at least it should be. Investing time and attention to a business plan and then shelving it for reasons of expediency defeat the purpose of having done the planning in the first place. But planning in any company involves many aspects of the company from human resources ensuring that there is an adequate pool of talent to be able to accomplish the mission, goals and objectives for the company, to those areas of the company usually having a high turnover, such as sales, where planning alone is not sufficient. You need to understand in greater detail why people are unproductive, or why they become disenchanted with the company.

Your business planning needs to involve all areas of the company. Having each area contribute still requires an in-depth understanding of how all the pieces fit and operate together. This brings up the subject of processes. The Figure (12) shown lists some functional areas of a hypothetical company with the understanding that at the top level is the business plan and all other areas take their lead from what is required of them as described in the business plan.

Each area will have their respective plans such as marketing, sales, manufacturing, and financial as examples. The plans for those areas need to not only reflect the core goals of the company but must translate them into actions and activities to show how they will be accomplished.

Figure (12) Contributors to the company business planning process.

Planning Activities

Business Plan Sections (each with goals, objectives, metrics)

- o Human Resources
- o Financial
- o Legal
- o Engineering
    - Manufacturing
    - Certifications
- o Product Management
    - Concept Design
    - Project Management
- o Marketing
    - Public Relations
    - Events
    - Collateral and Advertising
- o Sales
    - Opportunity Management
    - Competition
    - Direct
    - Channels
- o Support
    - Installation
    - Training
    - Help Desk

In too many companies to mention when I ask to see the business plan, I am shown a document that is far from living. It generally contains dated materials and does not reflect the reality of the current state of the business. However, the revenue and cost assumptions, the main drivers of the business are not tracking against the initial plans.

Some of those systems branched off into Customer Relationship Management systems while others became Enterprise Resource Planning and Management systems, and Product Lifecycle Management systems, while still others evolved into overly connective systems tying together the various groups in a company such as manufacturing, finance, inventory, sales, support, and others in ways that imposed additional process steps and more rules.

So, does your company have a formal planning process that drives both the development and maintenance of the business plan for the company and the plans for each group that detail how the goals, objectives, and other metrics will be met?

The end result of some plans are embodied in some more complex systems like SAP and Oracle and others that although they claim to bring order to the operation and make tracking the business plans more manageable they actually introduced gaps in the selling processes thus causing the selling process to be far more complex than it needed to be. Even a well-intended Customer Relationship Management (CRM) system such as Salesforce.com, SugarCRM or Microsoft Dynamics as mid-range applications tend to disrupt the business plans and the tracking that would indicate what areas of the process in the sales system need to be examined and refined or improved.

In the instance of Small and Medium sized organizations they benefit greatly from not being overly burdened with all that infrastructure and systems and yet they do benefit from understanding their processes and how to make them work even more effectively and efficiently than others so when they do grow the business rules and complex interactions are less. They stand a chance of being able to generate far more return on their sales and marketing efforts.

The counter-argument to this point is that management needs to make the micro-financial decisions to eliminate or minimize cost contribution to the price of the product, service, or solution. Without understanding the cost contributors in excruciating detail you cannot manage the successful delivery and profit on the product, service or solution delivered.

If you are defense contractor or sell to a defense contractor then it may be necessary to provide higher levels of detail and cost tracking due to regulations and government accounting practices. Otherwise, if your company wants to gain full control over the selling processes you might consider how to isolate the selling processes in ways that highlight the specific processes that contribute to the sale and assign value to them when reviewing them as a part of process improvement efforts.

There are Three Critical Factors that Contribute to Results.

Contrary to the popular belief that results can be fully planned for an achieved, reality demonstrates another set of results confused by diverse choices that could significantly increase or decrease the outcomes and entail certain risks generally outside of the expectations.

Results need to be driven and not left to fall in to chaotic behaviors. Achieving results requires all three of the critical factors listed are addressed and managed. Although they are straightforward, an investment in time to understand the interrelationship between them and vigilance is required to derive the most benefit from them including modifying them over time as needed.

- *Concepts* drive the most productive processes internally or externally.

- *Processes* improve the ability to communicate what is needed, when and why, and the sequence of actions required, to implement the process.

- *Discipline*, starts at the top and is required for any process or method to achieve results. An organization that does not understand process is ineffective short and long term.

Look at Figure (13) to observe the interrelationship of the component contributors.

Figure (13) Essential contributors to driving of results.

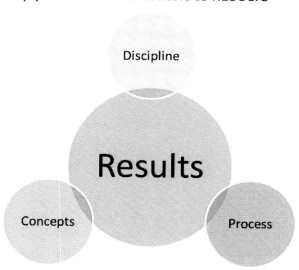

(3) Essential Contributors to RESULTS

Discipline

Results

Concepts

Process

Source: SW Consulting, 2011

Most processes work best if they are connected to a concept framework that can move towards achievement of a goal or an end result. The framework for those concepts may show the need to have multiple sub-processes or intermediate steps that are required to complete the implementation of the concept to move towards the desired result. In most business operations, the model is plan, execute, and assess the results to make improvements to the process.

Processes, as defined earlier, entail the sequencing of interdependent and linked procedures that convert inputs (such as data, material, parts, people resources and time, etc.) into outputs. These outputs then serve as inputs for the next stage until a known goal, or a result is reached. As we understand our processes through exploration and examination during discovery and analysis, we begin to see the areas, inter-relationships, and linkages that can be improved wherever possible.

Bringing order out of chaos requires discipline and leadership. The senior leadership team needs to understand the concepts, the processes, and the operational workings such that they cannot only champion them, but they will be able to provide guidance and advice to keep them pointed in the desired direction and towards the appropriate goals. Metrics, once determined, will tell the team what is working and what is not.

Observing organizations where the difference is between having working and manageable processes, or not, the highest results are achieved when all three of these factors are aligned after understanding their inter-relationships.

Questions: What Comes to Mind When I Say Sales System?

Whatever your answer to this question is the answer becomes the starting point for our analysis and development of ways that we can improve whatever that sales system and the processes associated with it looks like. The purpose of asking that question is to begin the process of uncovering as much information as we can about your sales system, whether it is in its infancy or well-developed, so that we can discover ways of improving and reinventing your sales system to deliver better results for your product, service, or solution, offered by your company.

Question: when I say sales pipeline or sales funnel comes to mind regarding your particular sales system, as it exists today?

Depending on your exposure to various selling methodologies, you may use the terminology pipeline or formal somewhat interchangeably when describing off the available opportunities that your company is pursuing actively. The key word here is active. If there is no activity associated with the opportunity to the senior pipeline or funnel then perhaps it may not be worth pursuing, or it might be stuck somewhere in that selling process and that further analysis and understanding of why might be in order.

Question: what does the word qualified or qualifying mean in your organization?

Again, depending on your exposure to various selling methodologies the definition of qualified or the process of qualifying may mean something different to each of the members of your senior leadership team and to your sales force. At some point, most companies need a strict definition of both what constitutes a qualified opportunity and a description of what must be done to qualify a potential opportunity as it relates to your specific product, service, or solution.

Question: From the selling perspective, what does the phrase "product focused" mean to you, your executive team, and all of those in your organizations that sell or support sales?

A great many companies today do not consider themselves to be product focused, but may consider that they are very solution focused. There are several distinctions to draw here. The first is a general understanding that while what you produce may be a product or a service how it is configured, wrapped with additional services, or some other value enhancement, that constitutes a solution.

Second as we will discover the solution that we formulate may or may not match the concepts or image of the solution that will work best from each of the many participants involved in the buying decision making process.

Question: Assuming you have a business plan, can anybody draw a process roadmap to the customer, that points to a consistent, reliable, and productive sales result?

The challenge of great many companies have regardless of size will be starting at the customer and working backwards towards matching up with a product, service, or solution, that will solve their problems, meet their needs, and deliver the results that they need in a way that results in a win-win for everyone.

All too often companies that are strictly quota and revenue driven may seek to short circuit or bypass the necessary steps to ensure a significantly higher probability of success. What happens is they fail in the attempt because they did not understand the customer's concept image, and how to connect their product, service, or solution to the prospective people influencing buying who make that buying decision within their company.

You can assess a great deal, about how your organization operates by asking the simple questions and then discussing the answers and the possible consequences of both the question and the answers.

Some additional sample questions to ask people in your organization, and to then collectively review the answers as related to:

- Are there any specific sales plans of record and in use throughout the organizations? Are they tied in to an overall business plan/strategic plan?

- How long does a sale take and who is involved (number of calls, time, evaluations, references, demonstrations, negotiations, and the people involved and are there enough people able to contribute their time to the selling process from start to finish)?

- What issues are the clients trying to solve and does our solution address those issues directly and uniquely when compared to the completion?

- What process do you use to track progress (funnel, daily sales reviews, formal or informal reporting, CRM opportunity listing discussions, back-of-the-envelope approach, etc.)?

- What metrics do you used to define progress and success, and do they tie back somehow to the planning process?

- Do your sales and marketing groups understand who is responsible for what when and how to align marketing and sales efforts for maximum impact to address the customer's concept of a "best" solution for them?

- Are the portfolio of products, services, and solutions clearly emblazoned in the minds of all the participants in the sales and marketing processes?

The Old-fashioned Traditional Sales Cycle Approach to Selling

In the more traditional sales cycle approach to selling, a great many popular how- to books would lead you to believe that for a moderately complex products or resource solution the approach might appear to follow the format using the following familiar steps.

(1) Receive an inquiry

(2) Qualify and quantify the details

(3) Arrange the appointment

(4) Prepare for the customer appointment and visit them

(5) Arrange a discovery survey

(6) Conduct survey and evaluate the findings

(7) Formulate solutions and arrange presentation of proposal

(8) Conduct the presentation meeting, remove immediate obstacles, close the sale

I would say that today if you follow these eight steps your results would be less than stellar. What used to work in terms of old selling approaches does not work today or it works in such a haphazard "hit and miss" way with a low yield on results that people who have practiced it for years may cling to it for comfort only. More modern approaches to the selling method, depend upon your type of products, or the solution, and can be developed, refined, and implemented successfully, to become a part of the routine practice and conduct of company business.

Therefore, my advice is to urge you to learn a lot more about sales methodologies and why they work, and explore ways to implement either portions of a method or a complete methodology depending upon your needs and what your expectations are for results.

Watch Out For Conventional Wisdom and Thinking

During this exploratory journey to discover how your sales system works, there is a central theme. To discover is to ask questions about the information that you have, or do not have available to you, that you need to make decisions. You need to decide whether, or not, you will adopt, and internalize a more complete sales system as an approach that can be enhanced and improved upon through continuous analysis. You must determine which metrics will indicate success, or failure, and pinpoint what needs to be changed.

We will also explore brainstorming and strategizing as techniques to determine the best appropriate actions required to achieve results that our selected metrics will confirm.

Conventional wisdom and thinking however, even though a well-known phrase, may suggest that truly the definition of conventional means to continuously evolve in ways that improve results, obtained through a variety of newer thinking processes, and therefore a dynamic approach and not one that is static.

As business professionals, we would clearly like to achieve outstanding results for the efforts that we invest in any process. The values and expectations placed upon our sales organization in the selling processes that they use may have originated from traditional old-style selling methods, and we must always be vigilant to make sure that we keep them up to date and accommodate new selling ideas to keep pace with our customers and their buying decision making process.

It may seem like old history but traditional selling typically in the 1960s and 1980s timeframe is still found today as a method in companies. The reason you will still find traditional selling is most likely that the sale itself is not a coming more complex than when compared and contrasted to modern selling which needs to accommodate a greater degree of complexity. Traditional selling relied upon a highly standardized product whereas more modern selling deals with mass customization, or a highly customized and flexible product tailoring the product and service into a solution.

The sales function identified with traditional selling was that there is a sales person, more modern view of selling as a sales function is performed more by a strategic business manager or some other title, and a backdrop of additional subject matter experts that are there to assist with selling the complexity. In the traditional selling approach, the salesperson as a seller has product knowledge and based on experience how to apply the product to a great many situations.

Today, with more modern selling approaches, the salesperson needs to uncover strategic knowledge of customers' opportunities and know the implications and opportunities resulting from the application of their product, service, or solution, as it relates directly to the customer's expectations for results.

Another difference between traditional selling and the more modern selling approaches is that let's be clear prospective customers are all a lot better informed about potential products services and solutions that they might consider.

Clearly, the Internet and the other special-interest groups have stimulated the flow of knowledge to help make better decisions in almost every industry.

In a more traditional selling model a salesperson could state a value that represented what was judged according to the selling price as to be fair or not. Today's approach is to place a value now relates to a great many additional measures and metrics were value is assessed according to the costs to the customer and the financial implications such as return on investment.

In some companies, it is the impact on the corporation capabilities and other aspects that previously were not considered such as corporate social responsibility, or the prior impact of selected solutions, and any discussion of ethics and/or corporate culture impact. Value concepts today, have a completely different meaning when compared to the past.

Over time, the selling function itself has evolved from being purely a transaction that is effectively one-step removed from our concept of Stone Age and medieval bartering. Then appeared models that helped establish relationships and build trust popularized by Dale Carnegie among others, evolving from the early 1900s where continuity, consistency sustainability and other aspects of how a product, service or solution dealt with issues requiring trust be established with efforts expended to maintain that trust.

The greatest impact arising from the 1950s onward has been due to changes in management practices and the availability of information that helps make decisions a lot more easily based upon the fact or at least upon an analysis so that people could feel comfortable with a solution that matched what their analysis of what was really needed. These newer types of interrelationships have become more involved as the supply-chain model as has evolved.

The impact of both technology and training greatly accelerated the flow of new products and services necessitating better information handling. Information became a priority when any company is making a buying decision. Over the last couple of decades, the concept of the more sophisticated type of relationship building was transformed as buying roles were identified.

With the increasing fast pace of change both in the organization of customers and the markets they serve became more concerned about finding suppliers who would work with them in ways that could improve their time to market or the quality of the product to build differentiation from their competitors. Today, the evolving concept of formal partnerships is that they require an enormous amount of understanding, and cooperation, between both the seller and the buying organization at the highest levels.

A quiet revolution has been occurring with both the science, the art of sales itself based on the relationship trust and information handling associated with selling, and the continuous evolution of partnering arrangements as it applies to both supplying providers and also channels of sales that a company can use to reach additional customers.

The more modern approach indicates that there are sellers who are better equipped, trained, and have the ability to understand a customers' needs more sustainably and that we determine for those selling companies that do this in ways that make them more successful we identify as world-class and practicing sales best practices.

Sales best practices can only occur when you have excellent communication, real models that value the relationship and partnership between the selling of the buying organizations and that this concept of a win-win results from all parties benefiting from joint ventured development of understanding their needs and supplying those needs in the best manner possible.

Another textbook version of selling that is often quoted is identified as "seven steps of the sale." The seven steps terminology has been around a great many years and in recent years has achieved a much more sophisticated interpretation and application when we discussed selling processes. Recent interpretation requires that we expand and interpret more slowly and with flexibility certain key activities that comprise the selling process.

Those key activity steps are:

(1) Preparation -- the planning, researching, and strategizing, and approach to a prospective customer

(2) Introduction -- defining the key issues that will be important during the opening comments trying to establish a relationship between a prospective customer in the salesperson, and to establish credibility on the part of the salesperson

(3) Questioning -- the inherent ability to identify needs, ask questions that uncover answers that are needed, and to establish a horrible and intellectual rapport and trust with any prospective customer

(4) Presentation -- this is less about the lengthy PowerPoint presentation and more about how to properly convey an explanation of the solution as determined through conversations with the prospective buyer

(5) Overcoming obstacles and objections -- fundamentally before we can overcome objections we need to understand what the basic issues of our, that may be causing fear and a misunderstanding of the amount of risk involved in the decision-making process, and how we present our information and fine tune our solution to better match the concept image of the prospective customer

(6) Bringing to closure -- if effective communication has been established but concept of closing in order requires that both parties are in agreement and make a commitment and confirmation that they both understand what the solution that is being proposed can do for the buyer and why

(7) Follow-up -- increasingly after a sale we find that continued engagement in maintaining and developing further the relationship between the now customer and to work with that customer to fulfill all obligations and complete the win-win.

Those listed seven steps of the traditional sale model are considered by most to be relatively rigid as an approach to selling. The same can be said of many other sales methods that we find that are being practiced today, but they all require discipline at the core of their practice. Solution often talked about by those same people, address such key attributes as flexibility, accommodation, and improved communications.

Selling Is Personal (except when the Internet is involved)

If you attempt to generate interest or to start the sales process using the Internet you may have experienced several drawbacks from just letting prospective clients bump into your particular solution and then configure what they need within the confines of your product, service or solution.

Self-diagnosis and self-solution selling makes a lot of assumptions that people can identify what they need from what you promote on your website. There are, as experience points out, many selling process traps that your company needs to understand, and avoid to improve upon sales. Especially when using the Internet.

A long time ago, I used XEROX Professional Selling Skills courses to teach and mentor fledgling sales people and some who had sold for many years. It was all about the art of conversation patterns with prospective customers. The hardest sales folks to sell on the concepts were the older established sales person. Why? Because they assessed change was not a good thing for them and had ruled out the possibility that changing anything would alter negatively the outcome of a potential sale.

Of the hundreds of folks I have taught, I can relate to you that the ones who were open to new ideas, and considered themselves as change agents, because after all selling is about impacting a customers' environment, were more effective in their role. They agreed change is necessary, and became far more effective, and able to improve results from their investment in the new thoughts and methods. It is not about the method taught, as it is about what you will be doing with it. Can you make "change" work for you?

What Miller Heiman, the Sales Performance Company, has demonstrated for a great many years is that the fundamental truths arising from early research into selling and buying processes continue to have outstanding value. These are validated through observations and are not theoretical but practical for anyone who sells to improve their game. Keep that thought in mind. It is not theory, its practical understanding of the buying and selling processes that produces results.

For example, we ask sales people attending any of the Miller Heiman workshops to bring live examples of an opportunity they are trying to win. We then apply the elements of Strategic Selling and when they walk out of the workshop, they are armed with a concrete strategy to win the opportunities they brought to class. They leave with the potential to win by bettering understanding the elements that constitute what they need to know to close the sale.

In most instances, they are able to apply what they learned immediately to drive sales. Again, no theories, just practical guidance to better organize their thoughts, strategies, and actions to improve their chances of winning. We see it work every day in subsequent follow up calls to ask them how things are progressing with the opportunities.

Another concept to consider is that we want to focus our energies on the actual opportunity, by understanding it better and then developing strategies to win it. The approach must be straightforward and very easy to grasp how that can be a benefit of the approach to help sales professionals. In a small business just think of the improvement in sales that can be achieved from being better organized and positioned to win those opportunities we want to focus on.

Decision Making Processes -- Corporate and Individual Processes

High performance sales people understand that in order to win business it is imperative to understand the decision-making process within a company considering their particular product, service, or solution. Best practices in selling goes one step further, by identifying the most successful salespeople also understand that each individual involved in the purchase decision-making process has their own internal decision-making process.

If you have ever purchased a large or costly item, think about how you spent your time figuring out which products, or if you researched a solution to purchase and why. Take for example buying a new car. Just looking around in the marketplace we know that there are lots of choices and options when it comes to auto purchases it is in fact a complex selling situation compounded by personal choice and taste as well as technical or specifications for reliability or fuel mileage and reliability with regard to repairs and lower insurance costs. When we walked into the auto showroom, rarely do we have a clear notion of the final concept of what our purchase will look like?

The myriad number of choices for options for equipment, colors, types of vehicles and where we wish to purchase the vehicle and determining as well the financing options all tend to form a large cloud of confusion for every buyer and makes it hard to determine what exactly a "win" for buyer would look like based on all those variable.

How we arrive at the purchasing decision in the case of some purchases such as automobiles, or a high ticket item like a wide screen television, even though it looks like it is emotional and tied strictly to taste, yet there are also some factors involved that people consider during their decision-making process.

The astute car salesperson for example, understands that when an individual walks into their showroom that they may have done some research and may therefore have been farther along in their decision-making process. Nevertheless, the salesperson asks where are they in their hunt for a new vehicle, what do they know about the current models, and what are their thoughts about a particular vehicle that will ideally satisfy all of their requirements.

I think of the example where a husband and wife go to a showroom and they are looking at a sports car on the showroom floor. If the salesperson approaches them, thinking that all they are interested in sports car, they may ultimately not establish a good credible bond with those prospective buyers because they have overlooked perhaps an obvious piece of information.

We do not know unless we communicate effectively, and have conversations with any prospective buyer to learn what their interests, needs, and their reasons for considering purchasing. This is specifically about understanding the decision-making process, and how it becomes a critical, and distinctive factor, between good salespeople, and exceptional salespeople. In it they understand both the corporate decision-making process and who's involved for making a purchase of a product, service, or solution, and the individual decision-making process that each of the people involved in making a purchasing decision have the goes through to arrive at the best choice for their particular needs.

Problem Analysis vs. Decision Making

While we are on the subject it is important to differentiate between problem analysis and decision making processes. Your company will have some approach to a problem analysis and decision making process that you use to manage your business. It may be formal or more loosely implemented as an informal process.

Consider that your prospective clients are also using an analogous problem analysis and decision-making process in their business and likely have a variant of that they use for purchasing decisions.

Your company and your prospective clients both must perform a problem analysis first which involves gathering information that will be used in the decision making process. When referring to the distinct process of problem analysis there are generalized guidelines to improve the process including:

- Identify and inventory the internal and external information sources available to you that will contribute to the analysis.

- Analyzing the results or performance and assessing what the results should be against what was planned.

- The identification of problems means we look for the deviations from the anticipated results or metrics.

- In order to address a problem it must be precisely identified, described and the relationship to other processes noted.

- The objective of problem analysis is to identify what change occurred and why.

- A frame of reference from past performance or expected results aids in assessing those things that have changed versus those that have not.

- Change in and of itself may not be the problem, and the most likely cause of a problem will be the one that is explained by the facts uncovered during review.

Decision-making requires that we explore the options, with several choices to choose from, and that alternative actions be considered before we make the decision. Attributes of decision-making are:

- There need to be objectives and they need to be established first.

- Those objectives need to be classified and ranked according to their priority or degree of potential impact.

- A number of internal viewpoints must be considered from all participants in the decision making process and with assessing the impact of the decision.

- Brainstorming is needed to discuss, develop, and evaluate alternative actions.

- Any alternative must be compared and evaluated against the objectives.

- A clear alternative that appears to satisfy all of the objectives is the most probable decision.

- The most probable or tentative decision is more rigorously evaluated for any possible negative consequences on other objectives or processes.

- Once the tentative decision is selected and the corresponding actions taken then monitoring prevents adverse impact consequences and if appropriate triggers another round of problem analysis and decision making again. It is an iterative process.

- Keep in your thought processes that how you make decision and how your prospective clients make decision concerning your product, service, or solution both require an understanding and acknowledgement that these processes can dramatically impact results, both your business results, and your client's specific buying decision-making process.

Specific to observing the model process for buying decision making at a minimum the following steps occur within the buying organization.

- It generally starts when there is an event, a trigger, that sets in motion some problem analysis approach, that analyzes and determines a problem exists.

- The persons that are impacted and involved in the decision-making progress gather information from internal and external sources including the results of their problem analysis. At this point, some persons will be charged with collecting external sources of possible solutions.

- The appropriately impacted people involved begin a personal synthesis of information, beliefs, attitudes, fears, and motivations to for a concept of the solution to the problem. This is a cognitive and bias aspect of the decision making process.

- Collaboratively or collectively, each contributor to the decision making provides their assessment of the best solution and formulate a decision from the available information from potential supplier sources.

- At this point in the process, they entertain additional alternatives and thoughts through divergent thinking to consider the possibilities and consequences of the choices under investigation.

- The decision to purchase is either put on hold or made to proceed, and the appropriate supplier selected (or not if the solution is developed internally) with the intent of entering into a detailed purchase agreement.

- The purchase occurs followed by some implementation and transformation of results that correct or improve the problem being addressed.

- There is a period of positive post-purchase behavior or buyer's remorse (cognitive dissonance, they realize what they bought is not what they envisioned the solution to be) requiring some level of communications or resolution.

To embrace and understand these concepts and steps to the problem solving and decision making processes your company will be on the road to developing world-class best practices for improving your sales performance and with the operational efficiency in your daily operations.

The Importance of Communications – External and Internal

We take it for granted one of the most important aspects of selling, which is achieving optimum communications. In a truly customer centric selling situation, we have to put ourselves in the place of the customer to understand a great many things that we might otherwise have not even thought about.

We do this by formulating our communications, the conversations that you are going to have with the prospective customers. When you enter into productive communications, you are engaging in a form of consultative selling where your goal is to achieve a win-win for both parties.

An interesting aspect of communications involves word choices. Observe to people from the same area of expertise talking. They use terms and acronyms that they are completely familiar with using. They are after all subject matter experts. But when a third person is introduced in to the conversation if that new member does not know the terminology or the significance attached to the terms then there is immediately cause to think carefully about how to achieve understanding.

Quite often companies selling new solutions will use state of the art terms or their own branded terms that they know quite well but others may not. This potential communication hazard requires that we be mindful it exists and always cross check meaning and interpretations with anyone, we meet for an effective conversation to take place.

You need to have the thinking ability to use a process that allows you to see the problem from another viewpoint, from the point of view of your prospective customer. This is so you are more fully able to understand the concepts and terminology in their language. Then, to translate that information into the specific needs and concerns, so that you can in fact respond by addressing each of their concepts and concerns. If you put yourself in their place, you will improve your chances of winning the business especially when compared to the responses from other sources of competition.

During the course of the conversations with your prospective buyers you need to uncover and identify what they feel are the key issues and concerns of each of the parties involved in the purchase decision making process. To the extent that you are acting as a consultant helping your prospective client you will learn what results the client needs to achieve and tailor your solution accordingly so that you both mutually arrive at acceptable solution.

Along the way again in the role of a consultative salesperson, your task is to help with the identification and selection of options that will improve or enhance the outcome of the decision to purchase. You can only achieve Win-Win solutions with Win-Win procedures and processes.

Win-Win is not a personality technique or just a catch phrase. It is a total paradigm of conversation and interaction. Therefore, your goal in the communication process will be to obtain information from each of those people involved in the decision-making process and to understand through asking questions and getting information whether or not your product, service, or solution, can deliver the desired results were not. You must also work with the buying influence to achieve commitment to move the process towards completion.

Again, during the communication processes you will need to uncover any what might be called basic issues that the buyer has. These could be fears, reservations, or experience from past purchases that is causing them to hesitate and possibly consider alternatives that you might not know about. Obviously, a communication involves two parties it involves a dialogue but more so it involves whole lot of listening on the part of the salesperson to truly understand and grasp what are the prospective customer's needs.

Consider that several groups in your organization need to be aware and have at various times the need to communicate with existing and prospective clients. A functional communication process entails the source group initiating an actions or communications with a target who is an individual within prospective or existing client, a channel partner, or collaborator for example.

They need a response to be able to gather and process information and to make decisions about what needs to be done now or in the future to improve the situation.

Functioning Loop Processes For Each Group

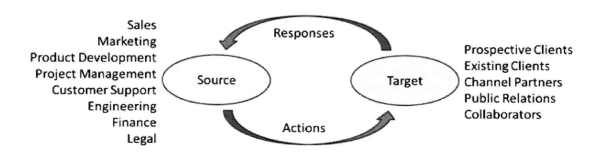

Source: SW Consulting, 2011

Nevertheless, sometimes any one of the source side contributors generates and action or communication to the targeted audience a response is not forthcoming. What caused the breakdown in communications becomes a more important consideration. Without a response, taking further actions poses a potential risk. Making decisions in the absence of information can compound the current situation leading to a loss of client or the loss of a current sale.

Failed Loop Processes For Each Group #1

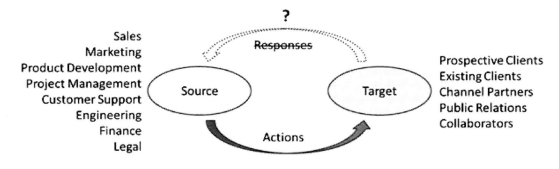

Source: SW Consulting, 2011

Another scenario is where the prospective client or existing customer is in fact communication with the various source side parties but nothing is generated in the way of an action. This failed loop process is dangerous for the selling company. It potentially shows the target side an unresponsive supplier of products, services, or solutions. This failure is usually disruptive to the relationship, and it results in a loss of credibility and trust, and may causes the target to consider other more responsive suppliers.

Failed Loop Processes For Each Group #2

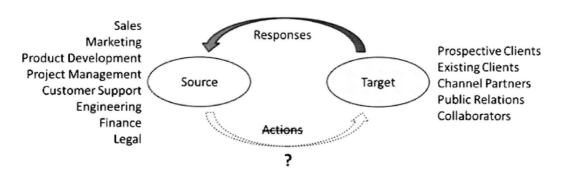

Source: SW Consulting, 2011

The bottom line is you need to understand the source-target communications process and the need to pay careful attention to it because it can greatly impact the outcome of sales efforts both short term and longer term.

How Well Positioned Are You?

When we are talking about position and positioning are not talking about how in the market place we up here. What we are referring to is in the eyes of our prospective customer how do we up here to meet their requirements, solve their problems, and deliver results that they desire. Therefore, the first task when you are communicating with your prospective customer becomes a series of dialogues to determine does your solution will fit the customers view, or their mental image, of what they believe will produce the desired result they need. A second question is that you need to determine in the eyes of your customer how well does your solution match they are image of the ideal solution and what evidence do you have two show that you are the best fit supplier.

The difference between customers and influential people involved in the decision-making process is that it is easy to determine on the selling side who needs to be involved in the successful pursuit of the sale, but it is less easy to determine who was involved with the sale on the client side. You can imagine inside of every company is they have a number of people who contribute to the buying decision for any product, service, or solution, that the company chooses to buy.

This buying process that goes on within a company involves a number of influencers who participate in and contribute to the decision-making process. We know from analyzing a great number of sales situations that the salesperson who fails to identify the influencers, their needs, and what they contribution to the buying process, becomes less successful than those who do pay attention to address each of the influencers needs.

A salesperson as a change agent as we have mentioned. However, as a change agent what they need to understand is the impact of the change on each of these people influencing buying that is contributing to the buying decision making. Within the company, there are a number of people, who participate in this purchase decision-making process. Each one of them plays a different role and has different criteria that need to be met in order for them to endorse any particular product, service, or solution, over another.

What matters to those people influencing buying is a thought process that they go through to assess and understand what differentiates one product, service, or solution, from another. These people influencing buying also need to contribute to the internal knowledge to help the key decision-makers, the ones who control the release of the funds and to prepare them to make the final decision.

Think of the company as a giant cloud, and in the cloud there are a number of participants. These people are influencing the buying, and each one of them is contributing to the decision-making process. In a simple sale, there are probably not as many of the people influencing the buying involved, and the degree to which they have requirements that must be met are less stringent.

Conversely, in a more complex sale, not only are there more people influencing buying contributing to the decision-making process but they have additional concerns viewers requirements and criteria that they will use to evaluate whatever product, service, or solution, that the company is considering buying and why it would be a good purchase.

Truly exceptional salespeople understand that there are a number of these people influencing buying and that they must identify them, communicate with them, and help them to refine their image of what the product, service, or solution, looks like. try to imagine that the salesperson is able to pull together a room full of these people influencing buying and in the traditional model would proceed to go through a PowerPoint presentation were some dissertation where they talk to at no ad nausea mop out the features and benefits of their particular products or resource solution.

The mental picture that's conjured up by this image shows the difficulty that the salesperson will have been satisfying the individual requirements for each of those decision-makers. As very few people think exactly alike because of their experience, knowledge, and opinions about which would be a good purchase or not, or have an impression of you or your company that may influence their decision. The task of the salesperson becomes very daunting in a group dynamic and is therefore to be discouraged because contrary to the popular belief of getting everybody on the same pages this is not the case and not the dynamic of what occurs in a group meeting.

The salesperson needs to work more methodically, and harder, to single out those people who have concerns and those that have issues with their particular products, or resource solution, and whether or not they can be satisfied by what is being proposed once the need is understood. This situational awareness requires knowledge and intuition.

Our sales system approach says that the salesperson will engage in dialogue, communication between them and the individual people influencing buying, to determine the need the sense of urgency and the concerns that the particular people influencing buying have. The salesperson will then bring that information to the attention of those people in their organization that may be subject matter experts, or engineers, or finance and other support people who can assist the salespeople with formulating a solution that more clearly matches the concept that the individual people influencing buying have.

The Customer's Concept – Repeat: Theirs, Not Yours.

Customers search for ideal solutions and make decisions once they have some idea what that ideal solution looks like. As a salesperson with a traditional background, my experience was always to learn all about my product, service, or solution and all of the features and benefits of that product to show how it could be useful to any prospective clients that I would engage in conversation with. I became very adept at picking and emphasizing the features and benefits and why they would be important potentially to any buying influence for any company. Over time, and through a lot of trial and error, I was able to determine that my knowledge of features and benefits although necessary, turned out to be inappropriate to dump on every single buying influencer who is contributing to making a purchasing decision.

What I observed, and learned early in my selling career, was that by understanding more precisely what each of those people who influence the buying was all about, their needs, their fears and reservations, of specifications that they needed to have met, and the sense of why or what trigger event was causing them to make a purchasing decision. I came to realize relatively easily that it was this concept this mental image of what the best solution was that each of those buying influences had that was my secret weapon. To be more successful both the seller and buyer need to be on the same page for thoughts and ideas and effectively communicating with each other.

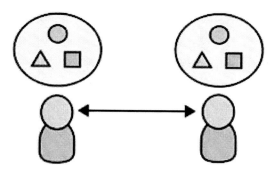

The sales process is not full of secret weapons, tricks and magic bullets, or additional ways to hypnotize prospective clients into buying your solution. It does involve starting and building productive communications though and making observations that might otherwise be overlooked. What I am referring to is the fact that this concept or mental image of the solution within each of the buyers who influence the decision to purchase is something that is transient, in need of refinement and subject to change as more information and interactions with other buyers with influence in the course of the decision-making. It takes precise communicating to synchronize the understanding for all parties involved in the process.

One obvious question to be asked is, are prospective customer and we using the same terms to describe the situation, and the concept of their needs? Can we understand their concept of just what the product, service, or solution looks like that they perceive is the best fit for them at this moment in time?

I am sitting in a room with one of the prospective buyers, and I am engaged in conversation with that buyer. I am listening carefully after I ask a question to start the dialogue, to get them to tell me as much as possible about the concept of what they need, why they need it, and what they were attempting to accomplish with it. Or if there were other things about the situation that I need to understand that could help me as the salesperson propose better solutions to help them accomplish what needed to be done.

I learned through prior experiences, that it was not always my products, or my resource solution with its features and benefits that mattered so much. What mattered more was my ability to understand better, and to portray precisely how my solution could in fact, resolve their particular problem by meeting needs, and delivering to them the type of results that they required of their preferred vendor. It is a learned process to be sure.

Back in the 1980s, I worked for a company that was a pioneer in telecommunications equipment. The company for years was a primary competitor to AT&T in all areas of telephone equipment. This company had a reputation for producing advanced and reliable communications equipment, and was instrumental in bringing to market many new breakthroughs in telecommunications. I was hired as a part of an elite team of industry specialists to help launch and sell an entirely new product.

This new product was very advanced compared to what was available in the marketplace at that time. Not only was the product clearly superior to anything on the market but it was clear to prospective clients but that product addressed a great many areas where they had needs, and held the promise of being able to deliver significant increases in productivity while reducing the costs of buying communications equipment.

There were two problems with this new product. One problem was it was as recognized by the prospective clients themselves, a very sophisticated piece of equipment that could in fact solve a lot of their potential problems. However, not all customers had a number of the problems that needed to be solved all at one time with one solution. The second problem was that the product for all its sophistication, was an extremely complicated product to manufacture and manufacturing was unable to produce a reliable product.

So here, we have a buying contradiction in terms presented by a telecommunications product. The product was the exact opposite of what you buy a telecom product for, which is for its reliability, but this one was too sophisticated for the clients and therefore they felt that somehow there must be hidden costs, or that this product would be obsolete very quickly because the complexity would need to evolve further. The clients were right.

My fellow sales people and I as a part of our elite team sales operations were able to pre-sell many millions of dollars of equipment on the premise that it would work reliably reduce costs and greatly enhance the customer's ability to improve their communications capabilities. We did our job. We were able to identify those clients that were willing to take the risk and adopt this cutting edge solution image that we put before them as being very helpful and productive for them to use. The point in mentioning this is in rare circumstances where you have a product or service or solution that sets a new paradigm for customer expectations you have to find those customers that are willing to take the risk before the product has essentially earned a positive reputation for reliability for cost or savings for proof points that are real.

Let us talk about your pipeline or follow of opportunities. One big advantage of having a sales system is that you can optimize for selling time using the follower pipeline model. Let us compare the traditional approach of the sales system approach. The traditional approach starts with the universe of potential opportunities we are there is an audience of prospective clients but we have not identified who would be likely candidates for our products or resource solution.

This universe consists of an initially everybody without distinction for whether or not they can benefit from the use of our particular solution. As we search through this universe by whatever means we use either marketing or sales call, mailing, advertising, or other means to seek them out, we need to consider how big the universe is and how to optimize our scarce resources to pinpoint those that are more probable or likely suspects in that universe.

In the traditional approach, we move from looking at the universe and trying to sub select from the universe those who we consider prospects. Our marketing department may have been able to produce leads from our website, advertising, e-mail campaigns, public relations, or through some activity that resulted in a call to action in action taken by a prospective customer that we identify as the lead.

These are followed up on by various people, it could be a call center, or it could be the sales professional himself or herself. Appointments are set, and usually visits will result in presentations after some number of visits per salesperson may feel they have been qualified enough to deliver a proposal.

After some initial discussions, and a few more additional clarifying discussions we move towards the negotiating close of the opportunity, and then the delivery and follow-ups. This traditional approach from start to finish as a win-loss analysis or a win-loss ratio associated with it. The ratios for many companies are typically very low.

The main reason why the prospecting and lead generation on the front end does not always match the specific application of the solution for the product, or the service that our company has to sell is that we are most likely not using good selection criteria for identifying the prospective customers. In this instance, our marketing efforts are generating leads that go nowhere. A common problem in business is the expectation that just be performing some marketing or sales activity that leads will appear. That assumption gets a great many companies in to a time wasting scenario where the investment in marketing and the return are not what is needed to sustain the business. The messaging or the information developed for marketing purposes may appeal to many people, but they were not the people influencing the buying, or are experiencing the pain that is making them search for a solution. This can be remedied.

In the sales system approach, we define the universe the same, but applied against that universe we develop a best customer profile. The best customer profile consists of either current or former clients, that we judge to be good customers. Those customers may have experienced the best of a win-win situation with us, or they purchased our products and our relationship is rather tenuous but nonetheless they purchased from us. Marketing best practices also does a more precise job with regard to matching the specific information needs of those with a pressing problem that needs to be solved.

Therefore, we determine what are our customer profiles look like by selecting criteria that we had data to show what constitutes a best customer. Once we have determined that best customer profile, we test against the universe that profile, and pinpoint those prospective customers that we think are a good match. For those that are matched we use the resources that are available to us either in the form of marketing campaigns, or telephone campaigns, to generate additional points of contact within the targeted best customer profile.

Additional research on our part into market activities and the need for our product, service, or solution, will help us in refining our best customer profile continuously so that we may increase the accuracy of the leads generated. Some organizations rely strictly upon their website to produce prospects and leads. In the sales system approach because the salesperson needs to know a lot about a particular company and needs to use the best customer profile that when the lead for a price that is received they need to compare and contrast that best customer profile against the information that is collected for that particular lead. Once a lead has been identified, the salesperson needs to plan for any further communication or interaction with that prospective customer. The preparation is required will consists of thinking about the customer's situation, events that are impacting them, data from various research sources such as Google or Hoover's to better understand the situation that is faced by that prospective customer.

The astute salesperson will recognize that they need to do their homework in advance of making any calls by trying to identify those issues and/or questions that are likely to be a trigger event within that prospective customer. A well-prepared salesperson with questions also will be able to generate far more interest that is precise by understanding early on, how best to proceed with that particular contacted buying influencer.

With the information learned from research plus having conversations with the prospective people influencing buying to determine what their image or vision is for a solution we can now start to strategize what a win for both will look like.

The winner has to accommodate the result that is desired by the buying influencer, and must accommodate other aspects related to the sense of urgency, and if there are other, basic issues and red flags present in the customer. The more we learn and the more we strategize, with the information that we have and continue to accumulate, we start to understand the customer's concept and can move towards our consultative approach being able to improve the communication if more fully understand the people influencing buying concept of what is needed.

The salesperson who has prepared, who has done the strategy based on information that has been accumulated through conversations, and who understood the customer's concept, will be able to propose a solution that more closely matches the image of the solution. Additionally, they will be able to help the prospective customer in the refining of their image to determine what the best solution will look like. After presenting the information to the buying influencer and other people influencing buying who are involved in the purchase and decision-making process we will better understand what needs to be done to complete the sale at this point.

When we have convinced the buying influencer who has control over the funds and the other people influencing buying that are solution in deed solves their particular problem then we can move towards negotiating and closing the opportunity. Next comes the delivery, implementation, and follow-up that is required to continue to develop a relationship, and to yield a win-win for all parties concerned. Using the sales system approach, the win-loss analysis looks considerably different. Why? Essentially because we start with a better universe of refined, prospective customers, when using our best customer profile, and we move the opportunity forward through better internal communication, and an understanding of what is driving the people that are influencing buying to consider that our solution is the best one for them, and make a purchase.

What is also interesting is when comparing the two different methods, that companies practicing a hands-off, or unstructured sales system approach, can run into all manner of roadblocks and hurdles that interfere with closing the business. Alternatively, that unstructured introduces delays, which cause the loss of the business due to the company demonstrated degree of responsiveness. Those organizations with a well-developed sales system, and sales processes, will achieve greater sales results that are more manageable, consistent, and achieved through better utilization of appropriate supporting resources.

The Importance of Perspective

The concept of perspective playing a role in the buying and selling processes requires that we follow the guidance learned from putting ourselves in the place of our prospective clients. Walk in their shoes so to speak. We can learn so much from the simple perspective shift and yet it is an underutilized technique.

For many of my clients and in my professional sales life I witness that when I can see from their perspective I am usually better able to understand and address their needs. Consider we need to practice this technique frequently when engaging clients with new products, services, or solutions.

It is true your perspective matters where appropriate, but the most significant perspective is clearly that of the prospective client. Always keep that uppermost in your mind and discussions.

Examples of Perspective

If we perform an analysis of how well our viewpoint and customers viewpoints align we should be able to determine how large the gap between these viewpoints is, and help us formulate a plan for reducing the gap. Frequently analysts cite the Magic quadrant of Gartner where we segment results into four boxes or quadrants of the possibilities.

This method is frequently aligned with strengths, weaknesses, opportunities, and threats assessments. Comparing differing viewpoints is used to test whether differentiation is being recognized by prospective customers. The discussion of differentiation is always in the eyes of the customer, and it is critical to understand their viewpoint and perception of our company, our solution and of the people involved in the selling process.

Likewise, understanding the competition is also critical from the perspective of the customer's viewpoint. As a part of our workshop, we will perform an assessment of alignment between the customer's view of our competition, and our view of the competition.

Why is this perspective so important? Because if we perceive our competition as weak or ineffective, and our customer, the people influencing buying, perceive our competition differently especially if they perceive the competitor as stronger in some areas, this is valuable information that we need to tailor our strategy and tactics to respond to the situation.

Therefore, there really are two questions that we need to ask of our prospective customer's perspective, the first how they view our company, the second how they view other alternative providers of the product, service, or solution. These two differing perspectives, and the gap between them, define how much work we have ahead of us to win the business or to improve our chances of winning the business.

It is an interesting and highly productive exercise to see how your viewpoint on the compares and contrasts with those of your customers view of the value you deliver for the price paid. Rarely does the internal view match the external views held by customers. The wider the gap between your view and their perspective the more likely they are to have a misalignment of how you have differentiated your product, service or solution from others competing for your business.

For example, your company assesses that the price paid for the product. Service or solution is viewed by the customer because your differentiation, that which the perception of value is based upon, is superior. Your customer's view on the other hand is in the diagram Figure (14) is that their perception is your solution is higher priced, yet delivers a middle of the road type of value in their assessment. Your company wants to believe that the customer's view of your solution value to be higher with a lower price point.

This gap effectively is what needs to be closed for aligning with the perceived value and price to be favorable when they assess your solution against those of the competition. You close the gap by recognizing what contributed to the perspective and work to improve and close that gap through conversations, education, proof points, and references to improve your position and credibility.

As a useful technique, this type of visual representation of the gap between one set of views and another can be applied to any number of circumstances and assessments of viewpoint. You can compare and contrast the differences on topics as well as concepts to represent alignment. Create a set of questions that both parties representing the viewpoints would answer and compare the two audiences.
Later on in the book, we will explore using this method to assess the alignment of sales and marketing, the company view of the competition versus the customer view of the competition, and the most typical conundrum of price versus value. Any number of scenarios can be evaluated using this methodology.

Figure (14) Alignment of Viewpoints, Customer and Company on Price vs. Value.

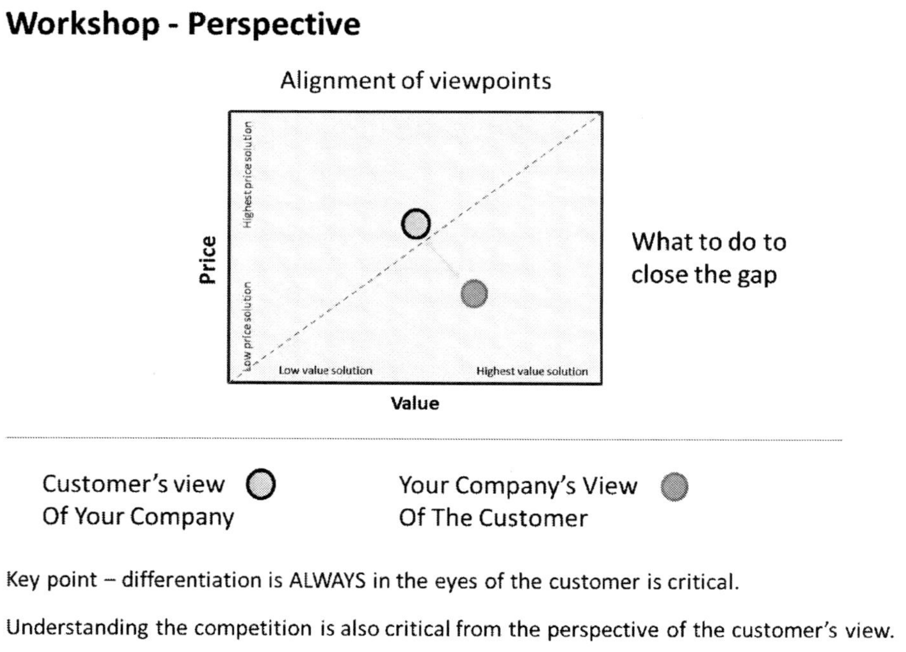

Workshop - Perspective

Alignment of viewpoints

Price / Value chart with axes: Price (vertical, from Low price solution to Highest price solution) and Value (horizontal, from Low value solution to Highest value solution). "What to do to close the gap"

Customer's view ◯
Of Your Company

Your Company's View ●
Of The Customer

Key point – differentiation is ALWAYS in the eyes of the customer is critical.

Understanding the competition is also critical from the perspective of the customer's view.

Source: SW Consulting, 2011

In the second perspective viewpoint workshop, you will assess your company position versus the competition for price and value and put yourself in the shoes of the customer as to how they view the competition. A misalignment of how the customer sees your solution or capabilities versus the competition or how you assess yourself against the competition could yield valuable insight into what you have to do to improve your differentiation from that of the competition.

In the example shown in the Figure (15), your customer assesses your competition to be able to deliver much higher value than your solution at a moderate price point. Your company for some reasons that need to be explore further assess that you view the competitor delivering what appears to be less value for the price point. This gap from the customer's point of view could mean that they do not value your differentiation or that when they assess your competitors' primary points of differentiation yours are not recognized as having value to them. Your team of people in contact with the customer can contribute to the assessment of how the customer views the competition, and how your company sees itself against the competition. Understanding the situation more fully is valuable input to have.

Your team will also want to identify and develop some action responses based on these assessments to increase your chances of winning and to better position yourself with other potential clients as well and especially if the same competitors are present in the opportunity situation . Your sales processes or how your sales systems interacts with customers might be a source of the disconnect producing the gap. Analyze the perspective from the customer's point of view and your will gain valuable insight to close the gap.

Figure (15) Alignment of Viewpoints, Customer and Company Competitor Viewpoints.

Workshop - Perspective

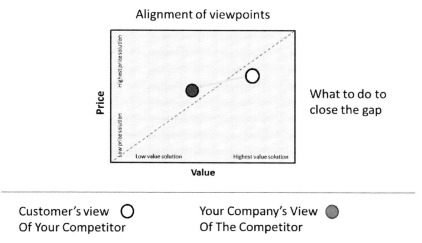

Key point – differentiation is ALWAYS in the eyes of the customer is critical.

Understanding the competition is also critical from the perspective of the customer's view.

Source: SW Consulting, 2011

The hardest aspect of this exercise for most people to get their mental images around is trying to assess how the prospective customer is feeling about the competitor and the situation in general. The value of the exercise is to change your perspective, view things differently, and see if there exists additional information about how your organization can be better than the competition. It is truly an eye opening experience for those who have never put themselves in the shoes of others to consider their viewpoints.

Once the assessments are made of how your competitor views your company and how they view your competitors, you use this information as you would another aspect of how to improve your sales system and the selling processes.

People Who Are Influencers and Their Impact on Sales

Your executive team needs to understand your sales professionals and the tasks that they need to accomplish in order to be successful, and more productive with the resources available to them. Your sales system and processes need the capability of dealing with lots of questions to formulate actions. If we draw a line between our salesperson and the company in the people influencing buying in the company that are making a decision to purchase, require something along the way there are many questions that need answers, and we need to take stock of what we know and what we do not know. Some questions needing answers as examples are:

- Who are all the people involved in the buying decision making process within our prospective company?

- What are the roles of those people influencing buying and how much influence do they have over the decision-making process question

- What was the trigger event that drove them to consider purchasing a product, service, or solution, and drives commitment to accommodate that solution?

- What is each individual buying influencer's personal view of the solution concept, and what your proposed solution will do for them?

- Can we identify a possible competitors and each of the buying influencer's perspective on that competition?

- What questions are your sales people going to ask of each of those people influencing buying and involved in the decision-making process, and why?

- What are your company strikes, your honor abilities, your differentiation from your competition, and what red flags are present at the moment that need to be addressed?

Understanding of the concepts from the perspective of a person influencing the buying will greatly help us connect our solution to that which is described in needed in the concept image of our prospective buyer.

In ever selling instance, there is a list of concerns and questions on the mind of each individual participating in the buying, and it typically depends on where they are in the decision making process. Some people who influence the buying are more concerned with their risks associated with the decision to purchase. Those that are risk averse will need to have different answers to help differentiate your solution from that of a competitor's solution. We understand that who we are talking to in the decision-making group does matter.

The exceptional salesperson will be an effective communicator and asked questions to draw out as many of the concerns that a prospective buying influencer has, to form a better picture of what the risks to their company is for selling a particular solution to that company. Rarely will you find all the people influencing buying on the same page with their concerns, or their needs for information to help them refine their concept of the image of the best solution for them, and their company.

The Role of Sales Channels

At some point, every company needs to perform an analysis and assessment of how their product, service, or solution, connects to prospective customers. The term channel refers to the ways in which a product reaches the users, buyers, NA Company. Some products are sold direct to those end-users, while others will pass through one or more intermediary or indirect channel partners on the way to the end-user buyers. There can be many arrangements.

Your company needs to consider if you require additional channels for moving your product, service, or solution, to achieve increases in sales. You need to determine whether your channel partner will provide additional value to that which you supply them, and how will they supply that value to their prospective customers to influence a sale.

Examples that come to mind are companies that produce software and hardware products that find they need the services of systems integrators, or specialty resellers such as independent software vendors, value-added resellers, value-added dealers, OEM, and other organizations, that in some way add value to the product, service, or solution, that results in a sale. Not all the times do these channels and resellers add additional value. Distributors for example, have the purpose to connect with customers through their various marketing methods to sell your product, service, or solution.

Commonly distributors are involved where there is a mass produced product such as a software package or a piece of hardware, and distributors fulfill the function of acting as a sales front for your organization. Distributors may also sell to any other intermediaries such that they may add value and resale your product to the end-user customers.

Your company must assess: (1) whether you need channels and what is the bottom line impact; (2) who would make good channel partners and why; and (3) whether or not your infrastructure can successfully support the needs of the various channel partners, because rarely are they self-sufficient, and able to adequately position your product and sell over some other competing product that they may also carry. Discuss each point carefully.

Channels – Multiple Pathways to Your Clients

Your sales system at some point may need to accommodate a strategy that includes selling through one or more additional channels beyond your direct sales approach. When using a channel approach, the focus is on understanding the channel partner, their concept of your product, and how they can sell that product effectively, to their best target customer profiles. When considering taking on a new channel a considerable amount of internal corporate analysis must first be done.

Our sales system, which traditionally will focus on direct sales to prospective clients, if it is well thought out, can accommodate multiple channels all at the same time. What you need to understand about your channel partner, is how they go about selling to prospective clients. We have talked about the buying, selling, and decision-making processes from the perspective of a client.

Your channel partner may however, not use the same approach and in fact may be still using traditional selling methods which depend strictly upon understanding the feature function benefit, and not the concept that the customer has of the best solution.

So as a part of bringing the new channel partner on board you need to understand their customers, how they market and sell to those customers, they are selling processes these, and their expectations upon you to assist with the sales process. Quite often, what happens is that a channel partner will find an opportunity, and then rely heavily upon their product, service, or solution partner to provide the necessary processes or support to assist with the sale.

For each channel chosen by your company, how you tailor the available resources, and processes for that channel, will impact your decision to bring on board that channel or that channel partner. Managing channel partners for some companies that have a more complex product, service, or solution offering, will be problematic for companies with limited resources. The challenge is to take your sales system and to make the necessary additions with regard to process to help reduce the impact of the resource requirements on the relationship. A goal of suppliers when they first bring a channel on board is to make the channel as self-sufficient as possible.

The trade-off they soon discover is that the channel partner may carry multiple product, service, and solution options, of which yours is only one potential offering that they can position in front of their clients. Consider that if a channel partner has a broad portfolio of products and services and solutions that your portfolio may not be the lead solution. To overcome this issue your approach to how you support your channel partner will help the channel partner decide what type of relationship you both will have. Some distributors counted as a channel, will only respond to an offer of greater margin than they will claim to be self-sufficient with regard to your resources.

A true channel partner relationship that is more manageable is to involve more members of the channel partner together with members and counterparts within your company, who understand how to make the selling process more effective for the channel partner.

Channel partners do in fact respond to differentiation from you as a supplier of product services and solutions. When comparing and contrasting other suppliers if the only differentiation is price, then selling a complex solution to their customer base may be more problematic. It is a well-known fact regarding sales that in the absence of differentiation or additional support services or some special program that will assist the channel partner, any difference between your product, service, or solution, and your competitors or other service providers may be lost.

To differentiate yourself from other suppliers you may need to create programs in support of the channel partner that make their job of selling your product, service, or solution, easier for their chosen client base. This could take the form of a sales support hotline only for your channel partner, or some form of additional services that can be a part of the relationship offered by the channel partner when they are engaging in sales to their client base.

Sometimes your concessions will only get you as far as getting a channel partner agreement in place. Those concessions may not translate into sales however, if the channel partner perceives your competitors products are a better fit for some customers than yours.

So consider carefully when you are thinking about adding a channel or bringing on a reseller partner as to what their needs are, and how they propose to sell your product, service, or solution, to their client base. You will want to ask them do they have a sales system for selling to their client base, what does their selling process look like, and how successful have they been with that sales system and processes.

Your position when considering a channel partner will be to identify those partners that have capabilities that when added together with your product, service, or solution, will differentiate from competitive solutions. From a marketing point of view working together with channel partner sales people, you will need to address the concept of the customer for the best solution with your sales materials and other support services.

Differentiation -- Part of the Customer Decision-making Process

Consider the picture if you will of the iceberg. It has a portion visible above the water line, and we know there will be a significant portion that is not visible, below the water line. Your company is on a course that you have charted to help you steer around the icebergs but in actual fact the portion of the iceberg did you see this clearly differentiated from that which is not visible and it allows you to make decisions about what to do. A part of the iceberg that is visible is the differentiation, it is tangible, and when comparing and contrasting it to companies and their capabilities these would be viewed as strikes that separate this particular iceberg from others.

The vast invisible portion of the iceberg is analogous to your customer thinking that if there is no differentiation between your solution and a competitor's solution that they as a part of their own individual decision-making process may lack the information sufficient for them to see any difference.

They may in fact invent or imagine unforeseen negatives that in their thinking maybe weaknesses or red flags about your product, service, or solution, in the absence of knowledge. Do not leave it to them to make assessments of you, your company and your solutions, communicate and show them how you are different responding to exactly what they are focused on for concerns. You need all the differentiation you can develop.

Building conceptual bridges between your solution and the prospective customer's view of what will help them best from their perspective. Buying and selling bridge building consists of good planning. It makes excellent use of questioning, and fact-finding, development of strategies for positioning your differentiation, and works to help all of the involved decision makers to thoroughly examine and consider how your solution fits with their conceptual solution view. Relationship bridge building increases your chances of winning, and for using the bridge for added opportunity development at some point in the future.

Change -- Its Impact Must Be Considered and Addressed

Change, or a trigger event, can occur at any time. This trigger event will accelerate and move the process of considering what needs to be done, or changed, to respond to improvements in the situation or to enhance capabilities and remove risks resulting from the need to change.

Change can also occur within a customer, or a market, and could be common to a large number of prospective customers in that market. For example, when in a recession when credit is difficult to obtain for all companies, it will impact their inventory and manufacturing position, or a new product line once introduced may have problems associated with it that will impact the acceptance of the product with current and future customers.

Perhaps in one good/bad example there would be the Yugo car, and its ill-fated introduction into the US market. Its entry in the United States was due to the company trying to take advantage of a need for low-end alternatives to transportation. It failed miserably, mostly due to quality issues. It did serve to change people's perspective on the low end, of what they would tolerate in the price versus quality aspect of buying a car.

Other forms of change can occur when one or more competitors introduce new products and services or solutions based on breakthrough technologies. This disruptive change impacts a lot of people not just the suppliers, but also the prospective clients who have to consider the merits of whether or not that new disruptive technology will help them accomplish or avoid a problem that they are experiencing in their company.

Your company may win a large opportunity that takes many years to implement, but the risk for the client is that during the course of that long-term implementation it is likely that if it's technology-based that it will evolve, necessitating changes to the operations within the client's environment. There are other change indicators that we see when comparing individual company market strategies, or visible in the tactics that they use when selling either new or existing products. The "new and improved" concept exemplifies change.

They may introduce for example, special programs with discounts attached for example, or they launch a new enhanced version of their product. As they release software enhancements there are companies in the market who will create market buzz, but not based on anything substantial in terms of a tangible improvement to any product, service, or solution. Therefore, they use the word "new" in ways that attracts attention but does not differentiate from those other competitors. Is the "new" item likely to impact and change something in the existing customers? Knowledge of the impact would be crucial.

You will also find organizational change to be a powerful force to be reckoned with because it is as disruptive in your organization as it is in your prospective client's organization. As described before the number of people involved as people influencing buying who are part of the decision-making process for buying any solution may change over time.

Your own organization made some internal change either in structure or in the roles and responsibilities of your people as your business continues to evolve. Frequently in sales, a sales person who created an initial relationship with a client will be moved to a different area where they have new client responsibilities leaving the existing client wanting to understand how to keep the relationship going in a positive direction with minimal effort on their part.

Strategy and Tactics

What is the purpose of having a strategy? What is the purpose of tactics? The answers to these questions will lie with how your company plans for, and then executes on strategies. So consider that the strategy is where we consider the options based on information collected and analyzed, and from that analysis will come the selection of potential and best actions.

We planned for tactics also by looking at what those actions are and determining what we will need to do to implement them. Therefore, tactics can be planned, or very dynamic, depending upon the situation and the requirements of the circumstances.

Tactics need to accommodate change as we discussed the topic of change. Now, when looking at your sales system and what it can do for your company, you need to identify what strategies you will need and the corresponding tactics required to be maximally effective. Strategy always requires that we have information and perform the analysis.

Strategy also allows us in advance to think of what differentiation do we have, what is the significance of our strikes, and what have we learned will be important for our customers when considering as a part of their decision-making process who and what to buy.

Loose Ends, Red Flags and Vulnerabilities – Approach With Caution

When selling to prospective customers the concept of loose ends is reflected in the old adage the "devil is in the details" accurately describes how out of control or well controlled the situation might be along with the true status of the opportunity and what must be done to improve the chances of winning.

Virtually every industry understands the concept of a red flag as a semaphore for something that is not right. Red flags can be very useful in a great many situations. When a red flag indicates that you are missing information needed to complete your strategy and analysis, that is a good thing. If we are guessing about a piece of information, we should always identify it with a red flag until we are certain of the significance of that piece of information. Guessing is a cause for concern.

To dismiss a red flag is to invite an increase in risk, and potential failure. For years people heard of an old selling tactic that was introduced by IBM which was known as FUD, "fear, uncertainty, and doubt." That translated to clients as selecting IBM was a low-risk alternative than to select some other solution.

Over time companies found that, the adage regarding selecting IBM was not necessarily true. IBM had lots to sell but whether the selected solution was the right one for the situation and a good choice for the buying company was only borne out over time.

In a customer centric situation where we understand more about those people influencing buying and our sales system has ways to accommodate the collecting analyzing and strategizing and how we perform the formulation of actions and best actions that we can be significantly more per adoptive and have a higher rate of return on our sales efforts.

Also it behooves any organization that they be sure to consider that any loose ends when working to understand the prospective client needs or gaps in our knowledge hinder our ability to pinpoint their requirements with a high degree of accuracy. Loose ends are the things that we think of later in the game or ignore altogether with varying potential consequences.

Vulnerabilities can take multiple shapes and if not thoroughly thought through in advance we likely encounter competitive pressure exploiting the vulnerabilities. Using our vulnerabilities against is could also be another reason why a prospective client feels we may not measure up to their standards if we appear to have vulnerabilities that cannot be mitigated or overcome in ways that neutralize those negatives.

The best way to assess vulnerabilities is to put yourself in the position of the prospective competitor and your prospective customer. Ask, does your assessment of the vulnerabilities line up with those either of the potential customer or potential competitor? You will need to address how to respond to those vulnerabilities in some sales situations so start thinking about the responses and the possible actions right now, because it takes a long time to appreciate if those vulnerabilities impact the sales efforts.

I worked for one company who will remain nameless for legal reasons that hired myself and other sales people and made us in to office automation subject matter experts. This was to prepare for the launch of a whiz-bang product, that was to revolutionize the way that companies handled their office needs. As the subject matter experts, we have a well thought out systematic approach and process to sell the solution. If was effective and we sold a bunch of them, literally. The only problem was the company could not manufacture the system. It was too complex. This big vulnerability resulted in the entire product line being pulled and giving people money back.

Our prospective clients and competitors alike will explore our products, services, and solutions for vulnerabilities. Some of the information they obtain will be factual and other information perhaps less so. If we have vulnerabilities, they are as much red flags for us in the eyes of our prospects, as they are opportunities for exploitation from our competitor's point of view. Attend to the loose ends, red flags, and vulnerabilities to increase your chances of winning in highly competitive situations.

One former aviator who as a pilot knew the risks involved with flying summed up the selling process experience to be like performing your first parachute jump out of a perfectly good plane while shortcutting some of the preparation and safety checks on your chute because you never thought they would make a difference. The possibility of a favorable outcome in this scenario tends to be slim and none. However, in sales we have the power to prepare, ask questions, perform assessments, and rely upon proven processes to give us guidance and to increase our chances of success yet so many companies do not do that.

The open mind approach is mentioned here because too often, what passes for a rigid process may not be the right course of action to take. If your sales system, consisting of several of those processes lacks the ability to accommodate new information and react accordingly then the results your get are likely to be imperfect.

For example, have your management team prepare the questions you would each ask the sales person and see how divergent they are as an exercise. Realize that much of our focus is forced to be on the macro view of how big the sale might be, and when might it materialize, but fundamentally, if the attention to detail and the loose ends are not attended to the outcomes will be like our poorly packed parachute.

This internal diversity of answers is precisely why you need to have a robust sales system and appropriate processes to follow and over time a playbook of tribal knowledge of what works, and what does not work, AND why the actions work or not.

Give careful attention to the processes you have uncovered and consider how they can improve your development of strategies, tactics and ways to reduce your exposure and risk of losing business by not being prepared or unable to flexibly adjust your game plans to accommodate the dynamic situations as you encounter them.

Again, failure to plan invites planning to fail time and time again. Fix the situations, record the results, and use them for building playbook that illustrates exactly how your process works and why.

Takeaways

The takeaways from this section are:

- Realize that every company that sells has a sales system consisting of several processes. Those processes need to address and align the decision-making processes of both your company and the prospective customers you sell.

- Perspectives are important. Your prospective customers have viewpoints that may or may not align with what they know about your company, your capabilities and what your product, service or solution will do for them. Understanding the role of perspectives and how to use the information to your advantage require making sure that your sales system and processes can accommodate that information.

- Concepts are drivers. Your prospective customers have a concept of what they believe will be the best solution for them either from you or from your competition. Your challenge will be to have your sales system and processes align with putting the information and contribution by members of your selling team that can help shape the concepts in your favor in ways that differentiate your responses from those of your competitors. Understanding the concept customers have and the assessment of perspectives as stated before combine to improve your chances of winning business.

- Communications that are able to connect the concepts of customers with the solutions you offer are a critical part of the communications processes. However, you either communicate in your marketing materials or through your understanding of the customer's concepts realize also that you are conveying to the customer what and why your solution is differentiated, and better than other solutions being considered.

- Sales people are change agents. Your sales system and the processes assist them in dealing with change in the market, in customers and their concepts of a solution, the impact of proposed solutions and the ability to cope with the ever-present need to be flexible to address situations as they arise.

- When channels are involved in selling to prospective customers your sales system and processes must accommodate the needs of the channel partners and align them with your direct sales and marketing efforts to garner the greatest return on the investments in them. All of the prior takeaways apply when working with channels and the challenge is to accommodate them to positively impact the opportunities for all parties involved.

SECTION (4)

Methodology

SECTION (4)

"*All truths are easy to understand once they are discovered – the point is to discover them.*" Galileo, the Great Master and Craftsman, Scientific Revolutionary

Methodology

This section suggests an approach for how to examine, document, and work to improve your sales system, and sales processes, and is divided in to three parts.

     (a) Prepare
     (b) Discover
     (c) Added Dimensions

The first part (a) is about preparing for discussions and offers definitions that provide a common language for some of the activities in the two remaining section parts. The emphasis is on brining into the thought processes those additional terms and concepts that frame the discovery and analysis of your sales system and process environment.

Part (b) details an investigative approach to discover your processes and follow with workshop activities, assessments, and evaluations of those processes and practices found in your environment. The exercises suggested will give insight into the mechanics, players and issues commonly identified in an organization that grapples with sales and desires to improve the operational aspects.

Part (c) provides additional activities that enhance the discovery methods and provide more dimensions to obtain greater insight into how to refine the understanding of the organization and the actions suggesting improvements. You can apply the information in other commonly encountered aspects comprising the sales systems as your organization develops the need.

Part (A) PREPARE

Some Useful Process Related Definitions

One of the stated goals of this book is that we believe better understanding of terminology helps get everyone on the same operational page. We attempt to alert the reader specific to where we want to ground the discussions around a common set of terms, definitions or concepts that everyone in your company should rally around when discussing your sales system and processes it contains.

The best place to start is with the most commonly used terms and descriptions of various processes from readily available sources. Here are six basic definitions of key process concepts describing business operations.

(1) Process – Broad Definition (businessdictionary.com)

"Sequence of interdependent and linked procedures which, at every stage, consume one or more resources (employee time, energy, machines, money) to convert inputs (data, material, parts, etc.) into outputs. These outputs then serve as inputs for the next stage until a known goal or end result is reached."

To read more about types of processes follow this link to a useful resource: *http://www.businessdictionary.com/definition/process.html#ixzz11gwdpBVb.*

From the description provided the point to consider is the interdependence of linked procedures. To reach the identified goals having procedures that assist are better than having some that inject confusion or encourage chaos serve to disrupt the selling process and the actions supporting it. In order to make adjustments and improve our processes we need to understand thoroughly the value each of them contributes to the sales cycle.

(2) Business Process – Definition (Wikipedia and businessdictionary.com)

"Series of logically related activities or tasks (such as planning, production, sales) performed together to produce a defined set of results". Also called, "the business function."

For more on this definition use this web address:
http://www.businessdictionary.com/definition/business-process.html#ixzz11gwusjVL

In context a business process or business method is a collection of related, structured activities or tasks that produce a specific service or product (serve a particular goal) for a particular customer or customers. It often can be visualized with a flowchart as a sequence of activities.

There are three general types of business processes:

1. **Management processes**, the processes that govern the planning and operation of a system. Typical management processes include "Corporate Governance" and "Strategic Management", quality control methods and practices.

2. **Operational processes**, processes that constitute the core business and create the primary value stream. Typical operational processes are purchasing, manufacturing, advertising, marketing, sales, and channel partnership and operations management.

3. **Supporting processes**, which support the core processes. Examples include accounting, recruitment, training, Call and service center, IT and Technical support.

A business process begins with a mission objective and ends with achievement of the business objective. Process-oriented organizations break down the barriers of structural departments and try to avoid functional silos.
A business process can be decomposed into several sub-processes, which have their own attributes, but also contribute to achieving the goal of the super-process. The analysis of business processes typically includes the mapping of processes and sub-processes down to activity level.

Business Processes are designed to add value for the customer and should not include unnecessary activities. The outcome of a well-designed business process is increased effectiveness (value for the customer), and increased efficiency (less cost to the company).

Business Processes can be modeled through a large number of methods and techniques. For instance, the Business Process Modeling Notation is a Business Process Modeling technique that can be used for drawing business processes in a workflow.

Note that the context here is related to business actions and not technical ones like product development, engineering support or professional services. The business process is more aligned with determining pricing, how to position value such as with marketing, and the actions of sales specifically.

(3) Business Process Management – Definition (Wikipedia)

Business process management (BPM) is a management approach focused on aligning all aspects of an organization with the wants and needs of clients. In addition to a rigorous planning set of activities, it is a holistic management approach that promotes business effectiveness and efficiency, while striving for innovation, flexibility, and integration with internal or external technology. Business process management attempts to improve processes continuously. It could therefore be aptly described as a "process optimization process."

It is argued that BPM enables any organization to be more efficient, more effective, and more capable of change than a functionally focused, traditional hierarchical management approach. In order for BPM to contribute to increasing the efficiency of the organization a deeper understanding the internal and external alignments of various operational groups, all which should be customer centric, needs to be internalized as an operating norm and not a one-off attempt at introducing improvements.

(4) Business Operations Process – Definition

(a) A business transaction that requests information from or changes the data in a database.

(b) A specific event in a chain of structured business activities. The event typically changes the state of data and/or a product and generates some type of output. Examples of business processes include receiving orders, invoicing, shipping products, updating employee information, or setting a marketing budget. Business processes occur at all levels of an organization's activities and include events that the customer sees and events that are invisible to the customer. The terms also refer to the amalgam of all the separate steps toward the final business goal.

(5) Sales Process – Definition (Wikipedia)

The set of steps aimed at initiating and supporting the identification and evaluation of likely customers (prospects), sales communications tools and the presentation portfolio, and the steps towards successful conclusion of sales activities. It requires a close coordination of people, equipment, tools, and techniques, and includes advertising and promotion.

The overall end-to-end process will consist of one or more steps more commonly labeled as:

- Prospecting and lead generation
- Researching and qualifying opportunities for a fit (understand the client's concepts)
- Investigate involved decision makers and the buying process, evaluate and establish needs, then decide if your solution is appropriate and to pursue or not
- Manage the opportunities and resource requirements
- Propose solution highlighting the areas of concern and technical merits
- Negotiate to refine pricing, terms and conditions and timelines
- Win the business and implement
- Post sale activities, support, relationship management

Your organization may have in place formal or informal processes to handle each one of the items listed above. What we are interested in exploring is how these processes and sub-processes can be made more effective and strengthen your sales system.

Sales Terminology

For example, in defining your process, you will need to know how these components relate to these basic sales process terms of art, and the quantitative metrics that apply.

- Leads - A lead is any person who may be interested in your products or services; for example, someone you met at a conference or who filled out a form on your Web site is a lead.

- Contacts - Contacts are all the individuals associated with the accounts you are tracking in whatever CRM system you use, and you need to distinguish a contact as a potential lead by asking and obtaining qualifying information, or just identify the contact for some future opportunity that needs to be qualified more completely. For each contact, you can store information such as phone numbers, titles, and roles in a deal.

- Opportunities - An opportunity that has been qualified to the point there is interest or a possible deal you want to track. Opportunities generally have more than one contact so it is important that the contact information be sufficient to develop strategies for developing or rejecting the possible opportunity. A group of opportunities builds to a funnel or pipeline that you can use for forecasting as it moves toward completion or elimination from consideration.

- Accounts - An account is any company, organization, individual that you have done business with or desire to track in the CRM system. Typical account profiles contain the information developed during the qualifying and closing stages of an opportunity, and may include additional details on competitors, and/or partners that may be involved. Tracking this information allows building and tracking ongoing account management plans.

- Metrics – The measures agreed upon by the organization that convey status, progress against plans or highlight areas for improvement. Generally each group such as sales, marketing, customer service and support as examples, will all have a set of goals and objectives defined by their contribution to the business plan and metrics indicate progress towards those goals either qualitatively or quantitatively.

- Channels – Alternative ways to get to prospective customers through intermediaries who represent your product or service and may deliver some service or expertise together with your product or service in ways that are recognized as added value by those customers. Channels can be identified by their external chosen role as that of reseller including retail operations, value-adder with subject matter expertise, systems integrators if your product is a part of a larger solution, or an agent or some other designation acting as a representative of your products, services, or solutions.

The Foundation for Results – The Discovery Approach

Business process discovery also known as "BPD" is a set of techniques, activities and workshops conducted internally that construct a representation of an organization's overall current business processes and its major process variations. It starts with discovering how well those processes and activities work in an organization.

These techniques collect evidence found in existing systems to show how the business processes operate within an organization and within the boundaries of how they are used. Some processes extend outside the organization and can greatly impact the resource requirements and the results. The processes that extend outside the organization are much harder to influence and control but need to be identified, examined, and structured according to needs.

Sales channels are one such example of outside processes and involve how you deal with your resellers or technical partners. We suggested an exercise to identify and map the channels in Section 3 as a precursor to discovering other information. We hope or assume that our sales and technical partners are working on our behalf towards some shared goal to aid us in selling our products, services, or solutions in ways that we both can win. Some channels require considerable efforts to obtain results while others do not.

The discovery process includes those processes external to the organization so that we can draw from the observations some conclusions about those external connections and if our partners are helping us in an optimal manner. If the business plan does not take in to account the full extent of the sales process including the efforts and resources required to achieve the plans then poor performance is the likely outcome and results will fall short of meeting expectations.

The use of the discovery method described in this book is a holistic way to begin to understand the connection between the business plan and the sales, marketing and support plans for our organization. That is why it is beneficial for all groups involved to participate. Quite often, the connection between the customer side of the equation and the business plan side fails to be adequate because of unrealistic or misunderstood objectives or situations that were wrongly scoped to begin with. Poorly thought out plans or the requisite support resources required as described in the business plans contribute to problems that can be identified by the discovery process using inputs and participation from all involved parties to the selling activities.

This discovery involves collecting, analyzing and determining through a series of questions and answers derived from the use of a workshop approach to show all of the identified areas interact with one another surrounding the activities in support of selling. You harvest the knowledge and tribal wisdom from internal sources and use it to refine how to make the process of sales more productive and effective.

Figure (16) illustrates the point that part of the discovery involves mapping your particular processes, activities, actions and the understanding that they should all tie back to be in support of business, sales, and marketing plans. They are interconnected internally among people who are in support of the sales efforts and externally through all the interactions with prospective and existing customers.

From the very beginning of how a prospective customer is identified or connected by some outreach of channel program, each process in support of the plans should be planned for, consistent, orchestrated and coordinated for maximum impact.

To get a clearer picture of how you operate is to also ask and answer questions about how the prospective and existing customers view your organization through the activities that connect with them. It is essential to learn and to understand the customer's perspective related to all that you do. We will explore perspectives further in this section.

Figure (16) the discovery process connects your plans to the prospective customers.

Workshops – How We Will Examine Your Processes

Why the Discovery approach?

Connecting the dots between the Business Plan and the Sales Plan is often an area left unstructured with potentially poor performance the result.

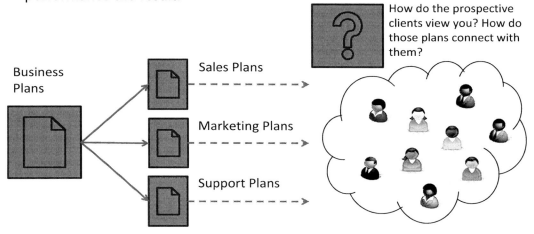

Source: SW Consulting, 2011

Process Definition & Mapping Guidance

To define your business process or processes, it is important to understand both the key terms, and how your basic processes currently work in your organization. That means: you will need to define in detail what happens at each step; what inputs are needed; who does what, when; and how to measure the results with appropriately determined metrics.

When defining your processes, it helps to follow this high-level conceptual approach:

- You will need to capture, catalog and understand basic process terms
- Identify the key characteristics or attributes of your process from end to end
- Do you currently link them to a CRM processes (SugarCRM, Microsoft Dynamics, Microsoft Outlook, Salesforce.com, etc.), specific to marketing, sales, order processing, finance, legal, manufacturing or engineering development, or to other processes describe the linkages and the conditions under which they are used
- Define and come up with a visual overview of your own process as a map

- Discuss and describe any new processes that would make the process simpler, faster, or done with less resources or repetition
- Map the overall processes from those customer related activities through the steps to the completion of the sale. If a loss results, map the process to review and debrief to learn from the loss.

What is a Typical Sales Process?

For most businesses, a basic sales process includes gathering information for the following steps:

- Generating Leads - Where do Leads come from? How do they get into the CRM (assuming you have one)? What happens next? What information do you want to measure about leads?

- Optimizing lead flow - How do you manage open leads? How do you check for duplicates and inaccuracies? How do you work through leads? How do you measure conversions and top performers? What do you do with rejected or failed leads?

- Identify the work that must be done for both parties to satisfy the client and move them along in the decision making process. How do you go about understanding their needs? How will you address those needs?

- Closing deals - How do you manage the sales funnel? How do you bring new customers into the CRM system? Alternatively, do you handle them differently? How can you measure top deals, closed business by the month, and month-to-date trending?

- Delivery, fulfillment, and follow up with clients once sold to maintain or build a stronger relationship for future business. Check for results and satisfaction.

The sales process includes understanding the roles and responsibilities of those who touch the prospective customer and what tasks need to performed and the associated timing of those tasks to accomplish the goal of a sale. Refer to Figure (17) for a graphic illustration of the concept.

Touch points are generally segmented by group or function within the selling company. Designations include engineering, finance marketing, sales, operations, service and support, channel management, product management, legal and human resources as examples.

Some companies fail to take in to account the impact of the interactions with customers from people within their own company. We hear of customer service issues, customer satisfaction issues and other issues that involve any number of people either pre sale or post sale. Knowing the activities and the impact on the customer and the sales situations can provide valuable insight in to those areas of the sales system that need to be modified or improved.

Figure (17) Touch point connections to prospective customers all contribute to the selling process.

Possible Touch Points Related To Customers

Marketing &
Public Relations
- Direct
- Indirect
- Campaigns

Sales &
Operations
- Finance
- Legal
- Bookings

Product
Management &
Engineering
- Manufacturing
- Development

Service &
Support
- Response
- Questions
- Remediation

Competition
- Resellers
- Channels
- Suppliers

Channel
Partners
- Resellers
- Integrators
- Value Added

Each touch point uses its own methods, processes, procedures
and policies for interacting with prospective or current customers.

Source: SW Consulting, 2011

Create Your Process Overview

The goal of this step is to come up with a visual overview of your process. You can use the default processes provided by salesforce.com as way to stimulate discussion. A good place to start is at the point when you have qualified a lead. Here is an example of a sales process map. It starts with the prospective customer and lists those who interact with anyone in the customer's organization. It lists the activities that each person performs in order to bring a sale to completion. Depending upon the nature of the sale the list of people and actions could be simple or more complex with many people touching the prospective customer at various times during a sale.

Discuss the sample process with the project team and modify it to fit your organization. If you don't have a defined sales process this will be the starting point for examining your processes and determining what type of CRM system you need and its requirements. If you already have a CRM implementation the output of examining the current processes and how they work with the system will likely lead to making changes and enhancing the system capabilities.

To set up your own sales process you would:

- Start with a listing of all possible ways you attempt to reach prospective and current clients, and list the ways the prospects and existing clients can connect with you.

- Then examine the point where a lead is qualified as an opportunity and the questions asked to determine how they qualify (best client profile).

- On a whiteboard, draw each step, as you ideally want the information to flow.

- Document your process with tools like Mindjet™ for future use and reference.

The Mind mapping approach using MindJet™ is shown on the next page in Figure (18). It is a technique that links the appropriate groups responsible for certain activities, and the activities performed. The central figure is the customer. The touch points for the customer shown are some of the most common describing the relationship between the company and the customer at some point in time.

When exploring your particular sale system start with the customer, identify the groups that have contact with or support the sales to the customer and the linkages between those groups. In some instances, the linkages will cross connect multiple groups if they participate somehow in the sales or support processes.

Some companies require that all contact flow from their company to the customers or prospective clients through the sales person. This places a tremendous burden on the time requirements each sales person has to find prospective clients and to work the selling process. Companies that are more successful are involving the supportive groups in the process from initial contact to completion of the sale and on into the support phase to ensure that the customer receives the appropriate care when it is most desirable and effective.

Analyzing each of the identified touch points, the parties involved, the list of activities and actions required to win a piece of business, affords most organizations a fresh perspective on the amount of resources required to generate a sale.

The investment a company makes to win sales is not just the sales people involved. It involves a great many more player, activities and actions required and when quantified produce a more realistic picture of the costs to make the sale. When the total resources involved can be recorded, a more meaningful return on investment in sales can be calculated.

As companies grow the cost of providing, the infrastructure often outpaces the revenue forecasts. Those who have responsibility for the company planning should include the investment requirements to generate sales and factor in the investments required to grow sales.

Figure (18) is a Mindmap diagram showing an overview example of the sales process, internal and external relationships, and how they are interconnected to customers.

SALES PROCESS RELATIONSHIP MAPPING EXAMPLE

Sales Contact Points
- Outbound Call Center
- Sales Direct Call
  - Quick Quote
  - Proposals
    - Legal (contracts, NDAs, licensing)
    - Finances (Ts&Cs)
    - Manufacturing/production
- Presentations
- Demonstrations
- Pilot Programs
- Channel Partner Joint Activities

Channel Partners

Competition

Prospective Customer

Service and Support Resources

Product Management
- Engineering
- Designers/developers
- Resource Planners
- Program Leaders
- Project Managers
- Programmers

Marketing Contact Points
- Web Site
- Collateral Mailings
- eMail Campaigns
- Advertising
- Trade Events
- Public Relations

Source: SW Consulting, 2011

Part (B) DISCOVER

Understanding the Architecture of a Sales System

The best place to start understanding a process is to start at what looks like the beginning of course. This requires gathering as much information as possible while identifying as many related aspects of your processes as you can by using the Discovery approach described. Not every company devotes the necessary time to exploring and evaluating just how things work in their company. All too often, they just accept what is present even without understanding why something works or does not work.

Every productive sales system has a foundation at the core that is based on a firm understanding of how things get done including assessments of what works well and what does not work as effectively. Once the foundation is in place, we strive to build a more robust framework and structure to have all of the functional parts working in concert to deliver the best results. We also need tools, the ability to perform assessments and a more formalized way of asking questions and determining answers and the appropriate actions to keep the system functioning optimally.

Let us look at one aspect of the business strictly based on where we are and what you are doing today. If your business is a start-up then sooner or later you will need to sell something. You start by performing a series of actions. When those actions reach, a more consistent level they take on attributes of processes involving several actions. They evolve relatively quickly over time and as more aspects are added, a sales system becomes apparent.

If your business is more advanced, then you will likely already have some set of prospects, and even a few at various advanced stages of the buying decision process. Your business could have been operating for quite some time and the routine cadence of activities and actions and have achieved some measure of a funnel of opportunities that can be monitored to determine what work needs to be completed to win the business. Your processes evolve somewhat slower due to entrenched process norms.

The Miller Heiman company is credited with first creating one of the most recognizable descriptions of how to characterize where opportunities are in the selling and buying processes and likens them to that of a funnel. Unqualified prospective opportunities are in the universe above the mouth of the funnel, while those opportunities that are just above the mouth of the funnel are in need of qualifying, when more is known about the opportunity and how to make it progress towards closure they are in the funnel where all the bases need to be covered and a possible order exists. Then, there are those situations where the opportunity has moved to clearly defined next steps, and appears to be at the order closure stage with little or no additional heavy lifting work required.

The funnel is useful as a visual aid but also useful to indicate whether an opportunity has been resourced and proper actions taken to win the business or not. The sales funnel concept is an example when taken as a whole of a sales system.

The simplest form of the sales system architecture will show all of the numerous activities, actions, and involvement of several people inside and outside your company. It involves working with prospective clients and managing them to completion that produced a sale, or not, if left undone.

The sales funnel concept helps to bring into focus the involvement of the sales people, resources, management, and the actions required to bring an opportunity to closure. Tracking the opportunities from prospect to closure gives us an accurate view of what business levels are present. If nothing is in the funnel, that is bad, and means we need to allocate more time finding, qualifying, and moving potential opportunities into the funnel.

Conversely, if everything is in the funnel and nothing is progressing we have identified a poor understanding of the opportunity to address a prospective customers' needs, the specific allotment of resources, or failed to adequately qualify or cover the bases for the opportunities. Movement is obtained by synchronizing the buying and selling processes through appropriate actions. If however actions are occurring and there is still no movement then something is not understood about the opportunity being considered either form the selling side or the buying side.

Funnel management is all about time allotments to each activity needed to build a healthy funnel and smooth out the roller coaster of no business to some business to no business again. Sales activities fall in to four general categories of prospecting; qualifying; moving opportunities forward or covering the bases doing pretty much what needs to be done; and most importantly, closing the order. Every business has some form of these activities in common and the allocation of time and resources according to the need for each of them. Some proceed with more process steps and some use a rigorous system of checks and balances to make sure progress is occurring.

Starting with the funnel concept will allow us to back track to a better understand how all the processes involved in selling fit together. If your funnel has nothing in it then we need to start thinking about creating opportunities. Let us look at activities specific to accomplish that.

At the earliest point, we need only to assume that our product, service, or solution we have to sell has a potential customer somewhere in the universe of prospects. This requires some validation by investigating the levels of interest in the product, services or solutions through various market research means available including surveys, panels of subject matter experts, face-to-face prospect discussions of your products, services or solutions. What is the process to identify prospective customers? There are a number of possible method choices. The goal is always to learn more about prospective the customers even after product development to learn how well your solutions are received.

A question to ask yourself is, for my given product or service, who would make an ideal customer for it. Ask yourself that question and then make sure to develop a profile of what your experience tells you are the descriptions of that ideal customer. The best target customers can come from searching information from prior sales histories, market research, or market sector trends to see who is adopting like or similar solutions to what you are selling.

Next, use whatever research tools you have at your disposal to identify a specific and targeted audience using the criteria you have decided will be to describe what a best customer profile looks like. If you have trouble finding any prospects because the selection criteria are somewhat restrictive then you need to consider broadening your criteria slightly. If the criteria are too selective, fewer prospects will be identified. If the criteria are, too general you will have too many prospects to reasonably deal with in an acceptable timeframe.

Assuming you are able to find some prospects that fit the what the best customer profile description, then choose a method to document ways that are used to reach out to them. Appropriate method examples are advertising and awareness development, the use of cold calling via door knocking or by initial phone contact, emailing if you have an address, snail mail with a flyer or marketing collateral piece that tells the prospect about you and why they might need your product or service, or advertise in a local or national venue. The list of possible ways is extensive but each comes at a cost and each has a measurable contribution to the business success overall. You need to assess each of those ways and select the most productive ones.

Additional variations on the methods include handouts, fliers, special promotions, word of mouth in the business community, social networking, your web presence if appropriate, and whatever is indicated in your industry as a means to use to cost effectively find prospects. There are scores of methods. Each of these methods has metrics as well that need to be assessed. If it costs a million dollars to find one lead, something is wrong with the approach used. Likewise, if you generate considerable leads or interest but no one buys the product, service or solution you offer then you need to assess what is actually causing them to respond and are those responses useful in any way.

At this point, you will begin to examine your processes more closely by an exercise in mapping those activities described above and others to build a process map. The purpose of the process map is to identify as many of the activities that have a potential impact on sales and the connection to the customers. Begin by drawing boxes with the name of the group involved and placing them on the map clustering them together to indicate who interacts with whom on the way to reaching the customer. You can include your sale channels or create a separate map only for the channels to show the relationships between groups and the channel customer access.

The Figure (19) is a template for identifying and mapping the methods in use to reach the prospective customer. The "single" customer segmentation designation stems from a narrow definition of what is found in your best customer profile. The narrower the focus on the single segmentation the more discrete is the analysis of what works and what does not work at a granular level. Segmentation, as a method of targeting opportunities, is by itself a common problem for many companies. Assume we start with the entire universe of potential customers and then select those markets where our product, service, or solution is a great fit for those prospective customers.

For example, your widget product is used by several industries because of its flexibility. The segmentation therefore is that portion of the market regardless of industry but perhaps related to a function within all those industries that you target. Your widget is a horizontal segment in this instance. Were that widget to be only useful in healthcare or banking for example, it would limit the segmentation to those vertical market segments.

Zeroing in the appropriate segments should also connect with the market research done for the business plans. It is hard to construct a sales plan from a business plan that assumes the broadest possible markets or segments within those markets. Care must be exercised to narrow the focus so that it is manageable by each of your sales, marketing, and support plans. Map the connections to the prospective single segment customers accordingly with as much detail as you can uncover.

Some background on the templates used extensively in this section and referenced in the next. Each of the templates, and example diagrams supplied, should be viewed as a full-page document for maximum effect and comprehension. They are to be used as focal points, tools for the workshop style activities, to position as many of the questions as possible that need answers. Use them to stimulate discussions that will drive a better understanding of how each part of an organization performs its functions related to the selling and the buying processes.

No two results will be the same for different companies in my experience, but that is a good thing, and expected if your company is trying to uncover and leverage differences from others in your market. If the identified areas do not work optimally, or just do not yet exist to support the sales system in its present form, develop a plan to change them. If you are willing to implement changes to those processes identified as needing change as a part of your sales system, expect improvement in your results. Good process practice is to allow some time to pass and then re-evaluate the implemented changes to assess the improvements or the need to revise some of the changes. It is an interactive process and rightly so if you want to achieve incrementally better results.

There is not really a right or wrong way to use them. Some companies will need to use them all while other may choose to focus on selected issues at the moment and leave some others to a later date. I encourage all readers to try them and continue to use them at intervals to drive the continuous process of improving sales performance results.

One last comment on the templates you will see upcoming illustrating various points discussed. They are the product of years of driving strategic planning, organizational change, and incremental improvements to processes across all corporate functional groups. I caution the reader that no one form or method accommodates the entire spectrum of companies that exist in business today. I am however, encouraged by the number of companies where the described discover approach gives them new insight into their business operations. In addition, by the fact that they are more empowered to uncover the "why" things work answers more regularly.

Figure (19) the single customer segmentation template for process mapping from sales to customer including all activities and connections to a customer from any point in your company.

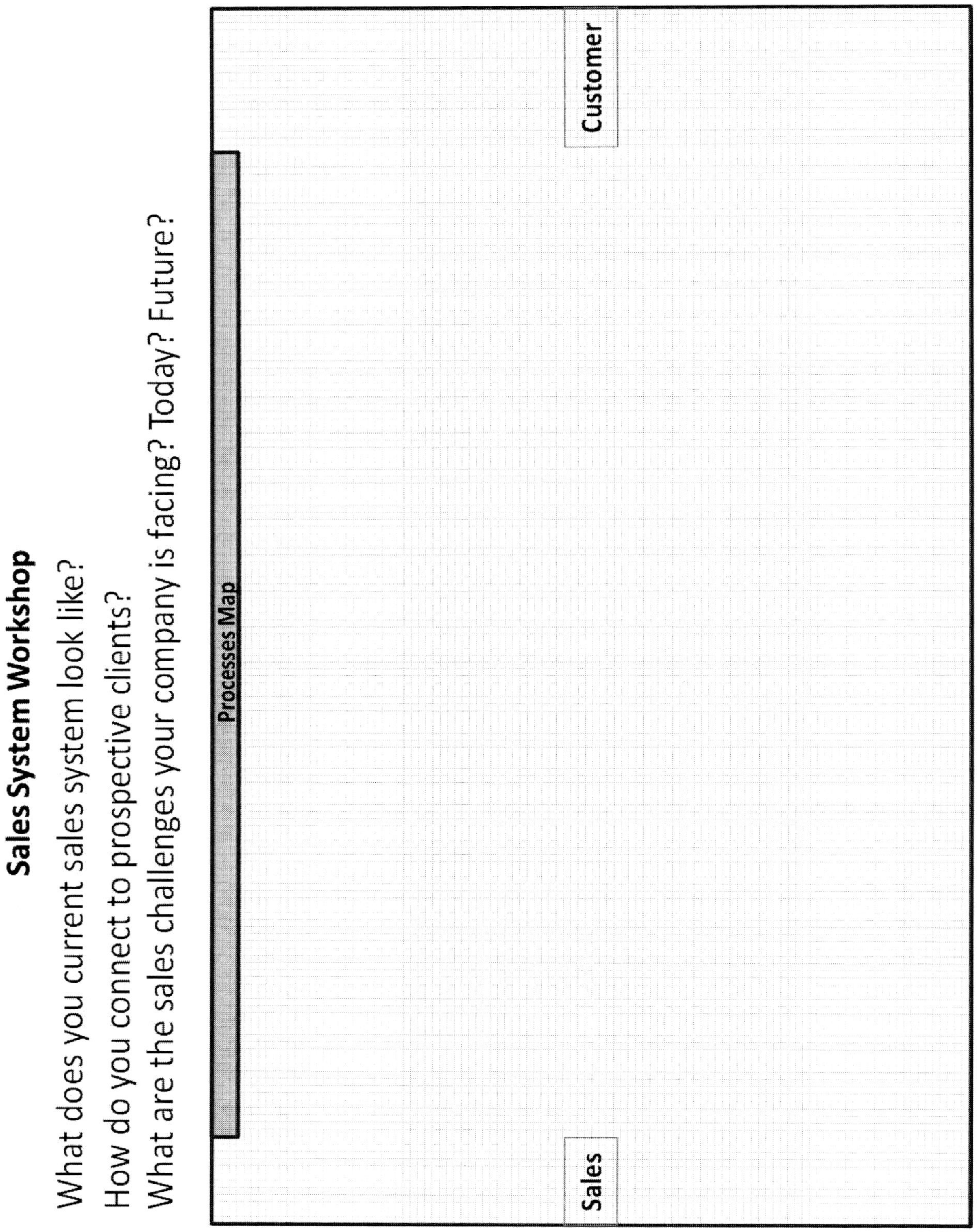

Sales System Workshop
What does you current sales system look like?
How do you connect to prospective clients?
What are the sales challenges your company is facing? Today? Future?
Processes Map
Sales
Customer

Source: SW Consulting, 2011

Figure (20) is an example illustrating some of the linkages and pathways from Sales to the Customer in your sales system.

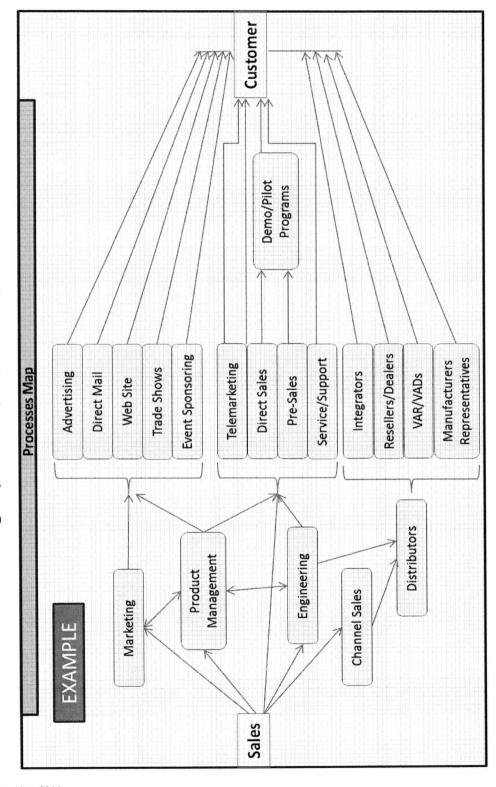

Channel Mapping

As a part of your sales system, channels play a critical role. The most common channel is of course the direct sales channel where your sales people or representative employed by you as agents handle the selling processes with the assistance of the various internal groups such as marketing, operations, and support. Other channels could be resellers, value added dealers, integrators or organizations that utilize your product, service or solution as a part of an overall solution they sell to their customers.

In section (3) of this book, we briefly mentioned the contribution of channels and how the sales organization utilizes them to reach additional prospective customers. The connection between the selling and buying processes, goes well beyond just the mere linkage of a sales channel to the customer, and includes the detailed processes in support of those efforts from selling to supporting.

As with our sales system templates, a part of our discovery needs to explore just how those channels work, and contribute to revenues. Identifying channels also takes in to account the internal groups that play a role in supporting the channel sales efforts.

The template supplied in Figure (21) is to be used for documenting each of those processes required from the selling activities that connect to the potential customers in a single market segment. It helps to make a top-level view such as the one in the sample-completed template Figure (22) illustrates the connections for the all participating representative groups and channels. Then, using that information for the single segment view list all of the set of activities and actions for each of the processes identified.

Most organizations engaged in selling activities have both a more normalized process and set of activities to capture the business from prospective clients, or they use an ad hoc approach wherein various individuals or teams are assigned to respond to the necessary challenges presented by the opportunity. The ad hoc method is disruptive especially when the opportunity is not well characterized and several resources are used to pursue an opportunity that stands a margin chance of success. Ad hoc methods of pursuing opportunities quite often fail to be accounted for in the planning process and are often dealt with outside the normal resource accounting thus driving up the investments required to win sales with any consistency.

Another aspect of ad hoc sales situations is they frequently take away resources that support existing clients in ways that reduce customer satisfaction with your product, service, or solution. If you find in your organization that you need to daily prioritize sales and support with available resources you definitely need to evaluate your processes and the activities that drive them with close attention to detail to find ways to streamline both.

Together, as a team, a channel partner can be a very powerful resource used for leveraging and improving sales results. However, for a great many companies they only examine the discount structure and not the topline contribution to increasing sales without thought for how to leverage the channel and how to develop what is needed to support the partner to produce more sales.

When building the case for implementing a new channel to reach more business in the same segment, or to increase access new market segments, the planning process will benefit from having thought through and mapped the current channels connecting to appropriate prospective customer audience in single or multiple segments. The costs of your channel support can be assessed, compared, and contrasted with those of each channel when making the business case. To lump them all together with assumptions that are quite possibly false, is to invite problems and a steep jump in costs without commensurate contribution to results.

Whether your situation is of the single or multiple segment type, consider when planning is performed, the outcomes will provide additional guidance on the need for creating, changing, or modifying internal processes to accommodate the necessary changes.

On the next several pages, you will see several template and examples for assessing, documenting, and mapping your channels. Figure (21) illustrates what is identified to be the single segment-mapping template as different from a multiple pathway template.

There are two major ways to map your channels using the template models provided. The first as shown in the example Figure (22) is a single customer segmentation version and it starts with the sales organization, and examines collectively all of the sales channel linkages reaching customers in a specific single segment. Appropriately, if you have multiple segments, another template model is used if you have more than one target market. If you sell software for example, your product might be sold into multiple market segments. Blank templates for single and multiple market segments are shown.

The multiple segment second channel map template shown as Figure (23) is for where you have potentially multiple channels but they cover a range of various sectors or subsectors of a market. The completed version is shown in Figure (24). For example, if you were selling a commodity such as batteries, your channel model shows you reach different customer types through multiple channels. This model is one that demonstrates all too frequently channels competing for business by offering different margins for the same product based on volume or some other aspect of sales. One way to resolve channel conflict is to map the connections, estimate the costs and revenue contributions for each, and decide which channel to modify or eliminate to cure the problem.

The cleanest example of what constitutes a channel is the single customer segmentation model template, shown on the following page. IF you have one channel direct sales to your customers, this template should be completed in as much detail as time allows. Complete the channel mapping exercises for both the single and multiple segments and drill down to explore your best segment.

You should keep in mind that as you itemize the activities, their commensurate costs, and the involved groups, the metrics for defining the "best channel" would emerge from the information related to costs and revenue contribution. Save this information for use in the next section covering the overall methodology to understand your sales system. The channel mapping exercise enhances management's ability to put in perspective the parameters and effort required to sell and support sales.

*Figure (21) shows the **single** customer segmentation-mapping template used to map the channels to a customer including the activities and connections of all involved points of contact from your company.*

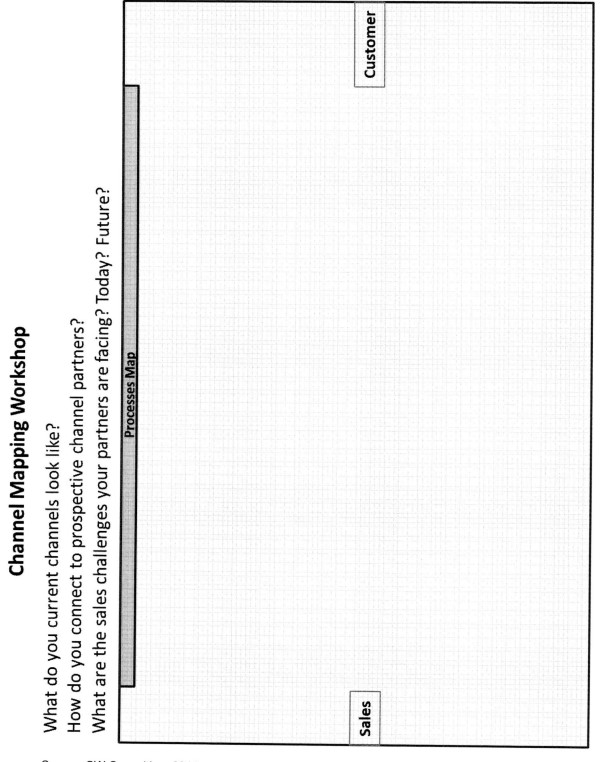

Source: SW Consulting, 2011

Figure (22) is an example of the single segment channel map of the connection points to the customer each would require support and harmonizing of sales and marketing efforts.

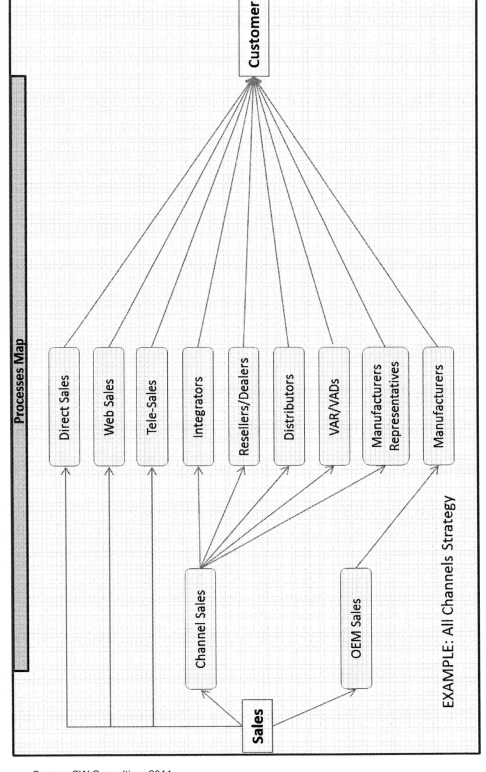

Single Segment Channel Mapping Workshop

What do you current channels look like?

How do you connect to prospective channel partners?

What are the sales challenges your partners are facing? Today? Future?

Processes Map

Customer

Direct Sales

Web Sales

Tele-Sales

Integrators

Resellers/Dealers

Distributors

VAR/VADs

Manufacturers Representatives

Manufacturers

Channel Sales

OEM Sales

Sales

EXAMPLE: All Channels Strategy

Source: SW Consulting, 2011

Figure (23) is the channel mapping to market segment template if you have multiple segments as a part of your business, sales, marketing, and support plans.

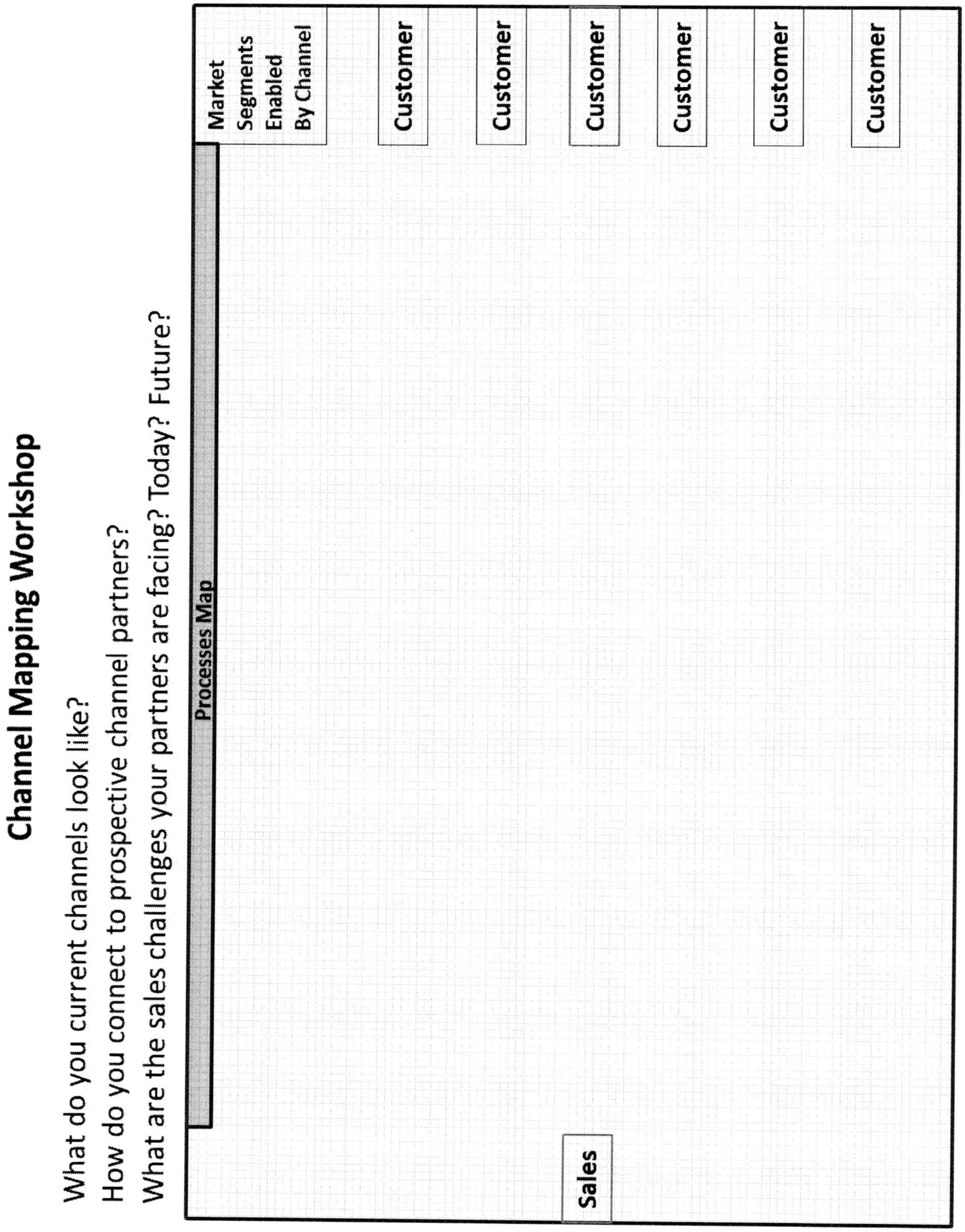

Channel Mapping Workshop

What do you current channels look like?

How do you connect to prospective channel partners?

What are the sales challenges your partners are facing? Today? Future?

Processes Map	Market Segments Enabled By Channel	Customer	Customer	Customer	Customer	Customer	Customer
Sales							

Source: SW Consulting, 2011

120

Figure (24) is an example of a multiple channel pathway with segmented customer targets showing connection points to separate market segments and customers.

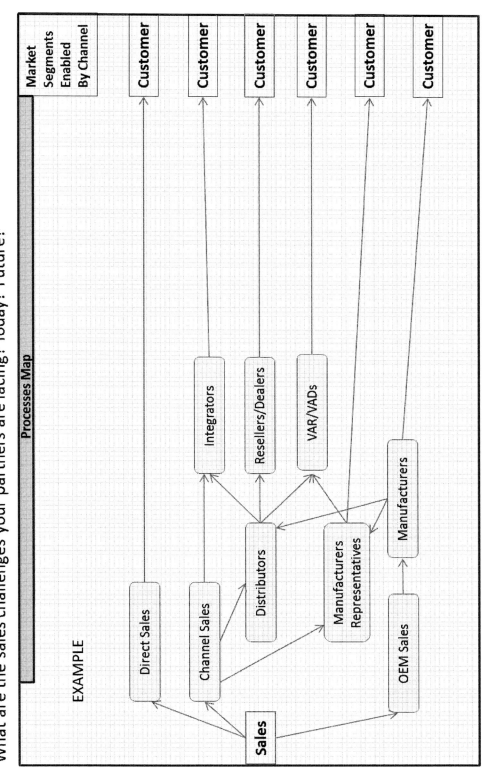

Multiple Customer Segment Channel Mapping Workshop

What channel partners connect to an identifiable market segment?

How do you connect to prospective channel partners?

What are the sales challenges your partners are facing? Today? Future?

Processes Map

Market Segments Enabled By Channel

EXAMPLE

Sales

Direct Sales

Channel Sales

OEM Sales

Distributors

Manufacturers Representatives

Manufacturers

Integrators

Resellers/Dealers

VAR/VADs

Customer

Customer

Customer

Customer

Customer

Customer

Source: SW Consulting, 2011

An Approach for All Sized Enterprises Using the Discovery Method

In the workshop version of this book, we discuss and perform workshops showing the methods and an approach that you will need to understand your own sales system. The method shows whatever that looks like today, can be greatly improved upon using this method and will show you where to focus your energy and attention to improve sales performance. Figure (25) illustrates the repetitive nature of the processes.

The method uses a set of activities structured into workshops consisting of a planning document that results in a template for improvements, and shows you how to create a roadmap for the activities that must be done to make improvements to your sales system.

During the workshop activities and in sections of this book yet to come we consider that there are several parts and additional activities that we will utilize to more fully uncover and evaluate your sales system, and to determine how to transform it to one that has higher sales performance.

Here are the five core steps from preparation to execution we will be discussing for analyzing your sales system and the processes related to it:

1. Collect the data from identified sources you will be analyzing
2. Analyze the data to learn about the activities and processes used
3. Devise strategies by brainstorming for appropriate ideas and metrics
4. Define what are the possible actions we can choose
5. Select from the total actions the set of best actions for implementation

Figure (26) shows some of the questions associated with the five core steps. Each of the core step sections requires you and your group to perform activities and short workshops to analyze ways to strategize and develop a focus on the identification of and selection of the best actions. You, your senior leadership team and those involved in the selling process need to be included at various times in the collection, discussion, and action plan development to ensure the appropriate level of understanding of the sales process. Prior to attending the internal workshops, the workshop exercises shown should be pre-assigned to the participating individuals and groups.

You should complete these activities and be familiar with the results prior to reaching agreement on the changes to be made and the direction to be taken along with the expectations from implementing any changes. The results of each exercise in will be discussed in detail in the workshop style environment and used to document the review process and outcomes as a part of the data sources and analysis. The actions decided upon will also be used to help you drive both appropriate metrics and subsequent actions for improving sales performance. Both the set of activities and the workshops themselves are intended for the senior executive leadership team. Quite often this team needs to be engaged, and they must fully understand what the sales capabilities are, the limitations of their particular selling environment, the techniques, and methods, that can be used to improve their performance overall.

Figure (25) the discovery method process mapping showing assessments and execution aspects.

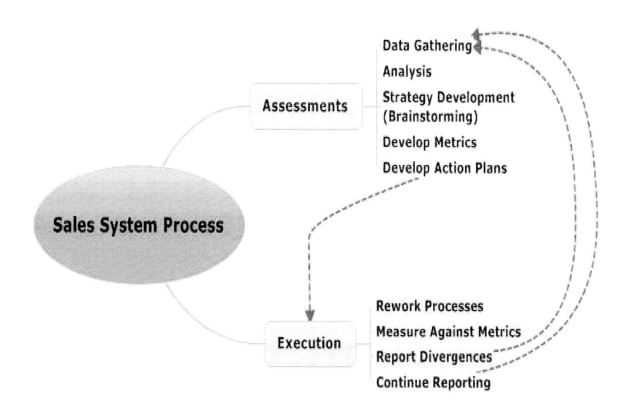

Source: SW Consulting, 2011

As a normal practice the discovery cycle moves from assessments to execution and back to assessments when new data indicates another analysis is required to develop and refine actions for implementation. Following the core steps means that once you begin the assessment process and determine the actions required to modify or enhance your sales system it becomes a continuous process. The collective knowledge from your assessments can continue to be a portion of the basis for actions when you take in to account the new information arising from ongoing evaluations and assessments reporting progress or the need to refine the actions.

The following is an example of Small and Medium Enterprise discovery template derived from a facilitator-led version of the key elements discussed in this book. It shows the five core steps, and some basic questions, that would be discussed, and resolved, during the step workshops.

Figure (26) Five step core discovery model and some of the activities and questions used.

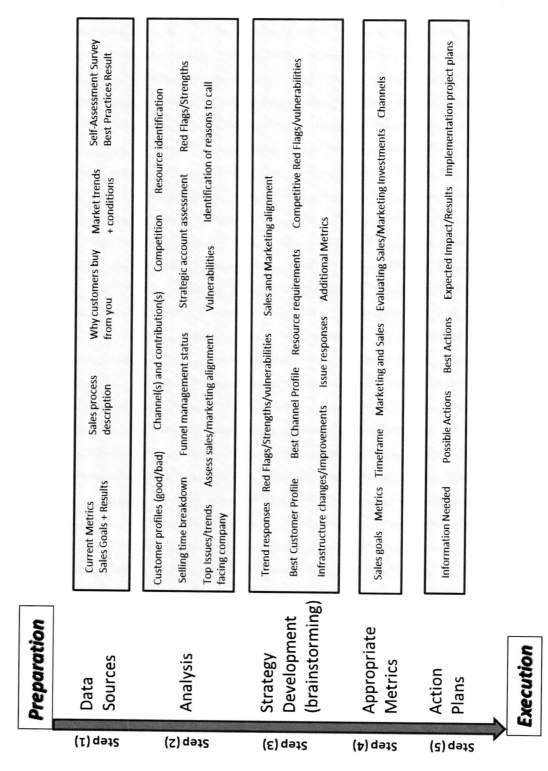

Source: SW Consulting, 2011

The Discovery Process Details

In the discovery phase of trying to understand our own sales system and the processes that are present now, we start with collecting data that we will then analyze, strategize for brainstorming, develop appropriate metrics, and then develop action plans.

STEP (1) GATHER DATA - The first step for data sources is to collect as much of the information in your environment and outside your environment about those prospective and existing customers that we have. Some examples of data sources in your company are your business and sales plans, marketing plans, your current metrics, your specific assigned sales goals, and current results against those goals.

Another data point is the data collected from face to face interaction with current and prospective customers and to have the senior leadership team and those people in the sales organization described the sales process provide sufficient detail so that the activities associated with selling using your sales system so that it can be analyzed. Ask the senior leadership team and anyone who is in sales and marketing the following question, "why do your customers buy from you"?

Make sure to consult additional data sources or relevant market trends and the current conditions in the market that you have targeted for the sale of your products, services, or solution. Take advantage of an available free self-assessment surveys that exist online by such companies as Miller Heiman, Richardson and CSO Insights so you will be better able to determine the best practices that your company has when compared and contrasted with other companies for best practices for processes.

Process Identification Inventory Activities

As a part of the first and second core steps, there is a need to perform a process identification and to inventory the roles, responsibilities, and action s of everyone involved in the sales system and with the selling activities. The template provided overleaf identified as the Process Identification Inventory Worksheet is used to capture the initial information about what group and individual and the types of actions they take.

At this point in the data collection and analysis steps, you should inventory and document the processes who contributes to them. Evaluate each of the respective contributing groups against the identified steps in the end-to-end process that results in a sale. Their contribution should be described in as much detail as space permits to understand their involvement in the selling process.

Essentially, depending upon the nature of the sales, more or less group member involvement may be required to contribute to the overall sales process. Make sure to examine sales that appear to be simple contrasted with sales that appear more complex and involve more internal contributors to achieve the sale. With this data, you can assess and assign value to those who participate, those who contribute, those who contribute on-demand, or those who have no participation in the selling process. They might as examples, be a back office accounting function or a quality assurance manufacturing action and not directly involved in supporting the selling process.

Your desire is to want to capture each and every activity or action as a part of the overall process, define who owns responsibility for that activity and whether or not the individuals are required or desired to participate. The objective is to collect as much information about who is involved and in what capacity related to the activity or actions.

Once you have listed the activity or action and identified all of the people involved you can examine if the activity is appropriate and warrants restructuring in ways that facilitate more productive use of everyone's time, and involvement.

The Process Identification Inventory Worksheet shown in Figure (27) overleaf is an example of showing the relationship between all involved parties for that activity or action. Your organization will likely be structured differently so substitute functional group names, activities, or actions as needed.

Refer back to the channel description and mapping activities from Section (4) as data points that will be taken in to consideration and be a part of the overall analysis activities.

Following the Process Identification Inventory Worksheet template is an example worksheet shown with the key labels that are added to show each participant and the appropriate actions they are responsible for or characterized according to the type of involvements they have with the identified activities. The results of this exercise are used to stimulate further conversations among all the participants and will highlight those involved in the overall sales system and the role(s) in the process they play.

The key labels used with the assessment are:

O - Owns the action

P- Participates in the action

C - Contributes to the action

ON - Is available on-demand to contribute when needed as a resource

M - Monitors the actions or in some instances is assigned to generate reports

NSP – No Sales Participation identifies those people without an immediate role with the selling process

Identifying the participants, the activities, and the actions required to complete a sale are essential elements for analyzing what works and what does not work as well in your sales system. Remember to include as many details about the activities and actions performed by individual contributors or leaders in the supporting the sales efforts. The greater the understanding of those activities and actions the greater will be your ability to brainstorm on improving them in an upcoming core step.

Companies will generally need to ask lots of questions to more completely describe the entire sales process from end to end, and whether it results in a complete success, partial success, or produces less than expected success. While performing the data collecting make sure to include information about how the competition, the marketplace, and the trends are impacting the current sales efforts.

A number of clients in my consulting practice use competitive intelligence to win more business. The actions of other competitors, or market factors that are impacting everyone in a market area, are ways to understand responses to changing conditions.

Organizations that are more sophisticated invest in a competitive analyst, and use the information they produce, to build more productive strategies to win more business. That same role can be fulfilled by a sales coordinator who monitors who the competitors are and mines that information for facts that can be useful to the sales team or those working together to win more sales.

Thus far as a part of our data collection activities, we have explored single and multiple channels used by the company to connect with prospective and current customers. Performing a deeper dive into discovering more about the processes includes having discussions involving every group that contributes to a sale identify what role they play and the activities they are involved in connected to the selling process.

The process identification inventory worksheet completed example shown in Figure (28) will assist with the assessment of each cataloging a contributor's role in the selling process and identifies the nature of the role they play. It also shows the potential relationship and possible dependency of one group to another.

You will note from the example of the process identification inventory quite a number of groups could be involved, The number of groups will vary considerably from company to company but the objective is to not leave out any contributors to the selling processes.

When it comes to labeling the type of action each contributor makes participants can play more than one role and frequently do as their responsibilities cross groups or if they lead one or more of the identified functional areas of your company.

The NSP or No Sales Participation designation identifies those people that have limited involvement or they are rarely involved in the selling process itself but might play a role in certain circumstances. An external consultant is an example of this type of person. The NSP role differs from the people whose role is that they are routinely expected to participate on-demand as a resource perhaps due to their subject matter expertise.

At the conclusion of identifying and completing the process identification inventory worksheet the scope of your sales system and the processes will be much clearer. It becomes easier to have discussions concerning modifying those roles as the template is completed.

Organizations using this process identification inventory also find that they may wish to add more groups or reduce the number of groups in order to optimize the utilization of resources. Completing this assessment for specific projects may also provide more insight in to the cost to support the opportunity and impact the resource planning activities. Once the exercise is completed keep each one with an overview of the nature of the opportunity such as how large, what did it consist of and what were the milestones for the opportunity to make a comprehensive playbook for handling the larger projects more effectively.

The inventory helps to characterize the overall company involvement in selected opportunities, or the operational norm that is associated with the sales system and its processes.

Figure (27) shows the Process Identification Inventory Worksheet template for assessing roles in the sales process.

PROCESS IDENTIFICATION INVENTORY WORKSHEET

MATRIX	Groups											
Actions	Marketing	Sales	Sales Management	Senior Executive	Engineering	Finance	Training Support Service	Manufacturing	Legal	Channel Partner	SME Consultant
Awareness Development											
Lead Generation											
Lead Qualification											
Opportunity Scoping											
Opportunity Development											
Resource Planning											
Solution Proposal											
Negotiating Contracting											
Implementation Delivery Fulfillment											
Training Support Service											
Ongoing Relationship Management											

Keys: O (owns), P (participates), C (contributes), ON (on-demand), M (monitors), NSP (No sales participation)

Source: SW Consulting, 2011

PROCESS IDENTIFICATION INVENTORY WORKSHEET

Figure (28) Showing the Process Identification Inventory Worksheet example completed.

MATRIX Actions	Groups Marketing	Sales	Sales Management	Senior Executive	Engineering	Finance	Training Support Service	Manufacturing	Legal	Channel Partner	SME Consultant
Awareness Development	O – Sam K.	P	C	M	P	NSP	C	NSP	NSP	O – Goff D.	NSP
Lead Generation	O – Sue B.	P	M	NSP	NSP	NSP	C	NSP	NSP	O – Goff D.	NSP
Lead Qualification	O – Sue B.	O – Al M.	P	M	NSP	C	NSP	NSP	NSP	O – Goff D.	C
Opportunity Scoping	M	O – All	P	M	C	C	P	P	NSP	O – Goff D.	C
Opportunity Development	M	O – All	P	M	C	P	C	P	P	O – Goff D.	C
Resource Planning	C	C	O – Bob L	O – Jill O.	O – Hal P.	O – Paul D.	O – Sally W.	O – Sal T.	O – Jill O.	O – Goff D.	NSP
Solution Proposal	C	O – Jim W.	O – Jim W.	M	ON	P	P	C	ON	O – Goff D.	ON
Negotiating Contracting	NSP	O – Jim W.	O – Jim W.	ON	C	C	C	P	ON	O – Goff D.	P
Implementation Delivery Fulfillment	NSP	P	P	NSP	O – Todd H.	ON	ON	O – Sal T.	M	M	ON
Training Support Service	NSP	P	NSP	NSP	C	NSP	O – Sally W.	NSP	NSP	M	NSP
Ongoing Relationship Management	M	O – All	O – Tom G.	ON	P	ON	M	NSP	NSP	O – Goff D.	NSP

Keys: O (owns), P (participates), C (contributes), ON (on-demand), M (monitors), NSP (No sales participation)

Source: SW Consulting, 2011

An equally simple method for exploring specific questions that need to be addressed or the decisions that are needed and discussions about the possible options is to employ a balance sheet approach. You write down the question then gather as a group to discuss the positives (pros) and negatives (con) and rate and rank the results. A sample assessment sheet template is shown below and a completed example overleaf.

Use the template shown as Figure (29) for questions, decisions that need to be explored, or for assessing the options for a specific action being contemplated. The template is a way to capture the thinking of the organization and discuss the merits associated with the topic being explored.

The purpose for quantitatively assessing the question is to assess the prioritization of the list of questions, decisions that need to be made and the options associated with each one. Once the assessments are scored by each question, decision, or choice of options, they can then be ranked according to a further assessment of the items to discuss resources necessary to complete the tasks.

Figure (29) Pro/Con Assessment Rating form template.

PRO/CON Assessment Ratings

Question/Decision/Option Analysis:			
Pros (for - advantages)	**Score**	**Cons (against - disadvantages)**	**Score**
Totals		**Totals**	

Scores are on a 1 (poor assessment) to 10 (good assessment) basis

In areas where you have multiple questions, decisions, or options to analyze use a single sheet for each one of them and then group together the most similar ones. If you find lots of similar questions or decisions covering a single focused or related are it may be indicating that the magnitude of that particular area is larger than previously thought and requires more brainstorming. Additional attention to that area will be needed, to thoroughly explore the nature of the issues before coming to any final set of actions.

Some of the questions or decisions will arise from the preliminary data collected. Here is one example of a specific question and the responses along with the scoring. It highlights that quite often the CON position can overtake the PRO on a particular issue. Participants need to contribute their thoughts to aid in clarifying both the question or decision context and if they feel the scoring is consistent with the observations. Use this technique to stimulate the needed discussions to try to get everyone on the same page with regard to the issue or question being examined.

Figure (30) Pro/Con Assessment Ration form completed example.

PRO/CON Assessment Ratings

Decision/Question/Option Analysis Statement			
Question: Why do we take so long for our organization to complete the sales cycle?			
Pros (for - advantages)	**Score**	**Cons (against - disadvantages)**	**Score**
1) careful consideration reduces errors and our potential risk	7	1) our competition gets more time to react to the opportunity	8
2) there are multiple levels of sign off so everyone understands the level of commitments being made and their role	3	2) our prospective client involved parties changes with time	6
3) we want to allow sufficient time to qualify and evaluate the opportunity to decide how much effort and priority to assign to the specific opportunity.	5	3) our legal and financial evaluation processes are time intensive	1
		4) it takes us much longer to assess the potential risks/rewards adequately	2
		5) our products are in a state of flux and need more time to evolve	1
Totals	**15**	**Totals**	**18**

Scores are on a 1 (poor assessment) to 10 (good assessment) basis

In the examples CONS outweigh the PROS with it comes to explaining the specific answers to the stated question. In instances where the PROS strongly outweigh the CONS, make sure you have sufficiently captured the sentiments of all of the contributors to the group who have opinions about the question. In this example the CONS are indicative of additional consideration in the specific areas mentioned in the specific named areas (legal and financial for example) to see if the information represents the need to more closely examine those areas individually through new questions about the corresponding areas (legal and financial).

Additional drill-down questions will routinely produce more specifics that can be used to build a stronger case for modifying the areas through more discussions. As you explore the additional questions, you should decide upon the course of action and the sense of priority that needs to be assigned to the area as a part of your action plans. Revisit the questions in the planning discussions often.

Figure (31) Data collection and analysis questions checklist example.

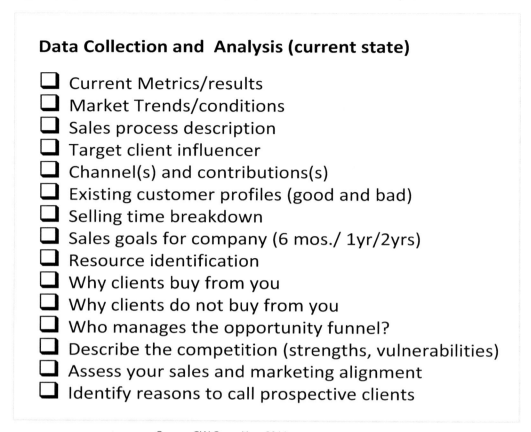

Data Collection and Analysis (current state)

- ❑ Current Metrics/results
- ❑ Market Trends/conditions
- ❑ Sales process description
- ❑ Target client influencer
- ❑ Channel(s) and contributions(s)
- ❑ Existing customer profiles (good and bad)
- ❑ Selling time breakdown
- ❑ Sales goals for company (6 mos./ 1yr/2yrs)
- ❑ Resource identification
- ❑ Why clients buy from you
- ❑ Why clients do not buy from you
- ❑ Who manages the opportunity funnel?
- ❑ Describe the competition (strengths, vulnerabilities)
- ❑ Assess your sales and marketing alignment
- ❑ Identify reasons to call prospective clients

Source: SW Consulting, 2011

This checklist shown as Figure (31) is to be used for collecting data (Step 1) discussed overleaf and to prepare for the analysis (Step 2) and the answering of questions which have been selected as important for understanding how your operational sales processes and the sales system interact and function.

Every functional area represented needs to bring data, the metrics that are in use and as much detailed information as possible about how the processes currently work as part of the sales system being examined.

Check the boxes only after discussing that topic point and making sure that any related questions are answered to the satisfaction of the group. Some may be flagged for further research and discussion to be revisited in a short window of time.

You may note from the nature of some of the questions that specific answers and understanding of the process area or problem associated with it are required for the group to be on the same page for subsequent discussions. Failure to answer or clarify the items on the checklist could result in false assumptions and lead to developing action plans that miss the mark and improve results.

Frequent use of the PRO/CON Assessment ratings method should clarify the position of the group related to the question, decision, or options to be considered prior to choosing the appropriate actions.

STEP (2) ANALYSIS - Step two in conjunction with the data collection is the grouping together and analysis of the data sources and information that we gathered in step one. This is also a good time to review the inventory of information collected thus far. It is also a good point to review any questions that arose during the initial data collection from various sources. Especially those areas or items suggesting more data is needed.

The analysis part is to pick apart the information and determine its validity and usefulness towards answering the list of questions.

From the data that we have, we should be able to determine the following:

- Do we have an existing business plan of record that has been communicated to the appropriate participants who have responsibility for the implementation and execution of the plans?

- Do we have clear customer profiles of what makes both good and bad customers? Do all of the sales process participants know the criteria?

- Do we know the channels and the contributions for each channel according to sales results? How are decisions for any aspect of those channels made?

- What do we know about the competition, and potential competition? How the customer and other competitors view our solutions?

- What partnerships, alliances, and other agreements with technology partners do we have in place now and how are we planning for properly utilizing their capabilities?

- What mechanism do we use to identify resources internal to our organization?

- Do we have a detailed look at and breakdown of our selling time which is defined by the amount of time spent searching for prospects, qualifying prospects and then understanding what it will take to close the business

- Somewhere in our organization, we need to determine the file management process and we can determine that from the metrics for sales. Do we have such a process in place?

- As a part of our analysis we need to look at how we would identify a truly strategic must have type of account, and what questions would be asked to assess them.

- What are the unique areas our company provides that differentiates us? Do we know how the customer feels about our differentiation compared to others?

- In our industry what are the top issues and trends that face us as a company?

- What are the top issues facing our prospective customers and existing customers and do we know what the impact will be of those issues on business decisions?

- We will assess sales and marketing alignment, from the aspect of how well marketing supports the efforts of sales during customer engagements.

- What vulnerabilities does our company have? In our products? In our services? Alternatively, in our solutions?

- We should be able to identify from the information available to us the reasons why we would call upon a customer and why they would be interested in our products, services, or solutions.

- Do we as an organization have a clear roadmap of how the product, services, and solutions portfolio will evolve over the next period and on in to the future?

The analysis step familiarizes and prepares your participants to handle the information, questions and requirements for additional information that will go in to the next step, the brainstorming of what the information indicates and where it fits in the overall scheme of your sales system and the processes that have been identified in step one.

STEP (3) STRATEGY DEVELOPMENT (BRAINSTORMING) - Step three is where we do strategic development and it requires brainstorming of that which we have collected for data sources and the analyses that we have performed so far to answer some basic questions. The best way to approach this is for each of the following topics to brainstorm on that particular topic as concisely as possible.

Some of the key areas for brainstorming our situation are:

- Responses to trends in the market, in the industry, and our customers

- How do we handle the red flags/strength/vulnerabilities that we have

- What can be done to improve our sales and marketing alignment if they are not already lined

- What does our best customer profile look like

- What does our best channel and channel partner profile look like

- Of the resources that we have now what can we do to leverage them to accomplish more

- Specific to the competition what are the red flags/vulnerabilities

- What infrastructure changes/improvements to our organization have we identified were need to identify for improvement

- If there are issues related to responses, or responsiveness we need to brainstorm

- We should also brainstorm additional metrics

- Define your differentiation in what must be done to achieve further additional differentiation

Simplified Brainstorming Process

Simplified actions associated with the Brainstorming activities:

1. Define and agree on the objectives
2. Brainstorm ideas and the suggestions will have an agreed upon time limit
3. Categorize/condense/combined/refine the ideas and suggestions
4. Assess and analyze the expected effects on results
5. Prioritize the option/right list the ones that are appropriate
6. Agree on the actions of the time frames to take
7. Select the best action and timeframes
8. Put in motion controls and monitor follow-up

You need to have some discussion centering upon the areas that impact your business the most. Typically, those areas include examining or re-examining your metrics, and how you select your goals during the planning process. Each time you have a planning discussion you will need to re-evaluate the goals, objectives and the metrics by which you measure progress in order to document clearly, what worked and what did not work.

Additionally, those factors that impact the business the most need to be assessed for the short term and long term contributions to results. During the brainstorming activities, no subject that is identified as contributing to, or inhibiting sales in some way should be taken off the table.

It is always a best practice to appoint a discussion facilitator who can be objective, and a scribe who will record all of the information from the collection to the final summaries and selections of those actions to pursue. The collective wisdom of the group also is a best practice to provide to the on boarding of any new employees who are involved in sales in any way. Use of common language and terms is encouraged throughout the organization.

The checklist shown in Figure (32) pertains to brainstorming activities and discussing the possibilities for actions based upon the data collected and the analysis performed in Steps (1) and (2).

Try to keep in mind the use of the suggested simplified brainstorming process. You want to collect as many opinions and points of views without judgment or prioritization and then move the discussions towards selecting those items needing prioritization. Make sure to capture all comments regarding the brainstorming and the prioritization as data points for future discussions. This information can also be used to benchmark progress and contribute to the overall understanding of the metrics that should be used to gauge performance at some future review date.

Figure (32) Brainstorming questions and checklist example.

Strategy Development (brainstorm possibilities)

☐ Discuss metrics for each process/subprocess
☐ Discuss trend responses
☐ Discuss areas of vulnerability/red flags/strengths
☐ Discuss best channel partner profile
☐ Discuss best customer profile
☐ Discuss selling time contributors (impediments)
☐ Discuss selling time allocations/priorities
☐ Discuss goal strategies
☐ Discuss resources strategies
☐ Discuss your unique differentiation
☐ Discuss critical areas needing improvements
☐ Discuss competitive responses
☐ Discuss short term tactics vs. long term strategies
☐ Discuss sales and marketing alignment
☐ Discuss additional reasons to make changes

Source: SW Consulting, 2011

STEP (4) APPROPRIATE METRICS - Step number four is to assess, and agree upon, the appropriate metrics. That means we are going to be looking at our sales goals, the specific performance metrics that we wish to select, and the appropriate time frames that we will measure as metrics. We also assess what activities do we look towards marketing and sales to accomplish, and how will the metrics impact them.

We need to clearly understand and evaluate our sales and marketing investments, to determine if we are receiving an optimal rate of return. We also must then assess our investment in the channels, and the return on investment that we plan to receive, as a contribution to the sales from the specific channels.

The checklist shown in Figure (33) provides a template for determining the appropriate metrics. First, identify the ones that are currently used, and then perform a group discussion as to whether they represent the best set of metrics to monitor. Second, try to determine how effective the sales processes are as measured by the metrics you have identified in use in your sales system.

Figure (33) Metric questions and checklist example.

Metrics (when, how much, pass/fail)

- ❑ Identify all the current metrics in use
- ❑ Have everyone describe what they believe the metrics to be
- ❑ What do the metrics indicate?
- ❑ Characterize – Is a metric indicating performance?
- ❑ Identify the most important metric(s)
- ❑ What is the timeline interval for the measurements?
- ❑ What are the channel partner metrics?
- ❑ Develop a list of metrics that indicate problems
- ❑ Are the metrics based on the business plan?
- ❑ Are the metrics based on the sales plan?
- ❑ What are the organizational goals (growth, profit, etc.)
- ❑ How is customer satisfaction formally measured?
- ❑ Are the metrics qualitative or quantitative?
- ❑ Do you measure the sales contribution by department?
- ❑ How do you measure individual sales performers?
- ❑ How do you measure sales support contributions?
- ❑ How often are the metrics reviewed? Revised? Communicated
- ❑ Do you benchmark against industry best practices?

Source: SW Consulting, 2011

Make a listing of the metrics by functional area in use in your organization. Sales might be measured on revenue, retention, gross profit, and cost of a sale or the return on sales investments for example. Marketing might measure lead generation or quality and conversion of leads.

STEP (5) ACTION PLANS - Step number five will be to take all of the prior steps and the key information and metrics that we have identified and use that that information to drive creation of actionable plans. If there is additional information that we think we need prior to doing the action plans we need to identify and make it a part of one of the activities that still needs to be completed.

From all that we have looked at thus far from data analysis, brainstorming and deciding on metrics, what are all of the possible actions that we can take focusing in on those activities that need to be improved and enhanced or modified.

Out of those possible actions we can select the best actions we want to refine the list and from those best actions what do we expect the impact to be on results, who is expected to perform the actions, and what decisions have been made on the implementation project plans that we need to develop.

To this point, we have described from preparation to execution a complete five-step process. Revisit your business, sales and marketing plans to re-assess what modification must be made to them, by whom from each area assigned, that will ensure implementation and on what timeline the actions should expect to be completed. Follow the checklist shown in Figure (34).

Figure (34) Action questions and checklist examples.

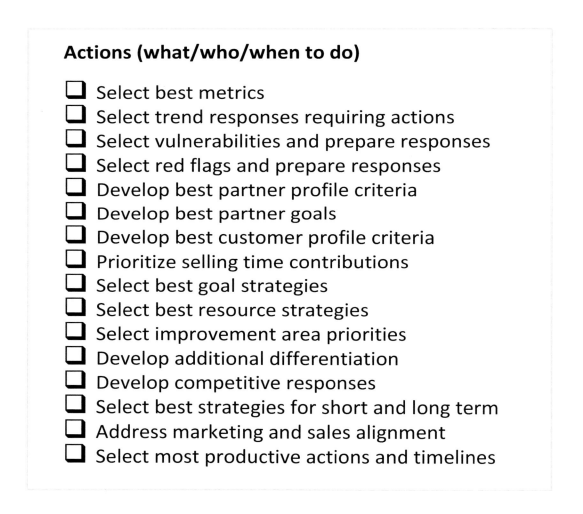

Actions (what/who/when to do)

- ☐ Select best metrics
- ☐ Select trend responses requiring actions
- ☐ Select vulnerabilities and prepare responses
- ☐ Select red flags and prepare responses
- ☐ Develop best partner profile criteria
- ☐ Develop best partner goals
- ☐ Develop best customer profile criteria
- ☐ Prioritize selling time contributions
- ☐ Select best goal strategies
- ☐ Select best resource strategies
- ☐ Select improvement area priorities
- ☐ Develop additional differentiation
- ☐ Develop competitive responses
- ☐ Select best strategies for short and long term
- ☐ Address marketing and sales alignment
- ☐ Select most productive actions and timelines

Source: SW Consulting, 2011

Discovery -- An Example

Try this exercise. Draw an amorphous cloud and in that cloud place some small circles that would indicate the people that will be involved in influencing the buying for any particular opportunity you might be pursuing. That cloud is the organization where those people influencing buying are, and we need to identify them as being a part of the decision-making process. If they have no impact on the buying influence the buying decision making process we need to identify that. So when we look at our cloud, one of the first questions we ask is what do we know about the organization, the company, the markets that that company serves, any indications that that company is experiencing either growth or trouble from annual reports, Hoover's, Google, or whatever source you feel comfortable as a reliable provider of information.

We collect this information and we will then analyze that information. By analyzing, we mean looking at patterns looking at facts, looking at trends, looking at indicators or metrics that can be used to gauge why a company might need to purchase a particular product, service, or solution, and with what sense of urgency is being driven by what trigger event.

When you draw the cloud and identify the decision makers, you look to your processes to connect the information and corresponding actions to satisfy each of those decision makers and improve your chances of winning. The more you know about the situation, and what your responses should be based on the understanding of what your organization is capable of handling so you will be better able to select and execute on the appropriate actions.

To be clear, the goal of your sales system and your sales processes is to be able to satisfy the concerns, the requirements, and specifications, and to take in to account any other hidden aspects of understanding what it will take you to win the opportunity. The more you know the better your chances. The actions you either routinely or in response to explicit situations should be well developed before you attempt to use them.

Actions can arise more purposefully when you understand the metrics, the desired outcomes, the factors that will affect your ability to perform the action successfully, and several other factors that should be accommodated by your sales system and the processes your company uses.

Frequently, actions are based on assumptions that may not be appropriate to the situation or to the stage of the buying process. Consider what actions your competition may be planning to negate the value your offer by trying to confuse the prospective customers. If you plan properly and deliver appropriate responses, you can differentiate your solution from the competition but it will become second nature if your organization builds and uses the most effective sales system.

Differentiation – Taking Inventory

Modern day selling quite frequently involves failing in to a number of sales people traps. The most common trap is failing to differentiate your product, service, or solution in ways that appeal to each of the decision makers. I frequently find it necessary to provide several examples to my clients to help them understand the concept of differentiation, and the potential impact, during both the selling and the buying and decision-making processes. If I draw a triangle for example, at the bottom third slice of the triangle there is no differentiation and all things are equal, then chances are bad things will happen as customers see no particular reason to choose your product, service, or solution, on anything other than the basis of price. They may further, invent perceived weaknesses in areas as a result of the salesperson not positioning properly any beneficial differentiation to match with the customers concept of what the best solution would look like.

Refer to Figure (35). In the middle tier slice of our triangle companies appeared to be me-to pricing is usually within plus or minus band with not a great or significant difference in range, but the primary characteristic of the middle is that there are visible things that the people influencing buying can research and determine on their own. That still is dangerous to us as the selling organization and reduces our chances of impacting the sale. At the top tier slice of our pyramid, we enter the zone of maximum differentiation. This area is where we clearly identify the differences between us and all other competitors that have relevance and significance to the people influencing buying show that they may make a more informed decision when we have given them this knowledge.

Figure (35) Conceptualization of differentiation at various locations on the value pyramid.

Differentiation – Those Attributes That Can Be Distinguished From All Else

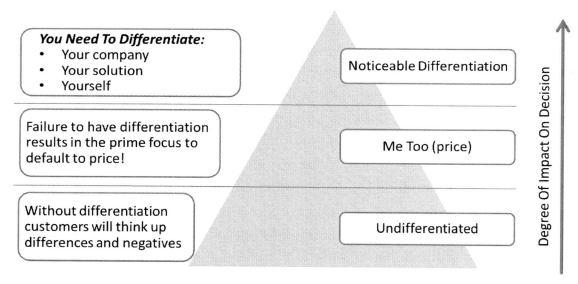

Source: SW Consulting, 2011

IF you have no real differentiation, I recommend some serious discussions take place about finding some. At the conclusion of collecting the answers to each listed above, decide what points won, or lost business for you, and how well your competition might fair against you at some future point.

Because differentiation involves individual perception, we need to validate that the differentiation is of value to the individual people influencing buying, and this can only be determined through good communication involving questions and answers to verify that they acknowledge our differentiation. If the people influencing buying do not understand the differentiation, or if the differentiation is of little or no value to them in their decision-making Ross says for this purchase only, then we reduce our chances of winning the business. Therefore, with each analysis of an individual selling opportunity, we must understand our differentiation, and what it means to the prospective buying influencer who will be making a purchase decision.

Here is an example of differentiation. Your prospective customer initially compares your solution to that of several others. Initially the comparison places each solution as equal or undifferentiated. During the course of several conversations with the prospective customer, your sales person uncovers that the prospective customer decision makers are looking for a solution that has significantly lower operating costs beginning shortly after initial start-up and depending upon exactly how the prospective customer implements the solution your ultimate cost savings becomes a clear differentiator in the selection process.

Differentiation most often occurs when your customer's perceive an advantage that at some point you have pointed out. If left to their own thought processes they might have missed it entirely or not included any hints in their initial project plans. In order to build as much differentiation into the selling process it requires the collective minds of several subject matter experts throughout the company to ensure that the differentiation is appropriate and relevant to the opportunity you are pursing. You should rely upon that which sales and marketing do together to identify and convey to the customer what your special differentiators are to win more business.

When discussing differentiation and whether you have it for any given opportunity try this approach. Gather the marketing materials, testimonials, accolades, and some proposals you have written in the past that, taking care to bring both winners and some losing proposals to the table for analysis. Take the information as a group and answer and record results for the following questions, then identify the most significant and consistent points of differentiation.

Questions to ask:

- What are our most significant points of differentiation in OUR view?

- What are the most important points of view on differentiation from our CUSTOMER'S view?

- What points of differentiation did our COMPETITOR'S bring to the table? (for wins and losses)

- For each point of differentiation ask: SO WHAT (answer the what's in it for the customer)
- For each point of differentiation ask: PROVE IT (what are the proofs for the differentiation)

Process Reviews

The discovery process is just one of explorations of how your company does things along with the identification and discussion of what works and what does not work well and why. Having these discussions should become a routine part of your operational culture. Continuous improvement methods generally state that to improve a process to get any measureable results you need to conduct reviews periodically and take the necessary actions as your people assess what needs to be modified or enhanced.

Following the discovery process to describe the mapping of channels, completing the process inventory assessments, and developing and understanding the metrics that are productive to monitor, will ultimately help you to arrive at the set of actions that will have the greatest impact. Utilizing the continuous improvement approach, in a more productive and interactive way, especially as it relates to understanding your sales system and the processes, yield ways to drive more business in your company.

As a consultant I recommend three types of reviews be used in routine operational situations.

(1) First is a metrics review or check for validity update. You determined the metrics as a part of your discovery activities. Put the most productive ones to use for conducting your reviews of the selling process end to end with all groups participating if they are involved in the selling activities. Again, the goal is to maintain a holistic approach to see that the sales system continues to be able to handle dynamic conditions as encountered. Set the metrics and make sure everyone understand what they indicate and why they are measured.

(2) Business planning reviews to connect all the plans. Where most companies get off course is where they do not formalize the strategic planning and treat the business plan as a living document updated to that each respective group can assess what needs to change in their organization to keep the entire sales system and working processes as productive as possible. The old adage of "if you fail to plan your plan to fail" is apt and unmistakably true. Make sure every group contributing to the sale process is involved in the planning and the review of both plans and expectations. Producing a business plan first starts with it being achievable and all of the contributors need to know how it going to be achieved and their roles and responsibilities to make it happen.

(3) Support the opportunity funnel review process. I find a number of organizations fail to conduct opportunity reviews in a positive, proactive and constructive manner.

Management always needs to set the tone of the reviews and supply clear guidelines what needs to specifically examined and in what detail to keep it from becoming a frustrating and less than productive exercise. The reviews are often focused on the wrong issues which is to say what are the resources needed, the priority in which they will be used and a clear understanding of where the opportunities are in the selling and buying decision making processes.

Process reviews are not your normal meeting. They should all be conducted like brainstorming sessions in order to uncover the best suggestions from the collective wisdom of everyone in the room.

Part (C) ADDED DIMENSIONS

Sales Objectives -- Keeping Your Eye On The Ball!

Our sales system must include a set of questions for us to determine both the buying influencer's interest and concept of what their vision for the solution looks like, and with each buying influencer we need to verify what the opportunity is that we are trying to position our product, service, or solution, to help them achieve some goal. Sales objectives need to be very precise.

As a part of our sales system process, those questions that help us refine and better understand the nature of the opportunity is a must. Questions that we need to ask about the opportunity are from the point of view of do we (a) understand what the opportunity looks like, (b) specifically from the perspective of those influencing the buying, (c) can we clearly articulate what we believe the nature of the opportunity, quantities and potential revenue and budget impacts are, and (d) that we have determined from communicating with the people influencing buying, a precise notion of the timeline involved, so that we know where we are in the buying decision making process.

Figure (36) is used to illustrate a Sales versus Plan example where the comparators are new sales, existing sales, the aggregate of the two, then compared against the overall sales plan. It points out various cycles of a roller coaster like pattern where the objectives, when they fall behind, rarely get caught up even in a cyclic business cycle. Sales planning, and the business plans, need to interpret these cycles in ways that could contribute to a more accurate, hence realistic, revenue cycle. If the plans fall behind examine all factors that are impacting the projections vs. results to see if other factors might be in play.

As to handling RFPs, if the notice is released containing specifications timelines and other information, it is highly probable we will have no time to make an impact on the buying decision-making, and therefore might be wasting valuable time and resources. On the other hand, if we understand the timeline, and we are able to early get involved with the people influencing buying we can assist in shaping their concept of the solution to our advantage. This may not sound like rocket science but I assure you unless it is a part of the routine operating process the productive opportunity yields will be very small, and the frustration very high.

Figure (36) Deconstructing the sales plan to assess new or existing client contributions.

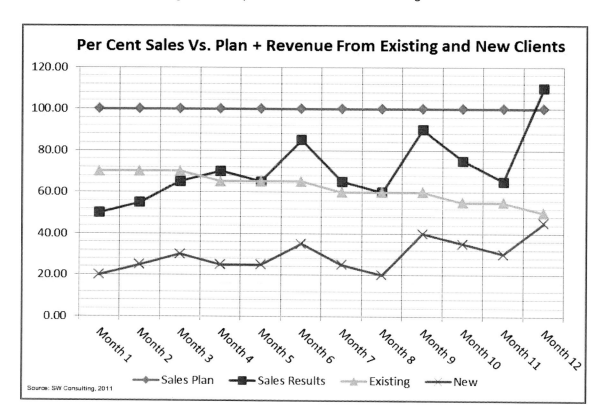

Sales Performance Questions

As a part of our assessment of the current state of our company regarding sales performance we need to ask first the question what, are the metrics that will assist us in both analyzing and proposing improvements or enhancements to our sales system to increase the sales performance. Each company practices sales and marketing differently depending upon the audiences that based and markets that they serve.

For each element of our sales system as we uncover them we will need to make sure that there is a corresponding metric by which we will assess their effectiveness and whether or not we are able to obtain significant improvements. Marketing may use as a metric the number of leads or qualified opportunities that are produced through their efforts. Rarely does marketing ever generate a report card for their collateral materials from the customer's perspective as to whether those materials are effective or not.

Therefore, this contrast points out that quite often we are concerned with top line metrics and often forget about qualitative metrics and other types of data that are useful to us in assessing what needs to be improved. When we talk about how we manage a sales opportunity once we have identified and qualified it then we count the number of new accounts acquired at this point but later on we may decide that they did not survive and we did not achieve the sale after following our sales current processes.

Companies will often distinguish between the acquisition of new accounts and the development of business within existing accounts. Still others made look at retention and not growth in managing to retain a client over some number of years. Which leads us to when we are attempting to manage the client relationship, what is a good metric? Often, it is an average of the amount of revenue, produced by the sales ongoing efforts, or an average account billing in any particular month, that continues to indicate either the account is remaining stable, or it is increased, or if it decreases, we immediately would want to know why as a metric.

When examining those metrics contributing to the sales process in our organization, we can assess an individual performer's quota achievement, against their assigned quota, and where they are achieving that on some timely basis. Alternatively, we can assess the achievement of sales according to the groups that have participated and support they provide to the selling processes. We would often look to our IT people to provide us with performance reports, and whether or not we have a Customer Relationship Management (CRM) system, we would hope that we are able to determine a forecast that has some degree of accuracy, such that we may plan with other areas of the company for production, or support resources.

Management often is only viewed from a metric point of view as overall quota achievement, overall margin achievement, or some level of increase in the business as a metric. So on the subject of metrics first understand that there are a great of them each of them should be geared to answer a question about whether or not we are making progress against our plans, and if they are giving us on our dashboard some indication that action is required and who should be taking the actions.

Therefore, the formula you could say is that revenue is associated with a set of activities and metrics at it as a part of our planning and budgeting process we will rely upon leaves metrics to determine if we are moving along to meet our goals or need to take immediate action to correct our course.

Therefore, as we explore your sales system we are going to ask several questions about your sales system, the metrics you use, and the tribal knowledge and wisdom that is your guide for the internal decision-making processes. We intend to dive deep into your sales system and uncover the processes that are currently in use, whether they were planned or not, and Stark thinking about not only what they contribute but how can they be changed to contribute to more sales results. During the course of collecting data and analyzing your sales system, we will be constantly vigilant to make sure we arrive at an understanding of how to enhance and improve our sales system and the supporting processes.

The key areas where we are going to evaluate and assess in our sales system are the areas that involve looking at both types of activities we perform today associated with selling, and engaging, with prospective customers. We need to look at the processes from the perspective of the prospective customers and compare and contrast those processes and activities that impact our sales efforts and outcomes.

Right from the beginning, we need to assess the role and responsibilities of both sales and marketing. Both play critical roles in different stages during the sales process, and moving the opportunity forward to closure.

Here are five key areas:

(1) Marketing and sales both contribute to the uncovering and developing of opportunities. They do this best by defining what the best customer profile looks like, along with the specific and most significant criteria to be used to determine a desirable profile. From there, they assess what marketing activities, or tools are needed to develop prospect interest to generate leads, and what specific info sources are readily available for either marketing, or sales people, to learn as much as they can about targeted prospective clients during the targeting process.

(2) Sales and marketing both contributes to the refinement and understanding of the opportunity the sales believes should be pursued by qualifying with appropriate questions of prospective client. A number of communication processes and dialogues needs to take place to uncover with prospective clients just what the opportunity is that they have a need to purchase and why. Obtaining that information allows sales together with or apart from marketing to establish strategies, activities and actions, that will aid in the better understanding of the prospective people influencing buying needs to purchase a product, service, or solution, and why.

(3) The essential communication that will take place with prospective clients occurs when the salesperson asks questions to assess needs, to try to understand objectives, determine the sense of urgency, and uncover the concepts of what the solution for the product, service, or solution, looks like to each of the prospective people influencing the buying. Marketing participates by supplying salespeople with appropriate information, tools and perhaps presentations or demonstrations that will aid the salesperson in addressing the information that is needed to help each buying influencer better understand what the optimum solution will be for them.

At this point, marketing often contributes white papers, position papers, references or develops some competitive intelligence to understand the potential competitors. That view of the competition will aid the salesperson in a detailed understanding of the competitors, and their capabilities, for this specific opportunity, to be used during discussions with the people influencing buying.

(4) At some point, the responsible sales person will need to have constructed a solution that will specifically address the concepts, concerns, needs, specifications, and the competitive questions the people influencing the buying. It must also clearly address the expected results from the purchase of any product, service, or solution. In some companies, it is marketing that provides support to writing the solution, and supplying necessary boilerplate where required, that addresses some of the technical people influencing the buying related to specifications and other required information.

(5) We need to assess the salesperson, together with their buying counterparts that are involved in the decision-making process, to be able to determine what works effectively and perhaps how best to negotiate the terms, and conditions, and to schedule the required follow-on activities that must be completed ensuring the success of the sale. Then, to prepare for the contract acceptance and necessary sign offs.

As we analyze our sales system, and ask questions in the key areas so we will need to collect the information to analyze all of the current practices, and determine what items are missing, or need to be improved. Once we have collected our data as we begin to analyze the answers to the questions asked and collected thus far, we will begin to form a clearer picture of what works, and what does not work, and why, in our sales system.

Sales Process – Top View Perspective

When I interact with my clients, I will ask them this question, when I say the word process what do they immediately think of. The most common answer is their perception of process is something that impedes progress, or is bureaucratic, and introduces delays. For those of us who study process, the things that organizations and people both like about processes, is that process can work well for them if designed and implemented to work for them. We also must understand what some of our own people's perspectives are, that is they usually just do not like process. Get them to tell you why.

What a great many companies like about having a process, and in this case, we are referring to the sales process itself for example, they immediately sense that by being systematic in this approach that we will gain repeatability, and that things will be much less chaotic and more ordered. Their perceptions are correct. Processes, and systems, bring order out of chaos in almost every situation.

That does not mean encumbered, or rigid, which is a common misperception of process. Some processes can be rigid, but those are where strict criteria must be applied with no exception. Other processes can sound much more like guidelines, and provide a degree of flexibility that can accommodate change, circumstance, and a multitude of trigger events. Other types of people state they like having a process to rely upon as it grounds them in where they are in any sales cycle. It is like a business GPS system; it tells you where you are located.

When they think about a sales process specifically that helps them to be more effective and more productive, they immediately understand why getting to know the people influencing buying in the prospective company has merit. Management enjoys what sales process can bring to them as a benefit, because it makes working with resources, urbanization, and reporting, much more manageable, and it helps them determine that which is outside of the norm and needs to be addressed quickly.

People who embrace process, including sales processes, understand that as a part of having the process in place, it will evolve. It will become a more refined, and enhanced process over time. Most people will claim they feel that if they have a sales process, that their conversion rates, in other words the effort to convert a sale, will be improved.

The common complaints about process, any process in business, especially the sales process from sales people, is this concept of any process involves more work than what is currently done, and more time will be required to do it. Although as adults, we have learned through our experience that by investing time in learning a process over time, the process itself does reduce the decrease in work effort and we hope to free up more time.

When we use the word *process* almost invariably I hear other concerns and frequently people will state that owe a process is less efficient than my total flexibility to act on my own and be independent. Some other participants in assessing sales operations have also commented that the need to bring in a process is to perceive that something is wrong, and they do not wish to be a part of the new process because their perception is that another process will just wind up like the first process.

One comment that I hear frequently from sales people when they position themselves as not in favor or open to embracing process is that they are the ones that are accountable for results and therefore they know best. Salespeople are an interesting group by themselves, as our sales managers because we have to balance skills, personalities, knowledge, and the other personal fertilization of activities against the productivity that we observe in the field.

As salespeople we can all relate to the story of the salesperson who is periodically asked by their sales leadership to say make an appointment and I will come with you to the call. The typical salesperson immediately turns to the Rolodex and appears to sort through and find a likely suspect for a potential visit that will make him or her look good in the eyes of their sales leaders. These are called "Howdy calls." And that is all they really are.

This is an unproductive sales activity, and is to be discouraged. It is disruptive, and uses resources with no expected outcome. A more pragmatic approach is that the sales leaders make their valuable time available, and they are willing to commit when called, to go on a sales call with a sales person that needs the expert advice of the sales manager.

One point to add is about process as something to viewed with a positive attitude and ultimately as a contributor to the potential differentiation between your company and some other. Prospective and existing customers respect processes especially if they are designed to help them in some way. A helpful process is not viewed as bureaucratic, and rarely with contempt. If on the other hand the process is cumbersome, unproductive or disruptive then it clearly needs to be analyzed and reworked to streamline what it does, or eliminated altogether.

If you have ever worked in a large company, you know what a process-rich environment looks like. The assessments of whether a process is good or less than optimum should always be from the point of view of those it impacts either internally or externally. Getting it right may mean the difference between success and failure, or satisfied customers versus those who are not pleased with how the processes treated them.

Sales Processes - Clarifying Questions

A procedure: a particular course of action intended to achieve a result; "the procedure of completing a purchase"; "it was a process of trial and error" as related to the processes associated with sales. Additional descriptions.

- The sum total of the steps taken in the sale of a product or service.

- A sales process is a systematic approach to selling a product or service.

- The performance of some composite cognitive activity; an operation that affects mental contents; "the process of thinking"; "the cognitive operation of remembering"

- A sustained phenomenon or one marked by gradual changes through a series of states; "events now in process";

- A set of linked business activities that take one or more inputs and transform them to create an output

- A business process or business method is a collection of related, structured activities or tasks that produce a specific service or product (serve a particular goal) for a particular customer or customers. It often can be visualized with a flowchart as a sequence of activities.

- A Business Process is the execution of a sequence of related steps in response to an event that leads to a clearly defined deliverable or outcome. A number of role-players may contribute to the execution of an end-to-end Business Process

- Gathering, managing, and analyzing event-based data on roadmap of conditions/experiences

- A defined set of business activities that represent the steps required to achieve a business objective. It includes the flow and use of information and resources. These should be high enough level to be understood by the users and managers of the process.

- A set of one or more linked procedures or activities that collectively complete a business objective or policy goal, normally within the context of an organizational structure defining functional roles and relationships.

- A Business Process is a collaborative activity closely linked to a business purpose.

Understanding Metrics

Here are some questions you should be asking yourself about the sales capabilities your company possesses and how to potentially evaluate them for improvement. On the subject of sales performance, are you satisfied with the level of sales performance in your company? On the subject of forecasting, are your forecasts accurate, are they consistent and manageable as well?

On the subject of effectiveness, are your sales people effective at uncovering and managing opportunities? Moreover, with regard to the return on effort, is your sales organization producing at the highest return yields possible?

On the subject of competitiveness, do your salespeople have actionable strategies for winning the business and how do you measure their effectiveness in any particular situation? On the subject of internal support, you need to know how well aligned your sales and marketing are with understanding prospective customers. In addition, what it will take to win the business and who inside of your organization is required to make sure you win. These are but a few of the questions every company needs to ask internally, not one time only, but on a continuous basis to ensure optimum results.

Here is a list of some common sales performance issues facing any size company.

- Do you have only one contact point in the account or prospect?

- Are you having difficulty gaining any traction in an account or prospective client?

- You cannot tell what the best prospects look like for the solutions that you offer.

- You have no strategy or plan for what it will take to win the count.

- You have not yet identified someone in the account, to act as a guide or coach to assist you through the decision-making process.

- You do not understand who the key players are their roles or the importance they play in making the business decision to buy.

- You do not know where your prospects are in their own buying process or where you are in the selling process to win them as an account.

- You do not understand how you are positioned or viewed in the account to be a viable solution provider.

- You try to sell a solution that is a poor fit, the proverbial round peg in a square hole sales model.

- You try to sell a solution where there is no perceived need, or the account appears satisfied with things just the way they are now, and not interested in changing to accommodate your solution.

- You do not know what your strengths or perceived deficiencies are within the accounts.

- You fail to identify the red flags and you ignore those danger signals in your discussions with the prospect.

- Your salespeople are not comfortable talking to senior executives in the prospective account for a variety of reasons.

- You follow a traditional sales approach and focus only on the perceived features and benefits of your product, service, or solution, and expect a change in results.

- You find yourself needing to discount as a way to get orders in many situations.

- Do you know how to gain internal support for the most challenging prospective accounts?

- If your approach to sales is undisciplined and it appears you would rather shoot from the hip then analyze and develop an account plan or strategy then no wonder your sales forecasts are inaccurate.

- Your salespeople generate a lot of activities but with less than expected results.

- Your sales organization is experiencing a higher loss to win ratio then you are targeted to achieve.

- Some of your salespeople are hired actually do not fit the characteristics of successful sales performers.

Therefore, if any of these aforementioned issues and questions point out problems, or are part of what you encounter in your daily sales activities, then it is necessary to diagnose what is and is not working, why, and what you need to do about it to correct the situation. Miller Heiman conducts a survey annually into best sales practices of companies of all sizes. Small and medium sized enterprises are in some ways, quite capable of performing equal to, or better than, their global counterparts. Areas where small and medium enterprises excel deal mostly with communication, availability of senior leadership to participate in the sale, and in their relatively close-knit infrastructure that takes advantage of the expertise of everyone in the company.

Another differentiator of small and medium enterprises from their global counterparts is the fact that the sales and marketing are more closely aligned, have fewer touch points to confuse a prospective customer, and consequently the messages are cleaner and perhaps better qualified than what you find with the larger global companies.

Yet another concept that is exploited in small and medium enterprises is that of collaboration. It is far easier to imagine in a small company that collaboration occurs more naturally than it does in a larger corporation where there are more layers and organization of vertical stovepipes. Therefore, the distance between the customer and the CEO is relatively short when compared to larger companies.

In the small and medium companies, it is also important to note that the resources are typically scarce and that there are not a lot of support and enablement tools available for use in the small and medium enterprises. What the small and medium enterprises use are more commonly identified as Customer Relationship Management system (CRM), and this system is used primarily to track contact information and perhaps documentation of contacts or conversations. The reliance and use of the CRM system does in fact improve certain aspects of the productivity of a salesperson in the smaller company when the results are compared to the more complex CRM system of a larger enterprise. Between small and larger installation the most significant difference is with the cost of the tools and the upkeep, required to keep the operation performing as needed.

Evaluating Someone Else's Solution – Who Are Your Competitors?

The diagram showing our perspective client as a cloud and in that cloud there are several circles that identify people influencing buying involved in the decision-making process around the opportunity that we have identified by working together with them. But what we need to establish, is who else is likely to provide or has already provided information about a solution, and what do the people influencing buying think about that proposed solution. Does the alternative solution appear to be a better match their concept of the solution, or does ours?

Just imagine that on any given day, there may be a parade of solution providers, all of them presenting to the audience of people influencing the buying and claiming they have "the" solution. When it is our turn to present our solution, it will be apparent to the people who influence buying who came better prepared to solve their problems.

If we are properly prepared, which means we fully understand the concept of the solution from the people influencing buying point of view, and we have successfully matched our product, service, or solution, to those needs and the concept of the solution, then we will be perceived as being a less risky and perhaps better choice.

We must always be vigilant in our understanding of those we are competing against. As much as we can know about our competitors product, service, or solution, and how they differentiate themselves from others, including us, become prerequisite requirements to win. In order to do this, a part of our sales system process needs to be to ask the question for each involved buying influencer, what does the best solution from the competitor look like, in their opinion.

Therefore, if we understand the buyers who have influence, and the concept of the solution, their needs including the results they expect to achieve, and by putting ourselves in their position and assessing the options of who to buy from, taken together they all become a critical aspect of our preparing to provide that optimized solution for their consideration.

Competition – Handle Them Differently Than Before

Competition is always an interesting topic when it comes to understanding the selling and buying processes. We have discussed the differentiation is a significant contributor to your ability to win business when compared and contrasted to a competitors solution. Once again, I will ask you to put on a hat of the individual buying influence or if you think about from their perspective how they view your competitor's solution and your solution.

A critical aspect for the client's perspective is to consider whether, or not, the nature of the solution being proposed forces them into a do-nothing state, challenged by internal priorities for funds or resources. It is helpful therefore, to create a version of the solution from any alternative information provider or competitor, comparing what you and your competitors would do, including the path of least resistance, which is to do nothing.

So again, the trick if there is one is in understanding your competition from a different perspective than you normally would have. Most companies try and assess the product, service, or solution of the competitor versus your own product, service, or solution. Just imagine that all of your prospective clients are people influencing buying from their perspective must review and assess and decide which one of the solution providers fits their concept of the solution better than the other.

Those same people influencing buying based on their roles and responsibilities in the decision-making process may have an internal agenda that they are working. That could mean they wish to take a solution internally using internal sources, or to repurpose funds on the basis of a shift in priorities, or they may ultimately decide to do nothing and have their reasons why doing nothing as an acceptable alternative to what is being proposed by you and your competitors.

During my traditional sales career, I found it important to build business cases with compelling arguments for why our product, service, or solution, was the best. Early in my career, I learned that vast was a relative term, and may not mean that I understood the buying influencer's position in perception of the best solution. Later I learned that through asking more questions when appropriate, that I was able to uncover their definition of best. Aligning my product, service, or solution, where possible with their understanding of what was best significantly increased my sales productivity.

The point of having a sales system and processes is that everyone understand what will be required to successfully win a piece of business, and what ways of dealing with the information, can help us make better decisions during the buying, and selling process.

Reasons Why You Lose Deals

According to CSO Insights, the number one factor for losing deals cited 80% of the time was the competitor's price and terms. Second in the list of top reasons why you lose deals, are the competitors existing relationship with the client where you are trying to unseat the incumbent provider. A third consideration that figures prominently in many sales is how well the competitors brand equity, reputation, and the investments already made by the buying company are viewed and valued versus the potential risk or reward from choosing your solution.

On the positive side, again from the perspective of understanding why clients by your solution or someone else's, the top three reasons cited for why companies we in our number one product superiority, number two the nature of the relationship with a prospective client, number three bus sales process itself, and tied with sales process are solid references attesting to the fact that your solution met not only their concept image but also delivered the results that they needed.

There are potentially a great many contributors to why you are losing lose deals, and there are different reasons why you win deals. It is better to know the answers to both outcomes. Your company should always do win and loss reviews as a part of the general monthly or quarterly discussions about the state of the business and results against plan.

An Additional Premise Behind Your Sales System

An additional perspective is stated in the following premise about what our sales system can do for us. Number one to achieve higher levels of results the simple truth is the more you know and understand the better off you will be an improved your chances of winning. Number two doing a thorough job includes understanding if you can win, and what you need to know, and how your solution will enable a mutual win for both parties. Number three the sales system as a framework guides you systematically through a better understanding of the processes involved in their contribution to successful win-win sales.

Selling Time -- Reality versus Best Practices

Each person involved in the selling process has a number of activities that need to be performed. Many of the activities are not productive, or contribute little to the actual selling of your product, service, or solution, directly involving people influencing buying. The market research company CSO Insights annually publishes results and analyze topsails effectiveness, and the contributors to sales success for a wide range of companies.

The first observation is that on a year-to-year basis the amount of time the percent of time selling face-to-face either with meetings or on the telephone with prospective clients is about one third of the time spent by the salesperson.

Dependent upon the sales system and processes in place, the remaining factors that contribute to sales time include generating new leads and researching accounts, 18.7% of the time, a broad category of other which includes travel training etc., 11.9%, account service calls which are not directly revenue producing, 15.2% and another large contributing category identified as administrative as it relates to tasks and filling out of forms, meetings internally, and other activities that do not directly relate to the selling aspect is being slightly over 20% of the time.

The most productive initiatives uncovered by CSO Insights focused on number one enhancing sales team communications as being the single largest contributor for approving sales effectiveness along with a tie for revisiting the sales process periodically to prove and enhance what is done.

The third most effective initiative stated by most companies was that for 31.9% of the companies surveyed working to align more closely the sales and marketing efforts contributed significantly to sales effectiveness.

Surprisingly lead generation programs and time spent realigning quota and compensation programs were viewed as not effective in contributing to improvements in sales performance. Another aspect uncovered by CSO Insights was that revising the type of salesperson hired contributed very little to the overall effectiveness of sales, and revising the sales team structure did not contribute what one might imagine.

Selling Using the System -- Time Analysis of the Selling Processes

Time is important to any selling organization. A curious observation is that if you ask a typical salesperson how much time they spend in selling they will tell you at least 50 hours per week. However, behind their assessment of how much time they spend selling are a great many other aspects of the selling process that require an investment in time.

If your company follows a pipeline, or a formal forecasting method, we know that through certain activities potential opportunities move in, or are excluded from our forecasts, sometimes based upon real-time assessments of progress being made with prospective clients. What everyone should realize is that the end-to-end selling process that we refer to consists of a number of sub processes, and the sub processes relate to where in the pipeline the prospective developing opportunity may be.

Words that you will frequently associate both with the selling and marketing groups are generating awareness and interest, prospecting, and use of terminology templates to aid in the qualifying of prospective buyers. Then the heavy lifting of getting answers to questions and uncovering what is needed to complete the selling process and to better understand the nature of what the people influencing buying' view of the product, service, or solution, that will work best for them.

The last major hurdle deals with removing any outstanding issues, impediments, or obstacles that are in the way between the prospective customer and us so that we can close the order and begin the execution and delivery against the sale.

To be sure, every professional salesperson handles these various stages of prospecting, qualifying, gaining clarity about the best fit for their products and services or solution with the prospective customers' image of what that solution looks like, and then the steps necessary to close the order, write the contract, and collect the funds.

Prospecting implies that we have first a universe of suspects for our product, service, or solution, that with a refinement of criteria and the use of a best customer profile as a filter so we will better be able to identify those who are more likely prospective clients than suspects. Companies can approach prospecting in a number of ways. Some involving marketing to generate leads from the universe of suspects, and others may use a part of the selling time of that a salesperson how much they spend researching the market place for target prospects that they feel fit well enough into the best customer profile, to at least put them on their list for further qualification.

In some companies, prospecting is done via the telephone and outbound call services to preselected lists of prospective companies or targeted people influencing buying whose names were obtained from a list source. You can imagine that the script that they outbound salesperson uses must resonate with prospective people influencing buying at least touch their concept of what the best solution looks like sufficient for them to want a follow-on conversation to occur.

Many companies, waste money, and time, spending to try and gain access to the mind of the buying influencer, with little or no effective results. The more technical and complex a product, service, or solution is, the less likely it will be easy for the telemarketer to connect with the mental image of a best solution that is held by the buying influencer.

Advertising is no less vulnerable to criticism because marketing is attempting to broadcast to the universe messages that they hope will resonate on their own with prospective people influencing buying who may be looking for additional information but not yet able to form in their mind what an ideal solution looks like. I am a similar nature and the use of a company's website to generate interest and leads that arise from inquiries about basic information may not be very productive depending upon the nature of your product, service, or solution, and the best practices in your industry for her communicating with the appropriate people influencing buying.

One of the next most critical steps will be during the qualifying stage, determining what questions will be asked of the perspective buying influencer to uncover where they are in the decision-making process to purchase a product, service, or solution, and what is driving their the purchase. When entering into the qualifying phase, a sales people need to prepare for any substantive communication with the prospective buying influencer.

Sales people, who are adept at contacting prospective customers, know that they clearly need to state their business purpose for calling, and why it will be important for the buying influencer to listen. The chosen topic is what the salesperson believes after researching the person he or she will be calling to find something that will resonate with the prospective buying influencer. If it resonates, they gain additional time to conduct more communications to more thoroughly understand the concept image in the mind of the buying influencer. Perspective is the most important key. Know your prospects.

This is an example of where your sales system might not be working effectively. Quite often, companies invest considerable in marketing efforts. This might include outbound telemarketing efforts, and other means to blanket the universe with ads or website links to uncover potentially interested parties. These contacts, or potential leads, are then used by a salesperson to have a conversation to uncover potential needs. What management needs to understand is that investing in marketing requires that we establish metrics to determine early on, what works, and what does not work, and to make a business case for the continued use of whatever marketing practices are in place within their company.

Everyone on the management team needs to understand clearly that marketing, even though there are more scientific means available today to develop accurate metrics, and to measure performance from various perspectives, that there are no silver bullets for precise targeting that matches any sense of urgency. Every buying influencer may have a differing sense of urgency. It is also incumbent upon the management team to understand for their chosen industry and market sector, what the norms are, and best practices associated with the industry for generating the highest rate of return on investment in marketing.

As the opportunity moves from the qualifying stage, during which at least some concept image has developed of what the people influencing buying feel a workable solution looks like. We then continue to refine the questions that we ask. How we process the answers, and our next set of actions, working in a consultative selling approach, will be to improve the influencing buying image clarity of their solution, where we position our product, service, or solution, more precisely to match their needs.

What marketing does in this particular instance is to support the efforts of the salesperson. Often they need white papers, presentations to educate and answer questions, pilots or demonstrations, testimonials, and other factual informative along with instructive tools that help the salesperson with the process of educating the people influencing buying, and to position your company's products, services, and solutions, for maximum impact.

As we are reviewing the sale system, we need to consider if there are other channels of access to prospective customers that our company uses. The support of a channel will require a different set of processes, policies, and programs to improve the chances of the channel contributing to our overall sales efforts. The impact on direct salespeople becomes a critical question even before a new channel is considered and brought online.

Quite often companies will assign a salesperson to a new channel role whose skills may be more of a direct nature. Then, through working together with a channel partner organization, they work to achieve sales results. So now, we need to assess if our marketing materials, programs, and other support mechanisms, need to be different for each channel, and the type of salesperson and their role. This may not seem to many people like new information, but as we are analyzing our sales system, and the processes involved with making it more successful, we must accurately map out how we deal with our channel partners, and what will they contribute to our overall sales efforts.

Since your channel partners operate their own sales systems, and as a part of your due diligence, we need to consider when developing an entirely new channel how to recruit the new channel partners. We also need to understand the nature of their sales system model, and how it can be connected, and integrated with our sales system and processes.

 The better we understand the model, the better able we will be to align our products, services, and solutions, the programs, and the pricing and support to meet their needs to be successful selling to their prospective clients. In instances where a channel partner carries your product, service, or solution, in a broad portfolio that may also include potential competitors, we will need to understand how much differentiation will be required to make our solutions better, or for our channel partner to position their prospective clients to generate a win-win-win for all situations we work together.

Frequently, the subject arises of business cannibalization, which for many meant that when you introduce a new pathway a customer could use to buy your product, service, or solution, that you take away a potential sale from either your direct sales force, or some other channel partner model.

Therefore, during our analysis of our sales system and channels, we need to feel comfortable asking the pointed question about whether there is any potential for conflict between the current and new pathways of sale to prospective clients. If we uncover a conflict, how do we address and resolve the conflict expeditiously.

An added topic of interest regarding selling time and resource allocations comes in the form of looking at those companies that are persuaded to take on a new channel after analyzing the impact. Say for example Manufacturer's Representatives (MR) as a prospective new channel. Manufacturer's Reps are authorized for some product, service, or solution in a designated territory, or in a specific vertical application area. The question is whether their activities by their very nature, take away direct sales business for us, or whether they provide incremental revenue opportunities for our company. They may require considerable channel support time, which translates in to added resources.

I can relate to you a for one small company that was looking to expand, and to reach a broader base of customers. They had outgrown their direct-to-customer sales channel, and were entertaining bringing on MRs as channel partners whose job it would be to uncover new sales. The problem was, the MRs worked together with yet another level of channel partners who were the specialty dealers, value added resellers, and systems integrators. The small company was overwhelmed supporting the intermediaries sold through the MRs.

Initially, when they considered bringing on MRs to enable them to find dealers, specialty resellers, and systems integrators, they had neglected to assess the impact on their current direct customer base. This small company found rather quickly, that in competitive selling situations where price until a local presence of a sales organization could mean that their product, service, or solutions, would be discounted in ways that were counterproductive to developing long-term successful relationships with clients.

Within a short time, the small company judged that because they had not thought through the possibilities caused by bringing on these additional channels that they were fast losing control of the price and support of their products. Therefore, their image of quality, service, support, and functionality became confused by the very selling organizations that they had enlisted to increase their sales. At the end of two years, they reassessed their entire channels strategy and determined it for their purposes and because of new products and services that they had created in the interim that they would abandon all other channel approaches other than direct. The only exception of teaming together, where appropriate, was with systems integrators who would add substantial value to their product.

As we analyze our sales system, we uncover precisely how we prospect for new business. We assess the talents and resources of both marketing and sales, which leads us to understand the process of qualifying these prospective clients, and the nature of the questions that need to be asked to determine whether they will be viable opportunities for our product, service, or solution.

Then, once we have qualified by ask the appropriate questions to learn the people influencing buying what the best solution picture looks like to them, we can determine whether or not our product, service, or resource solution matches, and will appear to the customer to be a best fit even when compared and contrasted against our competitors. Then we can focus on streamlining how we go about closing the business, negotiating, and executing the delivery of contracts.

Although greatly simplified this view of selling time follows pretty much true to form once we identify those processes in some processes that we need to understand and change them accordingly if needed. Our metrics, which we will have analyze and strategize about will help us determine where to put our energies to change those areas that need improvement.

Sales Performance -- Some Final Pointers

We judge sales performance on a number of factors or metrics. Obviously, revenue is one of those metrics. A marker of our sales system that we view as important is that not only do we establish the metrics but also we assess what we will use the metrics to accomplish our name indicators of problem areas, or are they indicators that just contain a feel-good factor and therefore are not indicative of where we are achieving our goals.

Our sales system from the first that we examine it, to the time that we make changes and improvements, requires continuous reassessments and audits, and not just the establishment of metrics, but also the guidelines of what to do if the metrics are not indicating what we need. Each and every individual in a selling company needs to be aware of what is going on with sales. This can only occur if there is transparency, and communications, at all levels of the company that are required to participate in support sales efforts.

I always find it fascinating that companies that stovepipe knowledge, experience, and information that could be beneficial to the improvement of sales performance continue to exist without attempting to eliminate those barriers and inhibitors to sales. Every day I am amazed at situations internal to a company that interfere and impede the processes of making and supporting a sale.

Miller Heiman as a sales performance company each year conducts a survey of best practice and identifies world-class company practices. In this best practices study of companies Miller Heiman uncovered an interesting fact, one that should not surprise a great many people know, is that as companies grow communications quite often decline, or their effectiveness is greatly reduced.

These lines of communication decline as layers of management and infrastructure increase. Companies will also experience as they grow that if they have implemented a good set of processes and methods that can accommodate the growth that they will continue to export its effective and efficient operations.

For those companies that reach a certain size and begin making sweeping changes without thinking through the consequences of implementing those changes, they see their effectiveness decline and they are suddenly in awe of why this is occurring while they are attempting to improve the situation. I for one find it amusing that what was uncovered in the Miller Heiman's survey was that small companies in addition to being more responsive and less bureaucratic have developed both formal and informal processes for communications that accommodate the needs of the organization.

Medium and larger size companies, on the other hand, as they grow often lose contact with their prospective and existing clients. The smaller company may know every client that participated in the buying decision-making on a first name basis and have a solid working relationship with them that continues well into the future. Whereas, the larger companies tend to distance themselves from their customers quite often to the point where they no longer rely on their front-line salespeople to communicate they are forced to use secondary means of communication such as newsletters and e-mails and things of that type. Once that event occurred, the burden of maintaining and developing the relationship seems to fall on the marketing person, which is an unfair place to align the burden of responsibility.

A chronic lament I hear when I go out with individual salespeople is it marketing no longer listens to my needs as the salesperson, but it appears that they have stopped listening to the customer needs and therefore I find them as the salesperson to be ineffective. So marketing becomes a bone of contention within companies in this speaks to the importance of aligning the sales and marketing activities to focus on the completion of the sale by providing the proper information to the people influencing buying who must make the buying decisions. Again, it is not rocket science to see how this approach can work effectively for any size company.

To CRM or not CRM -- That Is The Question

A number of companies rely upon their customer relationship management systems. The expectation of what that system is capable of contributing to sales effectiveness is often overstated. The largest contribution from having a Customer Relationship Management system is (CRM) that it improves communications between all parties involved in sales, and does contribute to improving the accuracy of forecasting sales.

Referring to CSO Insights studies of the contribution of the customer relationship management systems, interestingly they found that the CRM systems themselves do not contribute to the creation or tracking of strategies to pursue each opportunity in greater detail. However, the other myth associated with the use of CRM systems is that it shortens the sales cycle, improves win rates, or somehow contributes to improvements in the order processing accuracy, or that it significantly increases the revenue and improves the support of channels, or that in some way it increases margins. CRM systems do not create strategy, nor does it explore and assess how well processes work when dealing with customer as knowledgeable sales people do. CRM reporting systems do just that. Provide reports based on the information entered in to them.

Dashboards and Funnel Management

The subject of dashboards comes up frequently during the course of consulting with clients on ways to improve their sales performance and I want to share some thoughts with you on this topic. A dashboard is a management-reporting tool that highlights past, current, and perspective or forecasted future results, in some way that has a graphical representation designed to convey the state of the company using results against metrics. Dashboards are very useful tools once you have determined which indicators and metrics are the most appropriate ones to provide you a sense of well-being and progress of your business. I have been shown by many executives who were proud of their dashboards that they were generally well informed about their position against their plans.

When shown a dashboard I first acknowledge, "hey that's great you have a dashboard." Then I set about asking a few succinct questions about what the dashboard is indicating to them. My first question is always "are you getting the results that you need", and the usual answer is no. My next question to the executive showing me their dashboard is "how did you determine what metrics and indicators you would follow that could show you the state of your company regarding sales."

That question generates some thoughtful discussions usually indicating the metrics and indicators were determined in a haphazard manner relying upon suggestions from the dashboard tool provider, and less often, because the management team had developed an agreed-upon the appropriate set of researched and proven indicators and metrics, along with when, and how, they should be measured and used.

For those of you who have ever attempted to navigate using a compass you realize that the difference between a compass and a GPS system is that one is a system, and that it is a sampling of multiple points of reference to determine more precisely your position. Few among us can remember not using a GPS system, and fewer still may remember the use of a magnetic compass to determine our location. The point of illustration here is that we have far more accurate ways of determining our position today, but they still require that we understand what the indications are trying to tell us and potentially what are our options to alter our course.

Dashboard software providers generate a range of tools that can be useful to indicate selected information in a manner that is graphically representative of our position based on the indicators and metrics. Some of the dashboard tools are capable of providing graphic representations of your sales pipeline or your sales funnel, depending on your preference, but few of those tools demonstrate to you, which processes, as a part of your sales system, are operating correctly and efficiently.

Throughout this book, we explore concepts that you may not have internalized into your daily operations, but you might consider them in light of any new information that is conveyed by reading this book and gaining any new perspectives or insights.

Organization and Structure -- Consider Some Changes

At some point in the discussion of a sales system and the associated processes, we need to assess your own organizational structure, and how it is designed to operate. Good business process development, or redesign, requires that we analyze the organizational reporting structure and the specific contribution that each position can make to our sales system, and the processes contained in it. If for example, your company, even though perhaps small and less bureaucratic than others, introduced certain internal checkpoints did they in fact, impede, or restrict sales, even though initially they were perceived as necessary. Some checks and balances impede the a way that sales were pursued.

For many companies, engineering becomes a hurdle because engineering has to validate every aspect of the solution that will be provided to clients. This ensures integrity, quality, and supportability. While this example is only one aspect of our potential hurdles, it does point out that not only do you need to have a workable process, but you need to have one that is effective, and can contribute to the improvement of specific sales with customers. Another example may be that your company has a highly configurable product. Because of the many possible permutations the product salespeople need to understand precisely what can work and what might not work in terms of acceptable configurations, or being able to meet the needs of a specific customer.

A quite common example is when a software company has a product, that must be integrated to bridge a client's legacy IT systems with the newer systems. In this common situation, it may turn out to be an extremely problematic one for the integration, and use, of the new product, service, or solution, for whoever is responsible for implementation.

How your company responds to routine "exceptions" is a measure of whether at a detailed level, your processes are operating in the most efficient manner. Although we often hear that checkpoints are imposed to keep the company from getting into trouble, frequently when a situation is encountered, and a salesperson has uncovered a need for an immediate response, the response may not appear to be encouraging to the salesperson.

I frequently hear the lament of the executive leadership team that "we need to sell what we have", and although that statement may indicate an ability to satisfy some audiences of prospective customers, it may indicate that you are not prepared to increase your sales by addressing what you do not have in some planned, and well communicated, long-term approach.

If your organization is founded upon collaboration, an open and honest discussion is encouraged at all levels, you will likely need to develop a playbook, or a set of descriptive processes, that will help with not only current sales efforts, but may be used as a roadmap guide for the development, and enhancement, of your products, services, or solutions.

I find that organizations, regardless of their size, if there are stovepipes, or turf boundaries, that as a part of the playbook work-a-rounds will need to be discussed and internalized to become a part of the overall process.

At one time, I went to work for an startup Internet search engine company. That company had developed, for all intents and purposes, the most accurate search engine available in the market at that time. As we were constantly on the lookout for new business opportunities, and because everyone in the company was selling the products, services, and solutions, we were uncovering a great many potential opportunities at every turn. That was the good news. We had our sales system. Our marketing and lead generation was working specific to our capabilities.

Each of us would bring a new opportunity for discussion with the executive team. We would discuss the merits, drawbacks, and size of the opportunity, and then the executive team would decide on the priority for resources that would be assigned to the selected opportunity. There was only one problem with this egalitarian approach. It was that in order to get the opportunities implemented, we needed to do demonstrations using customer-supplied data, which involved the use of resources to convert and process the data even prior to any ability to do a demonstration for a prospective client. That was the bad news.

On Monday for example, one of us would bring forward for discussion an opportunity for $10 million, and at that time, we all agreed to pursue that particular opportunity. We always needed to shift resources around, but then on Wednesday, someone else brought forward a $20 million opportunity and the executive team would reconvene, and adjust the priorities accordingly. That became the really bad news. We were not qualifying, prioritizing, and evaluating the opportunities using workable criteria. Our sales system failed us, and when the investor funding ran out we were unable to sustain the company, mainly because too many opportunities had passed us by.

Imagine how chaotic business planning and execution would be if every company adopted this approach to deciding on which opportunity de jour would be pursued. Yet, it is still the approach of companies that do not use their sales system to handle the selling processes effectively. You can say that this approach would be very dangerous to a small business in startup mode with limited resources. Why? Because having a demonstration of this new product, service, or solution, was not a guarantee that the company would win the business. Further, unless and until we knew with absolute knowledge what we were going to provide right off matching client specifications to meet their needs for a search engine aligned with the client's concept image, then we were less likely to win, and more likely to have lost ground by investing resources without any potential payback.

I use this example because there are other companies who have a far more stringent business case analysis approach, and who sift through the available or potentially available opportunities using different criteria than strictly size of the opportunity to determine its priority. Develop, apply, and track your criteria carefully. They provide good guidance when selecting, and prioritizing potential opportunities.

Therefore, as a part of our discussion of the organization and structure of your company we need to be clear on how you make decisions to pursue sales opportunities. As a part of our discovery process, there are a number of questions that we will ask of the executive team to uncover their understanding of how you arrive at such decisions in your organization and potentially assess the pros and cons of how those decisions are made and for what reasons they are made. Changes clearly needed to be made.

There are as many examples of how having a sales system helps, as there are companies, but be sure it works in your markets, for best opportunities for your company.

Takeaways

Some of the key takeaways from this section deal with the more detailed view of your sales system and the processes that are a part of it. From the section, you observed a number of exercises and activities that are recommended for your use to enhance the understanding of what works and what might not work as well as expected in your company.

Here are the major takeaways.

- The discover approach provides a framework for collecting, analyzing and making judgments about several aspects of how your sales system and the supporting processes operate. The discover approach presented you with several tasks each that when completed would contribute to a better understanding of what works, what does not work and why.

- This section provides some common definitions and techniques that are intended for use with the initial discover evaluations but should be internalized and used consistently any time sales performance is an issue either with the overall sales system being used or any of the processes. The point being, performance enhancement does not stop after a one-shot analysis. It is an ongoing process unto itself.

- Consider carefully the role and requirements that channel development and management place upon your company. Channel impact both sales and costs as everyone knows, but few people really examine in detail what the true impact of creating, implementing, and supporting a channel really entails. Solid evaluations, cost investigations and a deep understanding of what it takes to not only support a channel but to align it with the goals and activities of all sales and marketing efforts requires extra care and attention.

- Two tools are new to most people but are great ones to adopt and routinely integrate into the operation of your sales system are (1) the process identification inventory worksheet and (2) the PRO/CON assessment rating method. Both have value when deciding to pursue an opportunity or not, or to ask questions and drive towards a consensus of viewpoints on a topic or issue. Try them and see if they produce results better than driven only by informal evaluations.

SECTION (5)

Refining and Optimizing

SECTION (5)

"We are what we repeatedly do. Excellence, then, is not an act, but a habit."
Aristotle, Great Philosopher.

Refining and Optimizing

Optimizing and Refining Your Sales System and Processes

This final section of the book deals with a number of common issues found when a company performs and discovery approach and uncovers more questions than answers about their sales performance. Even though we have related throughout the book that there are selling and buying processes at play companies still tend to overlook the aspect of alignment as critical to improving their effectiveness. Additional optimization and refinement of your sales system and processes may be required to attain the desired improvements in results.

Here is an example. Company A performed the discovery approach including channels, mapping their sales system and the details provided by performing the process identification inventory to assess who is involved with the selling process and in what capacity. They analyzed and found that their internal groups were not responding in anything other than a standard way meaning that they used the same metrics, tools, and marketing materials regardless of the channel or the selling situation to connect with prospective customers.

Company A determined they were still losing business to competitors at a rate far higher than their business plans and the sales plans indicated. They were right to be concerned. The solution came in the form of performing some of the additional assessments and group exercises contained in this section relating specifically to alignments. The alignment being identified here is of the business and sales plans, of the sales and marketing groups and the messaging and materials provided to customers, and a clearer understanding of the prospective customer perceptions of them and their competitors.

This new information assists with the determination of precisely what needs to be done to improve both the sales system and the selling processes that are needed.

Company B integrated and extended the discovery approach to include a more detailed assessments of their channels, competitors, and selected appropriate metrics. This was to indicate where improvements in results were needed, and what was measureable. They also included a full set of assessments of alignments from top to bottom, internal, and external, to accurately gauge precisely how well they understood their customers, and how their sales system responded to various opportunities they decided to pursue. Company B easily determined for any given situation, how to respond by having conducted the more thorough reviews with added insight from assessing alignments.

Positioning -- Charting Your Course to Overcome Obstacles

If you as assess how prospective and even current customers perceive you then it becomes far easier for you to develop strategies and execute them to improve those perspectives and close gaps that may cause your sales efforts to be unproductive. This is assessing what appears to be your positioning for any given opportunity. It also assesses the perceptions of not only your position but that of your competitors in the minds of the prospective customer.

Positioning via marketing efforts to improve the situation may not provide the needed differentiation we spoke of earlier in our discussions, of how we appear versus our competition for our products, services, or solutions. Positioning is based on situation specific, and opportunity specific, understanding of the customer's situation and how our solution will help them. This approach is by its very nature highly individualized, but well worth the effort on the part of your company.

Let us explore some ways to determine how your company, and its solutions, are perceived through performing some additional assessments.

The first is a Sales and Marketing Alignment assessment. It determines how closely aligned are your sales and marketing efforts. By having participants representing each group, sales and marketing, answer a few questions we can establish the basis for the alignment and graphically represent this via a plotting of the results.

The second alignment determines how well corporate Business Plans and the Sales Plans are aligned. By having individual participant group representatives from management and sales answer a series of questions, and by plotting the results, we see if the alignment is close, not close, or wildly divergent. The questions then become discussion topics for deciding upon how to reduce or eliminate the gaps.

The third assessment of alignment explores the gap on how people in your organization and your customers feel your Price versus Value alignment appears to them, and how the competitors appear as well to you and your customers. This is accomplished by putting yourself in the position of assessing the competitors as your prospective customer might, and determining how your customers perceive your particular value, price or some other factors.

The intent of this set of activities is to show where there might be discrepancies between how your company, directly or potentially through channel partners, is perceived and where there may be opportunities to differentiate your solution from that of the competition in ways that increase your chances of winning the business. As mentioned earlier in the book, perceptions are exceptionally powerful and they work either for you or against your selling efforts. These activities should help stimulate the proper ongoing discussions relative to your position and the strategies and enhancements to your selling processes required to secure more wins.

Sales and Marketing Alignment

The diagram shown in Figure (37) is a composite that shows at the center the prospective customer, and since we understand what customer centricity is about we want to be perceived by the perspective buyer in ways that connect with what they are searching for as a solution. The alignment of our product, service, or solution, with the concept of the solution that the buyer has can be supported by making sure that we do a number of things to find in our sales system process model. The diagram also shows that it is important for us to understand how our competition is positioned in a similar manner, and that we understand differentiation from the eyes of the people who are influencing the buying. Our sales and marketing activities must be aligned and consistent to mesh with all of the people influencing buying and need for information and the types of information that will be of value to them in helping them through their decision making process.

Figure (37) Alignment of all Groups Connecting with Customers.

Sales and Marketing alignment also includes Channels and Support groups

Whatever way the Customer interacts with your company ALL messages and responses need to be aligned and consistent!

Source: SW Consulting, 2011

All too often, a salesperson will leave behind collateral and other materials with a perspective buyer with the assumption that somewhere contained within the materials are answers to questions that the buying influencer may have. A best marketing practice example is that the materials produced would focus, with precision, on addressing those questions that the target audience of people influencing the buying have. At a time when they are forming a clearer view of what their solution looks like, they need to understand what your solution will do for them.

A highly customized approach to marketing takes in to account there are other audiences that must have appropriate information provided to them to answer their concerns as well. Some of those people are responding to specific technical specifications, so to must the technical people be able to obtain precise answers to the solution. Everyone needs to receive the appropriate information to aid in selecting the best solution. Best practice marketing caters to each of them, individually.

Within the customer, those involved users must also be satisfied and will be looking for impact statements to show how the proposed solution will impact them in terms of productivity ease-of-use or some other attribute. The key decision making buyer who controls the authority over the money spending for the purchase will be interested in bottom line types of information related to cost savings, long-term operating costs, return on investment, and the timeline to get a return, and other performance factors that contribute to the decision-making process.

Therefore, when sales and marketing are aligned adequately, there needs to be the alignment of our approach and the concept image of the people influencing buying to improve our chances of winning.

Selling, as a part of the decision-making process, is where we continue to need to align all efforts towards communicating, and providing appropriate information, to the buying process participants. Perhaps now, you can visualize the value of having a clearer understanding the selling and buying processes, and how important it is for them to be aligned.

Thus far, you have been exposed to the notion that each buying influencer has a concept of what the best solution looks like for their particular situation, the sense of urgency, and what precisely they need to accomplish. When we have covered all aspects and information requirements of the individual buying influencer's decision-making process, we will have achieved the best chance of winning the business.

Through a deeper understanding of how each of these concepts relate, and by uncovering what we need to do to accomplish we will be able to develop, implement, and track improvements to results. As a part of activities to understand the selling system and processes used in your company, the next few pages will provide you with a method for determining the alignment of sales and marketing.

These activities include conducting a more conclusive assessment of sales and marketing alignment. It is achieved by having each respective representative of marketing and sales answer a number of questions that are used to determine the respective viewpoints.

From the respective viewpoints of both groups, examining the resulting data produces assessments of the alignment. The resulting view will be one that they might not have otherwise expected regarding alignment, and shows the degree of effort required to drive any improvements.

The questions a general in nature but the comparison of the answers often yield startling results when tabulated and plotted on a viewpoint grid.

Marketing should own answering these questions:

- Do we have a clear understanding of what the best-fit profile for prospective clients' looks like?

- Marketing has in place a system for generating and managing all leads used by the sales organization.

- Marketing performance metrics are clear and understood by all areas of the company.

- Marketing participates directly in the selling activities.

- Marketing receives support for its efforts from the sales leadership management.

- Marketing develops the collateral materials, specification sheets, and presentation used by sales.

- Marketing participates in opportunity reviews to contribute ideas and help position the products, services, or solutions.

- Marketing is responsible for managing the response to requests for information and request for proposals.

- Marketing has in place methods to collect, assess and report feedback on the effectiveness of the materials from the sales person's point of view.

- Marketing participates in win-loss review activities.

Sales should take ownership of answering the following versions of the questions:

- Does sales provide to marketing a clear understanding of what the best-fit profile for prospective clients' looks like?

- The sales group generates and manages its own leads and qualifying methods.

- Sales performance metrics are clear and understood by all areas of the company.

- Sales controls and manages who participates directly in the selling activities.

- The sales group receives support for its efforts from the marketing leadership management.

- Sales needs to revise, customize, and modify the collateral materials, specification sheets, and presentations used during the engagement with customers.

- Sales conducts frequently scheduled reviews of opportunities, events impacting sales efforts, and engages with marketing for advice.

- Sales, as a group, is responsible for managing the response to requests for information and requests for proposals.

- The sales group has in place methods to collect assess and report feedback on the effectiveness of marketing materials.

- The sales group members seek participation throughout the company in win-loss review activities.

We plot and compare the results of a simple sales and marketing alignment assessment workshop with the answers to those questions listed. The degree to which the answers reflect the actual operational norms of the organizations and reveals whether the two groups are using best practices nor not. Alignment of sales and marketing is more demonstrable in smaller companies where everyone has a role and a vested interest in contributing to the success of sales efforts.

Close alignment between the two is found more often in world class companies than in those who have silo like operating structures where a marked difference between then can be identified. When we examine the plotted results of the ten-point questionnaire in the simplest interpretation alignment is indicated by placement in the "aligned" quadrant. Any other position indicated by the results will require examining how to improvement the alignment through actions and to re-evaluate again after some passage of time using the same questions.

Rarely are both sales and marketing aligned on the first assessment, but if they are, it is an indication that some best practices may already be deployed, and working. as perceived from the marketing and sales groups.

As a generalization as companies grew and had to accommodate changes they become more internally stove piped and communication or collaboration occurs less often across the respective groups and the gap widens. A widened gap as viewed from the customer's perspective and an assessment of how the customer perceives the company alignment of sales and marketing can result in a disconnect between what sales presents as a solution and how marketing portrays the solution. This alters some of the expectations a customer may have upon the company. Poor alignment may also make the company appear out of touch with their clients for their product, service, or solution.

Figure (38) shows the questions for assessing sales and marketing alignment. Have each individual participant of the group answer the representative questions for whether they are answering for the Sales of the Marketing groups. You can plot the individual data points question by question using the top and bottom answers as coordinates, or you can ask people to summarize by adding up the total and dividing by ten to average the findings and then plot the results. Either way you will see a pattern emerge as to how aligned sales and marketing viewpoints are in the eyes of the participants in the exercise.

The results of comparing the results where marketing has answered the questions and sale's has answered the questions will show the alignment between their viewpoints. The sample figure shown is meant to illustrate that in order to close the gap between sales and marketing perspectives actions are needed on the part of both parties. If both groups were to align only at the midpoint (5,5) participants should review the questions to see which ones scored lowest and discuss actions that can be taken to improve the alignment such that both groups wind up in the top right quadrant.

Most organizations tend to be somewhat aligned but those areas where they are not clearly aligned are the areas that must be targeted for improvement. Have each team prepare and present suggestions obtained from a brainstorming session initially, then as a group continue the discussions and brainstorming to decide upon appropriate actions to impact the alignment.

Please note that the Alignment Templates shown as Figures (38, 40, 42, and 46) show the list of matching question pairs and a rating scale that is indicative of agreement with the statements. A low number (1) will indicate lowest agreement, to a maximum of (10) indicating the highest agreement. These templates are the alignment activities presented in this book, but with modifications for any particular set of matching questions the approach works well to determine the individual scoring alignment, and the group average scoring alignment.

Figure (38) The Sales and Marketing Alignment Assessment Template.

Sales and Marketing Alignment Assessment

MARKETING VIEWPOINT

Marketing should answer the questions:

#	Question	Rating 1-10 Scale
1.	Do we have a clear understanding of what the best fit profile for prospective clients' looks like?	1-2-3-4-5-6-7-8-9-10
2.	Marketing has in place a system for generating and managing all leads used by the sales organization.	1-2-3-4-5-6-7-8-9-10
3.	Marketing performance metrics are clear and understood by all areas of the company.	1-2-3-4-5-6-7-8-9-10
4.	Marketing participates directly in the selling activities.	1-2-3-4-5-6-7-8-9-10
5.	Marketing receives support for its efforts from the sales leadership management.	1-2-3-4-5-6-7-8-9-10
6.	Marketing develops the collateral materials, specification sheets and presentation used by sales.	1-2-3-4-5-6-7-8-9-10
7.	Marketing participates in opportunity reviews to contribute ideas and help position the products, services or solutions.	1-2-3-4-5-6-7-8-9-10
8.	Marketing is responsible for managing the response to requests for information and request for proposals.	1-2-3-4-5-6-7-8-9-10
9.	Marketing has in place methods to collect, assess and report feedback on the effectiveness of the materials from the sales person's point of view.	1-2-3-4-5-6-7-8-9-10
10.	Marketing participates in win-loss review activities.	1-2-3-4-5-6-7-8-9-10

Agree with statement   1 = Lowest to 10 = Highest   *Average of Marketing:*

SALES VIEWPOINT

Sales should take ownership of answering the following versions of the questions:

#	Question	Rating 1-10 Scale
1.	Does sales provide to marketing a clear understanding of what the best fit profile for prospective clients' looks like?	1-2-3-4-5-6-7-8-9-10
2.	Sales generates and manages its own leads and qualifying methods.	1-2-3-4-5-6-7-8-9-10
3.	Sales performance metrics are clear and understood by all areas of the company.	1-2-3-4-5-6-7-8-9-10
4.	Sales controls and manages who participates directly in the selling activities.	1-2-3-4-5-6-7-8-9-10
5.	Sales receives support for its efforts from the marketing leadership management.	1-2-3-4-5-6-7-8-9-10
6.	Sales needs to revise, customize and modify collateral materials, specification sheets and presentations used during the engagement with customers.	1-2-3-4-5-6-7-8-9-10
7.	Sales conducts frequently scheduled reviews of opportunities, events impacting sales efforts, and engages with marketing for advice.	1-2-3-4-5-6-7-8-9-10
8.	Sales is responsible for managing the response to requests for information and requests for proposals.	1-2-3-4-5-6-7-8-9-10
9.	Sales has in place methods to collect, assess and report feedback on the effectiveness of marketing materials.	1-2-3-4-5-6-7-8-9-10
10.	Sales seeks participation throughout the company in win-loss review activities.	1-2-3-4-5-6-7-8-9-10

Agree with statement   1 = Lowest to 10 = Highest   *Average of Sales:*

Source: SW Consulting, 2011

Figure (39) Using the Sales and Marketing Alignment Assessment Results Mapping.

Sales and Marketing Alignment Assessment

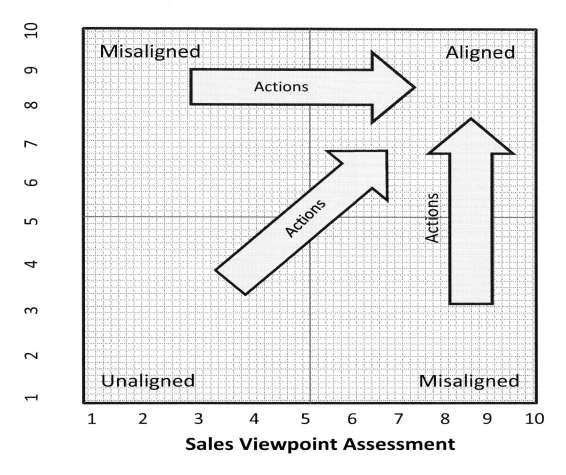

Source: SW Consulting, 2011

Draw the Figure (39) example chart on a flipchart or whiteboard and add the data points. Note that the lower right quadrant is labeled "unaligned." This is to designate that should the results obtained fall in this quadrant there is little evidence to support alignment. The corresponding actions should to uncover why the results are so low and to address how to increase the agreement on alignment.

Performing this activity once is not sufficient in the scheme of long-term business improvement expectations. Performing the assessment on some annualized basis or prior to the launch of any significant new programs or sales efforts can provide additional insight in to how the organization feels about the sales and marketing efforts at that moment. Best in class companies frequently assess their own organizations and check for sales and marketing alignment.

Aligning Sales and the Business Plan

Another aspect of alignment in the organization deals with how well aligned the sales and business plan actually appear to be. In organizations where the business plans are misaligned with sales, it will be more difficult for either to achieve the objectives. It is quite possible the objectives based on the assumptions for each plan are not synchronized or realistic.

For example if the overall business plan calls for a twenty-five percent increase in revenue there must be a corresponding estimated by sales of the amount of work, selling time and the length of the sales cycle and the usage of channels for sales and distribution that need to be factored in to the sales plans.

The starting point to determine the alignment is for each group, sales, and the business-planning group to answer the questions provided on the assessment template. Figure (40) shows the questions for both sales and management to answer. Once each group has answered the corresponding questions for their group, the results are plotted on the grid example shown in the figure following the questions.

The management team and those participating in the development of the business plans will have some concept of the goals and objectives that need to be achieved. Sale's is faced with interpreting those objectives and translating them into actions that will drive sales. Sales, as a group, will base its responses on the amount of resources, experience of the sales teams, the alignment with the marketing efforts, the competitive landscape, and the amount of time and effort required to complete a sale and realize the revenue from the maturity of the product, service, or solutions being sold.

You can see that without a set of well-known and communicated tribal knowledge, or without data to show the historic metrics of just how accurate the forecasting is, comparing the actual work efforts required to complete the sale results become uncertain and there is risk of an underachievement shortfall versus the plan.

World-class organizations using best practices for planning and for sales planning in particular understand the selling time and effort required to achieve the results but they also rely heavily upon their internal and external sales processes used in their sale system to accomplish the results.

Often observed in companies that have unreliable sales forecasts is the attempt to force fit the business plan goals into the sales plans. Another observation is that the business plan quite often is developed but not modified according to the actual results achieved over time. After all the business plan should be viewed as a long-term roadmap to success for the company.

If the road map is at odds with the actions that must be taken to achieve them the mapping plan is at risk. It is analogous to building a highway but forgetting that the bridges need to build and in place before the road can be used even if it were finished.

Performing the assessments will help to bring a more realistic dose of the achievable both in the planning process and in the process requirements to design, implement and modify the sales system that produces more consistent and reliable results.

Figure (40) The Sales and Business Plan Alignment Assessment Template.

Sales and Business Plan Alignment Assessment

EXECUTIVE VIEWPOINT

Executive Team should answer the questions relative to the Business Plan:

		Rating 1-10 Scale
1.	Does the Business Plan provide a clear understanding of what the intended target prospective clients?	1-2-3-4-5-6-7-8-9-10
2.	The Executive Team understands the sales and marketing efforts required to achieve the sales objectives?	1-2-3-4-5-6-7-8-9-10
3.	Does the Business Plan clearly articulate the metrics related to Sales and Marketing that will be measured?	1-2-3-4-5-6-7-8-9-10
4.	Does the Executive Team play a clear role in support of the Sales and Marketing efforts?	1-2-3-4-5-6-7-8-9-10
5.	What processes/methods/approaches have been committed to in the Business Plan by management?	1-2-3-4-5-6-7-8-9-10
6.	The Business Plan details Marketing's role and methods for development of the collateral materials, specification sheets and presentations used by sales.	1-2-3-4-5-6-7-8-9-10
7.	The Executive Team participates in key opportunity reviews to contribute ideas and help drive the solutions	1-2-3-4-5-6-7-8-9-10
8.	The Business Plan clearly states who is responsible for managing the response to request for information/proposals.	1-2-3-4-5-6-7-8-9-10
9.	The Business Plan clearly states the methods to collect, assess and report feedback on the effectiveness of sales	1-2-3-4-5-6-7-8-9-10
10.	The Business Plan clearly state the review process and ownership of the win and loss review activities.	1-2-3-4-5-6-7-8-9-10

Agree with statement   1 = Lowest to 10 = Highest   *Average of Marketing:* ☐

SALES VIEWPOINT

Sales Team should take ownership of answering the following versions of the questions:

		Rating 1-10 Scale
1.	Sales and Marketing are aligned to produce the best fit profile for target prospective clients'?	1-2-3-4-5-6-7-8-9-10
2.	Does Sales provide input to the Business Plan for the efforts required to meet the sales objectives?	1-2-3-4-5-6-7-8-9-10
3.	Sales performance metrics are clear and understood by all areas of the company.	1-2-3-4-5-6-7-8-9-10
4.	Sales controls and manages who participates directly in the selling activities.	1-2-3-4-5-6-7-8-9-10
5.	Sales is responsible for and manages its own processes/methods/approaches to sales and tracking of results	1-2-3-4-5-6-7-8-9-10
6.	Sales needs to revise, customize and modify collateral materials, specification sheets and presentations used during the engagement with customers.	1-2-3-4-5-6-7-8-9-10
7.	Sales conducts frequently scheduled reviews of opportunities, events impacting sales efforts, and engages with Management for advice.	1-2-3-4-5-6-7-8-9-10
8.	Sales is responsible for managing the response to requests for information and requests for proposals.	1-2-3-4-5-6-7-8-9-10
9.	Sales has in place methods to collect, assess and report feedback on the effectiveness of marketing materials.	1-2-3-4-5-6-7-8-9-10
10.	Sales seeks participation throughout the company in win-loss review activities.	1-2-3-4-5-6-7-8-9-10

Agree with statement   1 = Lowest to 10 = Highest   *Average* of Sales: ☐

Source: SW Consulting, 2011

180

Figure (41) Using the Sales and Business Plan Alignment Template.

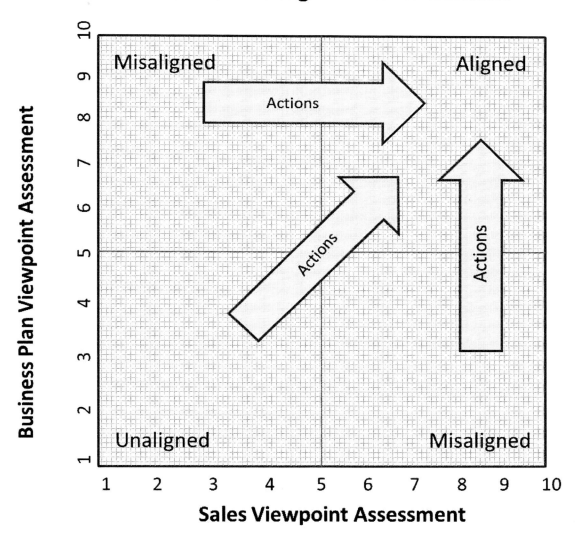

Source: SW Consulting, 2011

Figure (41) illustrates the graph template used for performing this assessment and plotting the results individually by data point or by averaging the total scores gives insight in to whether participants in the sales, marketing and operational areas of the business are in agreement and alignment. The closer to aligned they are comparing management views with that of the sales team often uncovers some previously unstated concerns or issues with the achievement of the business and sales plans.

Aligning Price and Value Viewpoints

As a part of your sales system, one of your tasks will be to develop and maintain a price and value assessment set of criteria. Quite often new companies have difficulty establishing a price for their product, service, or solution. The basis by which they construct their price may or may not be difficult to relate to the people influencing buying during the course of communications about the required solution.

A fallacy in thinking often is found in believing that your "value proposition" has any value to the prospective customers or will impact the outcome of your selling efforts for the current situation. The value proposition by itself is generally created in the marketing or sales departments and treated as though it were a silver bullet to be used with every customer and every buyer within the customer's organization. In fact, it is those buyers that assign the "value" to the proposition, and they see the value, or not, as it relates to the reasons they are buying your particular product, service, or solution. The results can vary considerably from one individual buyer to the next. Price is considered by many to be a component of the value judgment but the impression and perception of value needs to present them both together in ways the buyers can make sense out of the positioning of the components.

For example if you have a life-saving solution that costs more than other suppliers but if more effective at saving lives then the value assessment tips in favor of the value perception over price. If on the other hand you are selling a commodity product or service you need to more clearly articulate to all involved buyers why your solutions have merit that relate to the particular buying situation to balance out the perception of price winning over value.

A well-informed company will be constantly reviewing competitive insights into how others are performing in the marketplace. It will understand the impact of market dynamics, and availability of products, services, and solutions, in a price competitive marketplace. The company will also be aware, through conversations with prospective customers, the importance of those characteristics of the product, service, or solution, and how they are perceived as providing value to the client's company. Those characteristics are the telltale reasons why customers may view the value of your product, service, or solution more than those of your competitors.

Monetization of online services or Internet services in general is another example that approaches commoditization because of their availability through multiple sales access pathways or channels becomes difficult because the hide to each channel will be a pricing and a discounting method that may work against selling your product, service, or solution, on value instead of price. Even government contracts have the ability to specify best value over best price if the attributes are viewed by the buying organization, as having the value that they need is a part of the concept of their solution. If you are selling book online through multiple outlets the buyer will invariably explore the lowest possible cost options.

The value in this instance, beyond the lower price sought by the buyer, might be the ease of ordering or if free shipping is included, or some other valued attribute.

So the questions you need to ask are not just related to the pricing models in play at your company but equally pay attention to the concept of value from the customer's perspective. Ask your sales people, marketing, and management to answer these simple questions:

- Customers recognize our value, but on what basis?

- Customers view our value to be.......(in their words).

- What is it that or customers value us to do for them?

- Why is our value of importance to the customers?

- Customers say our value is .... compared with other competitors.

- Do our customers have suggestions on how we can improve the value of our products, services, or solutions? What are they?

- How do we measure our customer's satisfaction (loyalty, renewals, revenue, referrals, etc.)

The answers you obtain to these questions will yield a much better perspective on the views customers have regarding, price, and value, and where you both differ.

There are two viewpoints to consider. The first viewpoint when discussing value and price is how does the prospect or existing customer feel about the value and price your offer. You can assume or infer the information or more importantly actually work it into conversations with your prospects and existing clients. The second viewpoint represents how you and your people involved in the selling process view the prospective customer. In other words, your detailed assessment of them, and their needs.

To gain a more comprehensive view of how alignment of perspectives can contribute to understanding additional ways you can win you need to take a snapshot of how your prospect or customer feels about your company and compare that against how your company feels about price and value prospect or customer. Remember, it is not about how you feel about your company. It is how the prospect views you.

The value and price alignment assessment questionnaire, shown in Figure (42), is used to survey the feelings and viewpoints of how price and value are seen by your company and through your knowledge of how your prospective customer views, form their judgment, the type of value versus price you are offering.

Note that the questions are the same for both perspectives but putting yourself in the mindset of the prospective customer or existing customer for a particular opportunity can be used to produce a quantitative way of visualizing how aligned the two viewpoints actually are.

Figure (42) the questionnaire for comparing Price and Value from the Customer and Company viewpoints. Note the top set of questions represents the customer's viewpoint while the bottom set illustrates the company's view of the prospective customer.

Value and Price Alignment Assessment – Customer vs. Company on Competition

Customer's Viewpoint Of Your Competition

	Rating 1-10 Scale
1. How well does the customer recognize the value of what the competitor delivers.	1-2-3-4-5-6-7-8-9-10
2. Our competitor is seen as the price leader by the customer.	1-2-3-4-5-6-7-8-9-10
3. Our competitor is seen as the technical leader by the customer.	1-2-3-4-5-6-7-8-9-10
4. How well does the customer assess the competitor's marketing materials as relevant to their particular problem?	1-2-3-4-5-6-7-8-9-10
5. Our competitor's particular value is important to the customer.	1-2-3-4-5-6-7-8-9-10
6. The customer views our competitor's credibility as favorable.	1-2-3-4-5-6-7-8-9-10
7. The customer views the competitor's references as a critical part of winning the business.	1-2-3-4-5-6-7-8-9-10
8. Customer's speak highly of our competitor's value compared to our value.	1-2-3-4-5-6-7-8-9-10
9. Customer's understand the competitor's solution well enough to offer suggestions to increase it's value.	1-2-3-4-5-6-7-8-9-10
10. Customer's place high importance on our competitor's service, support and their satisfaction is measureable.	1-2-3-4-5-6-7-8-9-10

Average of Customer: [____]

Agree with statement   1 = Lowest to 10 = Highest

CUSTOMER VIEWPOINT

Company's Viewpoint Of Your Competition

	Rating 1-10 Scale
1. How well does the customer recognize the value of what the competitor delivers.	1-2-3-4-5-6-7-8-9-10
2. Our competitor is seen as the price leader by the customer.	1-2-3-4-5-6-7-8-9-10
3. Our competitor is seen as the technical leader by the customer.	1-2-3-4-5-6-7-8-9-10
4. How well does the customer assess the competitor's marketing materials as relevant to their particular problem?	1-2-3-4-5-6-7-8-9-10
5. Our competitor's particular value is important to the customer.	1-2-3-4-5-6-7-8-9-10
6. The customer views our competitor's credibility as favorable.	1-2-3-4-5-6-7-8-9-10
7. The customer views the competitor's references as a critical part of winning the business.	1-2-3-4-5-6-7-8-9-10
8. Customer's speak highly of our competitor's value compared to our value.	1-2-3-4-5-6-7-8-9-10
9. Customer's understand our competitor's solution well enough to offer suggestions to increase it's value.	1-2-3-4-5-6-7-8-9-10
10. Customer's place high importance on our competitor's service, support and their satisfaction is measureable.	1-2-3-4-5-6-7-8-9-10

Average of Company: [____]

Agree with statement   1 = Lowest to 10 = Highest

COMPANY VIEWPOINT

Source: SW Consulting, 2011

Prospective customers assess your value, and the price, based on the information that is relevant to the specific opportunity where they are trying to make a buying decision. If your value case is clear, but not relevant to their specific need, the perspective will favor your competitor's solution more than yours. If the value is perceived by the prospective customer to be more in line with their thinking, it can be used by the people participating in the decision-making process to provide a point of differentiation for your product, service, or solution and their view of your company.

Think about how this works. You have wonderful brochures, white papers, and detailed descriptions of your product, service, or solution. How are those materials relevant to their decision making process or the selection of the best solution for their needs? Companies will frequently need to draw from a collective body of information and tailor it to the specific needs articulated by those making the buying decisions. If it turns out the materials are not relevant they assess your solution as having a lower value. If cost is also considered as a factor and you have not made your value case you are perceived as offering a high priced non-fitting solution to their purchasing need. The decision making process and the assessment criteria they use may outright eliminate you from contention if that is the case.

The price-value perspective assessment questionnaire is for the Customer's View of Your Company versus Your Company's View of the Customer. Examine the price and value (with the axes shown as Company – Customer) perspective template shown in figure (43) and then have those staff members who interact with the customers directly answer the questions shown on the worksheet to see how your perception of price-value aligns with those perceptions of your customers. Have each member separately plot the results and then discuss the findings as a group. It pays to identify just where the viewpoints diverge and discuss the possible reasons for that divergence.

You could also segment the results by functional areas such as sales, marketing, support, etc. to see how diverse the perceptions are even among members of the same area.

For your organization to increase its chances of winning the business, you should take the assessment by having as many people who interact with customer provide their answers to the template questions and show how they rated the results for alignment. Make sure that you put yourself in the place of your prospective customer when assessing the customer's view of your company. Your assessment of the customer's viewpoint is to see how close you align with the thinking about value and price.

What is frequently an observed fact is that many people in your organization perform the assessment individually. Rarely is there a consensus on the alignment, and especially when your people perform the customer's viewpoint of your product, service, or solution, or value versus price. Those who are in the front lines with considerable contact with a number of people involved in the decision making process will provide a more accurate assessment of how the customer's view your company and the solution you offer.

Use the perspective template shown in Figure (43) as a visual display plotting the intersection of the question answer results for Customer's and Company's viewpoints.

Have team members fill out the questionnaire and tabulate their results on the two axes. As a suggestion, plot the results from the workshop with your team representing each participant's coordinates placed on the blank template or drawn on a flipchart as one method. Draw a rough circle around the cluster of the data points. Plotting each of the individual question results will show the scatter of the responses.

Figure (43) Perspective viewpoint alignment template, Company's vs. Customer's view of your Company.

Workshop – Perspective Template

Alignment of viewpoints

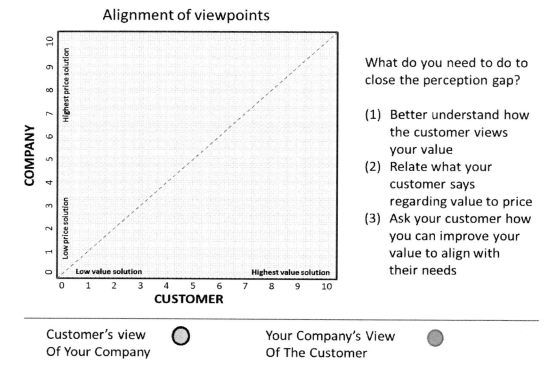

What do you need to do to close the perception gap?

(1) Better understand how the customer views your value
(2) Relate what your customer says regarding value to price
(3) Ask your customer how you can improve your value to align with their needs

Customer's view
Of Your Company

Your Company's View
Of The Customer

Key point – differentiation is ALWAYS in the eyes of the customer is critical.
Understanding the customer's perception of value is critical.

Source: SW Consulting, 2011

Plotting the averages of the scores for each participant shows the mean gap between the differing viewpoints and is another way to present the data points. Once the results of the questions are plotted by each of those members of your company involved in the selling or supporting the sales efforts, you will have a more factual appraisal of where the company is overall. The closeness versus diversity of results will get you thinking about what needs to be done to bridge that gap between your internal viewpoint, and that of a current, or prospective, customer's viewpoint.

The Figure (44) shown is a completed example of comparing and contrasting the value versus price perceptions of how your company views the situation versus how well your people assess the customer's perception.

Figure (44) Perspective viewpoint alignment example, Company's vs. Customer's view of your company.

Workshop – Perspective Example

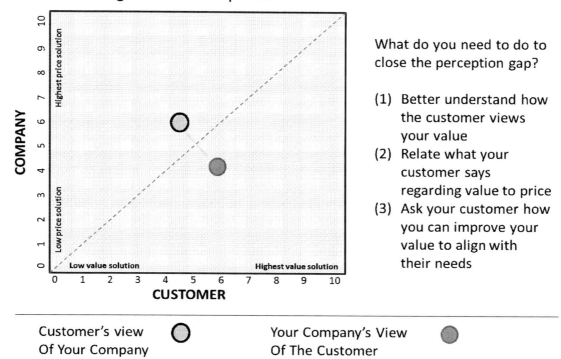

Alignment of viewpoints

What do you need to do to close the perception gap?

(1) Better understand how the customer views your value

(2) Relate what your customer says regarding value to price

(3) Ask your customer how you can improve your value to align with their needs

Customer's view ◯ Your Company's View ⬤
Of Your Company Of The Customer

Key point – differentiation is ALWAYS in the eyes of the customer is critical.
Understanding the customer's perception of value is critical.

Source: SW Consulting, 2011

Note the gap between your company's view and the customer's view illustrated in Figure (44). In this example, the alignment indicates the customer views your price is higher and the value is lower compared to where the customer is assessed by members of your company. The question is what you must do to close the gap between the perceptions of value versus price.

Closing the gap might result in a significant change in the marketing efforts. It might indicate the need for more white papers or case studies to provide proof points that sales can use more effectively in direct conversations to hit on the specific issues a prospective customer might have.

Assessing the Customer's View of the Competition

The next perspective to check for its alignment deals with how the prospects and existing customer view your competition for value versus price. The assessment questionnaire shown in Figure (45) identified by the heading contains similar questions to the first exercise just completed but they differ in the nature of the comparison which is how the prospect feels about your company versus the competition for value and price.

Figure (45) Perspective viewpoint alignment template, Customer's and Your Company's view of Competition.

Workshop – Perspective Template

Alignment of viewpoints

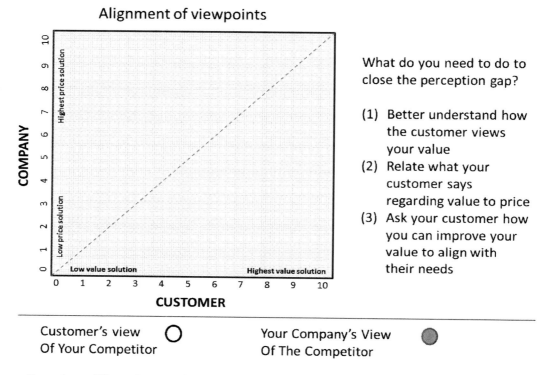

What do you need to do to close the perception gap?

(1) Better understand how the customer views your value
(2) Relate what your customer says regarding value to price
(3) Ask your customer how you can improve your value to align with their needs

Customer's view ○ Of Your Competitor

Your Company's View ● Of The Competitor

Key point – differentiation is ALWAYS in the eyes of the customer is critical.
Understanding the competition is critical from the perspective of the customer's view.

Source: SW Consulting, 2011

Frequently examining the viewpoint of how your prospective customer views the competition versus your view of the competition yields perspectives not previously experienced by those who are involved in or supporting the selling process.

Companies tend to superficially examine the competitor, without considering how the prospective customer feels about the competitor. When you compare and contrast that with your assessment the gap provides useful information aimed at modifying your strategies.

Figure (46) shown is the assessment questionnaire for Value and Price Alignment, Customer and Company on Competition.

Value and Price Alignment Assessment – Customer vs. Company on Competition

Customer's Viewpoint Of Your Competition

	Statement	Rating 1-10 Scale
1.	How well does the customer recognize the value of what the competitor delivers.	1-2-3-4-5-6-7-8-9-10
2.	Our competitor is seen as the price leader by the customer.	1-2-3-4-5-6-7-8-9-10
3.	Our competitor is seen as the technical leader by the customer.	1-2-3-4-5-6-7-8-9-10
4.	How well does the customer assess the competitor's marketing materials as relevant to their particular problem?	1-2-3-4-5-6-7-8-9-10
5.	Our competitor's particular value is important to the customer.	1-2-3-4-5-6-7-8-9-10
6.	The customer views our competitor's credibility as favorable.	1-2-3-4-5-6-7-8-9-10
7.	The customer views the competitor's references as a critical part of winning the business.	1-2-3-4-5-6-7-8-9-10
8.	Customer's speak highly of our competitor's value compared to our value.	1-2-3-4-5-6-7-8-9-10
9.	Customer's understand the competitor's solution well enough to offer suggestions to increase it's value.	1-2-3-4-5-6-7-8-9-10
10.	Customer's place high importance on our competitor's service, support and their satisfaction is measureable.	1-2-3-4-5-6-7-8-9-10

Average of Customer: [   ]

Agree with statement   1 = Lowest to 10 = Highest

CUSTOMER VIEWPOINT

Company's Viewpoint Of Your Competition

	Statement	Rating 1-10 Scale
1.	How well does the customer recognize the value of what the competitor delivers.	1-2-3-4-5-6-7-8-9-10
2.	Our competitor is seen as the price leader by the customer.	1-2-3-4-5-6-7-8-9-10
3.	Our competitor is seen as the technical leader by the customer.	1-2-3-4-5-6-7-8-9-10
4.	How well does the customer assess the competitor's marketing materials as relevant to their particular problem?	1-2-3-4-5-6-7-8-9-10
5.	Our competitor's particular value is important to the customer.	1-2-3-4-5-6-7-8-9-10
6.	The customer views our competitor's credibility as favorable.	1-2-3-4-5-6-7-8-9-10
7.	The customer views the competitor's references as a critical part of winning the business.	1-2-3-4-5-6-7-8-9-10
8.	Customer's speak highly of our competitor's value compared to our value.	1-2-3-4-5-6-7-8-9-10
9.	Customer's understand our competitor's solution well enough to offer suggestions to increase it's value.	1-2-3-4-5-6-7-8-9-10
10.	Customer's place high importance on our competitor's service, support and their satisfaction is measureable.	1-2-3-4-5-6-7-8-9-10

Average of Company: [   ]

Agree with statement   1 = Lowest to 10 = Highest

COMPANY VIEWPOINT

Source: SW Consulting, 2011

As previously mentioned, answers to the questions by each participant can be plotted as individual data points comparing the corresponding questions from the top half and bottom half of the questionnaire, or you could also total the results, calculate the averages, and plot them as a single pair of data points from one participant.

Figure (47) shows the graphical representation of averaged data. Try the plots with the individual results or the aggregate results as the points of intersection. The groupings may provide additional insight in the diversity of opinions resulting from personal viewpoint answers to the questions.

Figure (47) Perspective viewpoints, Company's vs. Customer's view of Competition.

Workshop – Perspective Example

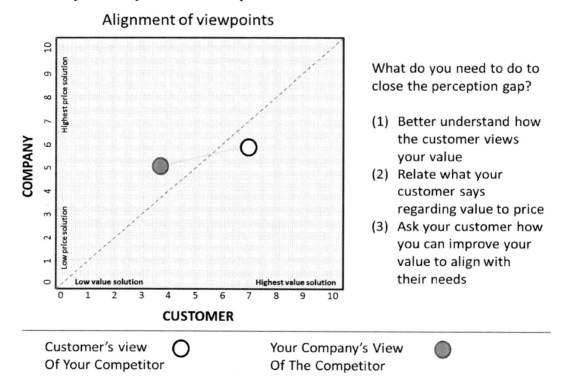

Source SW Consulting, 2011

Takeaways

This section of the book, we offered the reader a range of new options for assessing their position, and ways to understand the potential impact of perceptions. After utilizing the approach provided by the discovery method in Section (4), users can add valuable information and additional ways to uncover possible differentiation they can use to thwart competitors and to increase their sales performance by modifying the sales system to accommodate the findings.

The essential takeaways from this section are:

- Critical to the success of the organization is the alignment of the various groups in support of the selling process. The sales system used by your company can be improved by assessing the sales and marketing alignment to ensure that the most productive and useful information is effectively targeted to appropriate stakeholder decision makers in a prospective customer account.

- Alignment extends to having the corporate wide business plan aligned and in synch with the sales, channels, marketing, support and other plans in the organization. Performing the assessments of alignment is not enough. Each plan needs to be dynamic and have some tolerance for flexibility with regard to resources and priorities to optimize the returns on each of the investments. World-class companies use a best practice of assessing the alignment and correcting any gap between the perspective viewpoints in their organizations. This holistic approach is also focused on the metrics that are used to measure both progress and performance of the plans.

- When it comes to perspectives prospective and current customer's viewpoints are invaluable and provide insight in to the most competitive situations. This is especially true where perceptions of price and value are in questions or if a competitor presents a better price-value perception. Truly integrated and aligned organizations know the gaps and respond with new or better ways to differentiate their product, service, or solutions in the eyes of their potential customers. This subtle difference contributes to increasing sales performance perhaps more than any other assessment. Understanding your company and solution position compared to another's solution means you are prepared to respond to the situation assessment.

- Competitive situations are the norm in today's fast paced and highly interactive markets. Those organizations that can assess their competitors as the customer sees them are better able to understand why they would lose business if they did not respond. Customers always compare products, services and solutions, but today more customers make additional assessments related to differentiation and attention to specific advantages for choosing one solution preferably over another. All information gained during the assessments of perceptions, and of the alignments, will improve the chances of winning more business. The outputs should become a routine part of your sales system, and the sales processes.

Summary

At the beginning of this book, I stated a set of goals and takeaways I felt would provide a solid benefit to using the discussions, ideas, and materials presented throughout the five sections. I would ask the reader, and any participants who indulge in the exercises, assessments, discover workshops and related activities, to provide me with comments so that I may know how the information and approach worked for their particular set of circumstance. I ask this also to provide me with feedback to improve the concepts discussed in this work, as new input may be applied to other projects of a similar nature in the future.

The stated goals and takeaways were:

- Achieve incremental improvements in top line sales performance for your company.

  Commentary -- It will take time to measure the impact.

- Develop a deeper understanding of the buying and selling, and purchasing decision making processes that will motivate you to explore and implement improvements.

  Commentary -- Learning these two distinctly different processes, and how to work them effectively, is the challenge all organizations should face.

- Gain exposure to a methodology that if used and embraced by your company will put in place a solid foundation to accommodate the expansion of your business.

  Commentary -- You have been exposed to a variety of new concepts, ideas, and ways to approach your sales system through the materials presented.

- Gain a new perception of why a sales system and supporting processes can help your company to plan for and attain a greater results trajectory.

  Commentary -- I am hopeful you have a greater understanding of the sales system concept. You should also see how to make improvement to it, so that it works more effectively for your company.

- Gain improvements in your overall strategic and operational planning approach and execution.

  Commentary – Your planning activities can benefit from the additional insight gained through the activities discussed, especially related to tracking sales progress, and the areas targeted for improvements.

- Greater internal communications between all who are involved in sales using a common set of concepts and terms.

  Commentary – Communications should become more effective, merely resulting from a of sharing information while performing the exercise and activities.

- Understand what is required to enhance the position of your company with regard to competition, and to focus on strengthening your differentiation.

  Commentary – The more you differentiate your company, product, service, or solution, the more business you will achieve.

- Attain a closer alignment of your sale and marketing efforts to get a greater returns on investments in both sales and marketing.

  Commentary – The concept of alignment applies to many areas of your company. Examine, assess, and decide what actions, and metrics, are required to close gaps, and make the alignments produce better results.

In the end, your own particular sales system, and your understanding of the processes you currently use, and those that you decide to change, will visibly and noticeably contribute the improvement in your sales performance.

The final thought I wish to leave the reader with is this. Your company will not be the only beneficiary of the time, and effort, you put into those improvements. Your existing and prospective customers will also benefit greatly from your attempts at making the improvements. Periodically check in with them to determine if you occasionally, or more frequently, hit the satisfaction mark, thus reinforcing that their choosing your company was the right thing for them to do after all.

APPENDICIES

Disclaimer

This glossary is not intended to be a full compendium of terminology related to selling, process and the system but merely an introductory guide to additional sources of information related to selling methods. The reader is advised that a great deal of this material is available in many forms found on hundreds of web sites and no attempt has been made to provide full attribution to the origination of the terminology or to validate the currency of the links if they appear in this appendix.

APPENDICIES

Glossary of Sales and Selling Terms

This list is not exhaustive, and is not meant to be an endorsement of any of these techniques or terms.

Accompaniment visit/accompaniment report - when a manager, supervisor, or trainer accompanies a sales person while working on the sales territory, usually while meeting prospects or customers. Typically, the manager would complete an accompaniment visit report on the performance of the sales person, which would be discussed, and suitable follow-up actions or training agreed.

Account - a customer, usually a business-to-business organization; a major account is a large organization; a national account is a customer with branches or sites that constitute a nationwide coverage, which typically requires special pricing and senior sales attention.

Active listening - term used to describe high level of listening capability and method, in which the sales person actively seeks to understand how the speaker feels, and what their issues are, in which the type of listening extends far beyond common inattentive listening.

Added value - the element(s) of service or product that a sales person or selling organization provides, that a customer be prepared to pay for because of the benefit(s) obtained. Added values are real and perceived, tangible and intangible. A good, reliable, honest, expert, informed sales person becomes a very significant part of the selling organization's added value, as perceived by the customer, if not by the selling organization.

Advantage - the aspect of a product or service that makes it better than another, especially the one in-situ or that of a competitor.

Advertising/advertising and promotion/A+P - the methods used by a company to publicize and position of its products, services, or solution to its chosen market sectors. It includes product launches, image, and brand building, public and press relations activities, merchandising (supporting and promoting the product in retail and wholesale outlets), special offers, generating leads and enquiries, and incentivizing distributors, and agents, and sales people. A+P methods are sometimes described as above-the-line (media advertising such as radio, TV, cinema, newspapers, magazines) or below-the-line (non-'media' methods or materials such as brochures, direct-mail, exhibitions, telemarketing, and PR); advertising agencies generally receive a commission (discount incentive) from above-the-line media services, but not from below the line services, in which case if asked to arrange any will seek to add a mark-up.

Benefit - the gain (usually a tangible cost, but can be intangible) that accrues to the customer from the product or service.

Buyer - most commonly means a professional purchasing person in a business; can also mean a private consumer. Buyers are not usually major decision-makers, that is to say, what they buy, when and how they buy it, and how much they pay are prescribed for them by the business they work for. If you are selling a routine repeating predictable product, especially a consumable, then you may well be able to restrict your dealings to buyers; if you are selling a new product or service of any significance, buyers will tend to act as influencers at most.

Buying facilitation® - also known as facilitative buying, generally attributed (and registered) to sales guru Sharon Drew Morgen. Extremely advanced form of personal selling, in which the central ethos is one of 'helping organizations and buyers to buy', not selling to them.

Buying signal - a buying signal is a comment from a prospect, which indicates that he is visualizing to whatever extent buying your product or service. The most common buying signal is the question: "How much is it?" Others are questions or comments like; "What colors does it come in?", "What's the lead-time?", and "Who else do you supply?", "Is delivery free?" "Do you use it yourself?", and surprisingly, "It's too expensive."

Buying warmth - behavioral, non-verbal, and other signs that a prospect likes what he sees, very positive from the sales person's perspective, but not an invitation to jump straight to the close.

Call/calling - a personal face-to-face visit or telephone call by a sales person to a prospect or customer. Also referred to a sales call (for any sales visit or phone contact), or cold call (in the case of a first contact without introduction or notice in writing).

Call center - also called a contact center (US = center) - a department for outgoing and/or incoming (outbound/inbound) telephone calls to/from customers, commonly now extending to email communications also if useful for customer service, but not extending to email marketing. Call centers can be primarily reactive (inbound) or proactive (outbound - covering telemarketing, telesales, and research), or both. Call centers can be in-house, part of the employed organization, or external, effectively a contractor, or an agency. Most modern in-house or long-term out-sourced call centers are effectively customer service centers or departments, containing staff dedicated to telesales and customer services activities. Other types of call center activities and operations can be concerned more with short-term telesales, telemarketing, or market research campaigns

Canvass/canvassing - cold calling personally at the prospect's office or more commonly now by telephone, in an attempt to arrange an appointment or present a product, or to gather information.

Change impact and change management - in the context of selling and buying decision-making processes change is what happens when an organization makes the decision and commitment to buy a product, service, or solution. The impact of that purchase may have a profound impact on the organization and the people working within it so as a part of the selling and buying processes clear assessments needs to be made before the purchase and to look for ways to implement the purchase through appropriate change management processes.

Channel and channel management – channels are the conduit through which business is conducted and all require appropriate planning, execution, and management to be productive. The most common channel for a company is direct utilizing face-to-face selling. Other approaches include web purchasing, through reseller partners and integrators who ensure the fit and finish of the product, service, or solution sold. Channels can also tax the resources of a company if not properly planned for and managed. Channel and marketing need to be aligned in ways that do not detract from the direct sales conduit if present.

Close/closing - the penultimate step of the 'Seven Steps of the Sale' selling process, when essentially the sales-person encourages the prospect to say yes and sign the order. In days gone by a Sales person's expertise was measured almost exclusively by how many closes he knew. Thank God for evolution. See the many examples of closes and closing techniques in the Seven Steps section, but do not expect to kid any buyer worth his salt today, and using one might even get you thrown out of his office. Use with great care.

Closed question - a question which generally prompts a yes or no answer, or a different short answer of just two possible options, compared to open questions, which typically begin with who, what, where, when, etc., and which tend to invite much longer answers (also see "open question").

Cold calling - typically refers to the first telephone call made to a prospective customer. More unusually these days, cold calling can also refer to calling face-to-face for the first time without an appointment at commercial promises or households. Cold calling is also known as canvassing, telephone canvassing, prospecting, and telephone prospecting, and more traditionally in the case of consumer door-to-door selling as 'door-knocking'.

Collaboration selling - also known as, collaborative selling and facilitation selling - very modern and sophisticated, in which seller truly collaborates with buyer and buying organization to help the buyer make the necessary decisions to buy.

Commodities/commoditized (products and services) - typically a term applied to describe products which are mature in development, produced and sold in vast scale, involving little or no uniqueness between variations of different suppliers; high volume, low price, low profit margin, de-skilled ('ease of use' in consumption, application, installation, etc.). In a more generic sales and selling sense the term 'commoditized' refers to a product (and arguably a service) which has become mass-produced, widely available, easy to make, de-mystified, and simplified; all of which is almost invariably associated with a reduction in costs, prices and profit margins, and which also has massive implications for the sales distribution model and methods for taking the product or service to market. Commoditized products typically sell by the millions, whereas specialized products might only sell in hundreds or less. All consumer products and services become commoditized over time. Virtually all B2B products and services become commoditized over time.

Concession(s) - used in the context of negotiating, when it refers to an aspect of the sale which has a real or perceived value, that is given away or conceded by seller (more usually) or the buyer. One of the fundamental principles of sales negotiating is never giving away a concession without getting something in return - even a small increase in commitment is better than nothing.

CONCEPT Selling® - is a Miller Heiman method dealing with approaching the opportunity be uncovering through effective communication what the customer's concept is so that the salesperson can develop and refine the concept through a joint venture style of developing a solid understanding of the opportunity from the customer's perspective. A "green" sheet roadmaps the discovery plans for the meetings and communications necessary to gain, receive information and to gain commitment. The Miller Heiman Conceptual Selling® method has been used globally since the 1980's. When trained through the public or private course offerings using a Miller Heiman certified facilitator the user is granted a lifetime right to use the green sheet and methods learned.

Consultative selling (consultation selling) - developed by various sales gurus through the 1980s by David Sandler among others, and practiced widely today, consultative selling was a move towards more collaboration with, and involvement from, the buyer in the selling process. Strongly based on questioning aimed at gaining useful information.

Customer - usually meaning the purchaser, organization, or consumer after the sale. Prior to the sale is usually referred to as a prospect.

Customer concept – a term of art describing what the best-fit solution is as defined by the individuals who are making purchasing decisions and influence the decision-making. In the buying process, it is the point at which all individuals involved in making a purchasing decision visualize what solution they believe will best solve their particular problem. This concept is reduced to specifications, terms, conditions, and other attributes that need to be aligned with the response from the selling organization during the selling process.

Customer relationship management (CRM) - CRM is now a commonly used term to describe the process of managing the entire selling process within a department or organization. Computerized CRM systems enable management of prospect and customer details, contacts, sales history, and account development. Well known examples of CRM computerized systems are SalesForce.com, Sage's ACT!, SugarCRM, Microsoft's Business Dynamics, and Front Range's Goldmine. Chief elements of a CRM system (or strategy, since the term is used to describe the process and methodology as well as the system) are:

- Compilation and organization of data (prospects, customers, product, sales, history, etc.)

- planning, scheduling and integrating customer development activities and communications

- analysis and reporting of all sales related activities and data

Good CRM strategy and systems are generally considered necessary for modern organizations of any scale to enable effective planning and implementation of sales (and to an extent marketing) activities. CRM systems do not however, generate strategies for winning the business, sales people do. They do provide a platform for documenting information and can be used to develop and implement strategies.

Decision-maker - a person in the prospect organization who has the power and budgetary authority to agree to a sales proposal. One of the most common mistakes by sales people is to attempt to sell to someone other than a genuine decision-maker. For anything other than a routine repeating order, the only two people in any organization of any size that are real decision-makers for significant sales values are the CEO/Managing Director/President, and the Chief Financial Officer. Everyone else in the organization is generally working within stipulated budgets and supply contracts, and will usually need to refer major purchasing decisions to one or both of the above people. In very large organizations, functional directors may well be decision-makers for significant sales that relate only to their own function's activities. See influencer.

Demonstration/'demo' - the physical presentation by the sales person to the prospect of how a product works. Generally free of charge to the prospect, and normally conducted at the prospect's premises, but can be at another suitable venue, e.g., an exhibition, or at the supplier's premises.

Demographics - the study of, or information about, people's lifestyles, habits, population movements, spending, age, social grade, employment, etc., in terms of the consuming and buying public; anyone selling to the consumer sector will do better through understanding relevant demographic information.

Discipline - within the context of an organization this is similar to function, i.e., job role, although a discipline can refer more generally to a capability or responsibility, for example 'financial disciplines', or 'customer service disciplines', or 'technical support disciplines'. Discipline can of course mean separately 'control', others or oneself, which is certainly relevant to sales and selling, but not the reason for its inclusion in this glossary. In business-to-business, selling of a complex strategic nature looking at disciplines (capabilities and responsibilities) can help to explore the different ways that people are affected by a change or proposition, which generally accompanies the sale of a product or service.

Distribution/sales distribution - the methods or routes by which products and services are taken to market. Sales distribution models are many and various, and are constantly changing and new ones developing.

Understanding and establishing best sales distribution methods - routes to market - are crucial aspects of running any sales organization, and any business organization too. Sales distribution should be appropriate to the product and service, and the end-user market, and the model will normally be defined by these factors, influenced also by technology and social trends. For example, commoditized mass-market consumer products (FMCG - fast-moving consumer goods, electronics, household electrical appliances, etc.) are generally distributed via mass-market consumer distribution methods, notably supermarkets, but also increasingly the internet. The selling and buying processes are extremely short.

Empathy - understanding how another person feels, and typically reflecting this back to the other person. The ability to feel and show empathy is central to modern selling methods.

FABs – Features, Advantages, and Benefits - the links between a product descriptions, its advantage over others, and the gain derived by the customer from using it. One of the central, if now rather predictable, techniques used in the presentation stage of the selling process.

Forecast/sales forecasting - a prediction of what sales will be achieved over a given period, anything from a week to a year. Sales managers require sales people to forecast, in order to provide data to production, purchasing, and other functions whose activities need to be planned to meet sales demand. Sales forecasts are also an essential performance quantifier that feeds into the overall business plan for any organization. Due to the traditionally unreliable and optimistic nature of sales-department forecasts, it is entirely normal for the sum of all individual sales persons' sales annual forecast to exceed what the business genuinely plans to sell. See targets.

Functional roles - in the context of an organization, this means the job role or discipline, e.g., sales, marketing, production, accounting, customer service, delivery, installation, technical service, general management, etc. Understanding the functions of people within organizations, and critically their interests and needs, is very important if you are selling to businesses or other non-consumer organizations.

Funnel – a term of art to represent an image of where a single or multiple business opportunities are in the selling and buying decision-making process. See sales funnel

Influencer - a person in the prospect organization who has the power to influence and persuade a decision-maker. Influencers will be generally be decision-makers for relatively low value sales. There is usually more than one influencer in any prospect organization relevant to a particular sale, and large organizations will have definitely have several influencers. It is usually important to sell to influencers as well as decision-makers in the same organization. Selling to large organizations almost certainly demands that the sales person does this. The role and power of influencers in any organization largely depends on the culture and politics of the organization, and particularly the management style of the two main decision-makers.

Intangible - in a selling context this describes, or is, an aspect of the product or service offering that has a value but is difficult to see or quantify (for instance, peace-of-mind, reliability, consistency). See tangible.

Introduction - the word introduction has two different main meanings in selling: either Introduction refers to first stage of the face-to-face or telephone sales call or the term means a personal introduction - also called a referral - of the sales person to someone in the buying organization by a mutual friend or contact. Personal introductions of this sort tend to imply endorsement or recommendation of the seller, and since they are made by an existing contact, they help greatly in establishing initial trust. The value and potency of a personal introduction generally reflects the importance of the introducing person and the strength of their relationship with the buying contact. Networking is essentially based on using (sometimes several quite informal) introductions, to connect a seller with a buyer.

LAMP® - Large Account Management Process - sales acronym and methodology for major accounts management developed by Robert Miller, Stephen Heiman, and Tad Tuleja in their 1991 book Successful Large Account Management (see the books at the foot of this page). Note that LAMP® and Strategic Selling® methods and materials are subject to copyright and intellectual property control of Miller Heiman, Inc. Also, note that LAMP® and Strategic Selling® methods and materials are not to be used in the provision of training and development products and services without a license from Miller Heiman to do so for each participant.

Lead-time - time between order and delivery, installation or commencement of a product or service.

Listening - a key selling skill, in that without good listening skills the process of questioning is rendered totally without merit.

Major account - a large and complex prospect or customer, often having several branches or sites, and generally requiring contacts and relationships between various functions in the supplier and customer organization. Often major accounts are the responsibility of designated experienced and senior sales people, which might be formed into a major accounts team. Major accounts often enjoy better discounts and terms than other customers, because of purchasing power leveraged by bigger volumes, and lower selling costs from economies of scale.

Marketing - perceived by lots of business people to mean simply promotion and advertising, the term marketing actually covers everything from company culture and positioning, through market research, new business/product development, advertising and promotion, PR (public/press relations), and arguably all of the sales functions as well. A company decides what it will sell, to whom, when and how, and then does it by the process.

needs-creation selling - a selling style popularized in the 1970s and 80s which asserted that sales people could create needs in a prospect for their products or services even if no needs were apparent, obvious or even existed.

The method was for the sales person to question the prospect to identify, discover (and suggest) organizational problems or potential problems that would then create a need for the product. This selling method is no substitute for good research and proper targeting of prospects who have use of the products and services being sold.

Negotiation/negotiating - the trading of concessions including price reductions, between supplier and customer, in an attempt to shape a supply contract (sale in other words) so that it is acceptable to both supplier and customer. Negotiations can last a few minutes or even a few years, although generally it is down to one or two meetings and one or two exchanges of correspondence. Ideally, from the seller's point of view, negotiation must only commence when the sale has been agreed in principle, and conditionally upon satisfactory negotiation. However most sales people fall into the trap set by most buyers - intentionally or otherwise - of starting to negotiate before the selling process is aligned.

Networking - an increasingly popular method of developing sales opportunities and contacts, based on referrals and introductions - either face-to-face at meetings and gatherings, or by other contact methods such as phone, email, social and business networking websites, etc.

Objection/overcoming objections - an objection is a point of resistance raised by a prospect, usually price ("It's too expensive.."), but can be anything at any stage of the selling process. Overcoming objections is a revered and much-trained skill in the traditional selling process, but far less significant in modern selling. Modern collaboration selling principles assume that objections do not arise if proper research needs analysis; questioning and empathic discussion has taken place. In addition, the notion of using techniques or pressure to overcome what may be legitimate obstacles is contrary to principles of modern selling. Modern selling methods tend to identify objections much earlier in the process, and either to filter out the prospect at that stage and abandon the approach, or where objections arise from multiple decision influencers within the buyer organization, to agree collaboratively a strategy with the main contact at the prospective customer for dealing with objection(s) arising.

Opening benefit statement/OBS – (see Valid Business Reason) traditionally an initial impact statement for sales people to use at first contact with prospect, in writing, on the phone or face-to-face - the OBS generally encapsulates the likely strongest organizational benefit typically (or supposedly) derived by customers in the prospect's sector.

Open question - a question that gains information, usually beginning with who, what, why, where, when, how, or more subtly 'tell me about..' - as distinct from a closed question, for example beginning with 'Is it...?' or 'Do you...?' etc., which tend to glean only a yes or no answer.

Partnership selling - very modern approach to organizational selling for business-to-business sales.

Perceived - how something is seen or regarded by someone, usually by the prospect or customer, irrespective of what is believed or presented by the seller, i.e. what it **really means** to the customer.

Positioning - more a marketing than sales term, although relevant to experienced and sophisticated sellers, and related to targeting - positioning refers to how a product/service/proposition is presented or described or marketed in relation to the market place - with reference to customers, competition, image, pricing, quality, etc. Positioning refers to whether a proposition is being sold appropriately - in the right way, to the right people, at the right time, in the right place, and at the right price. A potentially brilliant business can fail because its products are not positioned properly, which typically manifests as sales people being unable to sell successfully. There might be little or nothing wrong with the sales people and their skills, and the product/service, but the venture fails because the positioning is wrong. Conversely, good positioning can rescue a less than brilliant product/service.

Preparation - in the context of the selling process this is the work done by the sales person to research and plan the sales approach and/or sales call to a particular prospect or customer. Almost entirely without exception in the global history of selling, no call is adequately prepared for, and sales that fail to happen are due to this failing.

Presentation/sales presentation - the process by which a sales person explains the product or service to the prospect (to a single contact or a group), ideally including the product's features, advantages and benefits, especially those which are relevant to the prospect. Presentations can be verbal only, but more usually involve the use of visuals, commonly bullet-point text slides, and images on a computer display or projected onto a screen. Can incorporate a video and/or physical demonstration of the product(s).

Process – a series of defined activities, steps, or events that occur while attempting to do something. Typically a process is repeatable, documented, and has defined boundaries. It is also well studied and the parameters once identified can be altered if the circumstances require.

Product - Generally, a physical item being supplied, but can also mean or include services and intangibles, in which case product is used to mean the whole package being supplied.

Product offer - how the product and/or service is positioned and presented to the prospect or market, which would normally include features and/or advantages and also imply at least one benefit for the prospect (hence a single product can be represented by a number of different product offers, each for different market niches (segments or customer groupings). One of the great marketing challenges is always to define a product offer concisely and meaningfully.

Proposal/sales proposal - usually a written offer with specification, prices, outline terms and conditions, and warranty arrangements, from a sales person or selling organization to a prospect.

Generally an immensely challenging part of the process to get right, in that it must be concise yet complete, persuasive yet objective, well specified yet orientated to the customer's applications. An outline proposal is often a useful interim step, to avoid wasting a lot of time including in a full proposal lots of material that the customer may not need.

Proposition - usually means product offer, can mean sales proposal. The initial proposition means the basis of the first approach.

Professional selling skills - see PSS

PSS - 'Professional Selling Skills' - highly structured selling process pioneered by the US Xerox photocopier sales organization during the 1960s, and adopted by countless business-to-business sales organizations, normally as the 'Seven Steps of the Sale', ever since. PSS places a huge reliance on presentation, overcoming objections and umpteen different closes. Largely now superseded by more modern 'Open Plan' two-way communication processes, but PSS is still in use and being trained.

Prospect - an entity as in a person, organization, or buyer, identified before the sale is made, i.e. a prospective customer. Any of the individuals within a company who would be involved in the purchasing decision making activities, and would have influence over the decision to purchase.

Questioning - the second stage of the sales call, typically after the opening or introduction in the Seven Steps of the Sale, but also vital to modern selling methods too, notably collaborative/facilitative selling approach. A crucial selling skill, and rarely well demonstrated. The correct timing and use of the important different types of questions are central to the processes of gathering information, matching needs, and building rapport and empathy. Questioning also requires that the sales person have good listening, interpretation and empathic capabilities

Referral - a recommendation or personal introduction or permission/suggestion made by someone, commonly but not necessarily a buyer, which enables the seller to approach or begin dialogue with a new prospective buyer or decision-maker/influencer. Seeking referrals is a widely trained selling technique, in which the seller asks the buyer (or other contact) at the end of a sales call for referrals, i.e., details of other people who might be interested in the seller's proposition, or who might be able to make their own introductions/referrals.

Research/research call - the act of gathering information about a market or customer, which will help progress or enable a sales approach. Often seen as a job for telemarketing personnel, but actually more usefully carried out by sales people, especially where large prospects are concerned (which should really be the only type of prospects targeted by modern sales people, given the need to recover very high costs of sales people).

Retention/customer retention - means simply keeping customers and not losing them to competitors. Modern companies realize that it is far more expensive to find new customers than keep existing ones, and so put sufficient investment into looking after and growing existing accounts. Less sensible companies find themselves spending a fortune winning new customers, while they lose more business than they gain because of poor retention activity.

Sales cycle - the Sales Cycle term generally describes the time and/or process between first contact with the customer to when the sale is made. Sales Cycle times and processes vary enormously depending on the company, type of business (product/service), the effectiveness of the sales process, the market, and the particular situation applying to the customer at the time of the enquiry. The Sales Cycle in an impulse commodity purchase is less than a minute; in more complex situations the Sales Cycle can be many months or even as long as a few years because more milestones and steps are required of the decision making process. A typical Sales Cycle for a moderately complex product might several stages and actions such as:

1. receive inquiry
2. qualify details
3. arrange appointment
4. customer appointment
5. survey in details the needs through questioning
6. evaluate potential solutions
7. present solution and options proposal and close sale

Sales forecasts - also called sales projections, these are the predictions that sales people and sales managers are required to make about future business levels, necessary for their own organization to plan and budget everything from stock levels, production, staffing levels, to advertising and promotion, financial performance and market strategies.

Sales funnel - describes the pattern, plan or actual achievement of conversion of prospects into sales, pre-enquiry and then through the sales cycle. So-called because it includes the conversion ratio at each stage of the sales cycle, which has a funneling effect. Prospects are fed into the top of the funnel, and converted sales drop out at the bottom after all necessary actions are completed. The extent of conversion success (i.e. the tightness of each ratio) reflects the quality of prospects fed into the top, and the sales skill at each conversion stage. The Sales Funnel is a very powerful sales planning and sales management tool. Also referred to as the Sales Pipeline.

Sales report - a business report of sales results, activities, trends, etc., traditionally completed by a sales manager, but increasingly now the responsibility of sales people too. A sales report can be required weekly, monthly, quarterly and annually, and often includes the need to provide sales forecasts.

Sales pipeline - a linear equivalent of the Sales Funnel principle. Prospects need to be fed into the pipeline in order to drop out of the other end as sales. The length of the pipeline is the sales cycle time, which depends on business type, market situation, and the effectiveness of the sales process.

Sales process – the collective activities that are required to accomplish the buying and selling alignment to complete a successful sale. Sales processes a regarded as components of a much broader sales system the encompass all aspects of activities, the who, what, where, and when that is behind the completion of a sale. See Sales System

Sales system – for most companies it is the sum total of all activities to generate sales through all of the channels in use and to the alignments of sales, marketing, the business plan and activities related to developing and maintaining business with all prospective and existing customers. The sales system approach and architecture in world companies using best practices for selling is repeatable, flexible, and easily enhanced to match changes in markets, customers, or situations. A part of many sales systems is a CRM system utilized for its documentation of the actions developed and executed. The CRM system does not generate the strategy but the sales system would make know to all involved in the sales process what the options were from the planning and results achieved points of view.

Sector/market sector - a part of the market that can be described, categorized and then targeted according to its own criteria and characteristics; sectors are often described as 'vertical', meaning an industry type, or 'horizontal', meaning some other grouping that spans a number of vertical sectors, e.g., a geographical grouping, or a grouping defined by age, or size, etc.

Segment/market segment - a sub-sector or market niche; basically, a grouping that is more narrowly defined and smaller than a sector; a segment can be a horizontal sub-sector across one or more vertical sectors.

Solutions selling - a common but loosely-used description for a more customer-orientated selling method than the Seven Steps; dependent on identifying needs to which appropriate benefits are matched in a package or 'solution'. The term is based on the premise that customers do not buy products, features, or benefits - they buy solutions (to organizational problems). It is a similar approach to 'needs-creation' selling, which first became popular in the 1970s-80s. Solution selling remains relevant and its methods can usefully be included in the open plan selling style described later here, although modern collaborative and facilitative methodologies are becoming vital pre-requisites.

SPIN® and SPIN® Selling - A popular selling method developed by Neil Rackham in the 1970-80s: SPIN® is an acronym derived from the basic selling process designed and defined by Rackham: Situation, Problem, Implication, Need, or Need Payoff. More detail about SPIN® and SPIN® Selling appears in the Consultative Selling and Needs Creation Selling methods section. Note that SPIN® and SPIN SELLING® methods and materials are subject to copyright and intellectual property control of the Huthwaite organizations of the US and Europe.

Steps of the sale - describes the structure of the selling process with regard to the activities performed, particularly the sales call, and what immediately precedes and follows it. Usually represented as the older documented "Seven Steps of the Sale", but might be five, six, eight or more, depending whose training manual you're reading or the complexity of the selling cycle.

Strategic Selling® - a Miller Heiman intellectual property selling methodology when used in upper case and/or in the context of Miller Heiman's Strategic Selling® methodology (which features in their books of the same name, first published in 1985) the Strategic Selling® term is a registered and protected product name belonging to the Miller Heiman company and training organization - so be warned. The Strategic Selling method employs development of a "Blue" sheet blue print to understand how to approach and plan strategies for winning of an opportunity.

Reference the book by *Robert Miller and Steve Heiman, The New Strategic Selling, Grand Central Publishing, New York NY*. For Conceptual Selling reference the book *The New Conceptual Selling, Robert Miller and Steve Heiman, Business Plus, Hachette Book Group, New York, NY.*

The third leg of the methodology is the Large Account management Process method, reference the book *The New Successful Large Account Management, Robert Miller and Steve Heiman, Business Plus, Hachette Book Group, New York, NY.* LAMP® and Strategic Selling® and Conceptual Selling® methods and materials are subject to copyright and intellectual property control of Miller Heiman, Inc., and again be warned that LAMP® and Strategic Selling® methods and materials are not to be used in the provision of training and development products and services without a license.

Strategic selling - you will also hear people (me included) referring to 'strategic selling' in a **generic** sense, and not specifically referring to the Miller Heiman methods and materials. In a generic 'lower case' sense, 'strategic selling' describes a broad methodology which began to be practiced in the 1980s, literally 'strategic' by its nature (the principles involve taking a strategic view of the prospective customer's organization, its markets, customers and strategic priorities, etc). When using the 'strategic selling' terminology in a training context you must be careful therefore to avoid confusion or misrepresentation of the Miller Heiman intellectual property. If in any doubt do not use the 'strategic selling' term in relation to providing sales training services - call it something else to avoid any possible confusion with the Miller Heiman products.

Strategy and tactics – Strategies are ideas, the conceptualization of how to reach the goal in as clearly an articulated picture as possible. Tactics are the actions you will take either planned or on an ad hoc basis to execute the strategy. Think about the problem, visual the idea to solve the problem, and then describe the actions to solve the problem along with any contingencies or past experiences that had an impact. Too often sales strategies do not align with marketing strategies and along similar lines, the tactics do not align either.

Target/sales target - in a sales context this is the issued (or ideally agreed) level of sales performance for a sales person or team or department over a given period. Bonus payments, sales commissions, pay reviews, job grades, life and death, etc., can all be dependent on sales staff meeting sales targets, so all in all sales targets are quite sensitive things. Targets are established at the beginning of the trading year, and then reinforced with a system of regular forecasting and reviews throughout the year. See forecasting.

Targeting - this has a different meaning to the usual noun sense of target (above). Targeting is a marketing term - very relevant and important for sales people and sales managers too - which refers to the customers at which the selling effort is aimed, hence targeting. In this respect, the term relates to 'target markets', or 'target sectors'. This is the customer aspect within 'positioning' of a product or service or proposition. Targeting is represented by the question: Who will buy the product/service? Deciding targeting on a company scale is normally the responsibility of a marketing department or agency, but each sales person and sales team as huge potential to develop and refine their own local targeting - to aim their efforts at the sectors or customers, which will produce the greatest results. For example - and many sales people, especially self-employed providers and traders - completely ignore the fact that sales generally come more easily from existing or previous customers than prospective new customers to whom the supplier is completely unknown. Similarly, size of prospective customer is another largely overlooked aspect of targeting. Any business will naturally have more amenable sectors of potential customers than other parts of the market. Targeting is the process by which the selling organization maximizes its chances of engaging with the most responsive and profitable customers.

Telemarketing - any pre-sales activity conducted by telephone, usually by specially trained telemarketing personnel - for instance, research, appointment-making, product promotion.

Telesales - selling by telephone contact alone, normally a sales function in its own right, i.e., utilizing specially trained telesales personnel; used typically where low order values prevent the use of expensive field-based sales people, and a recognizable product or service allows the process to succeed.

Tender/solicitation - a very structured formal proposal in response to the issue of an invitation to tender for the supply of a product or service to a large organization or government department. Tenders require certain qualifying criteria to be met first by the tendering organization, which in itself can constitute several weeks or months work by lots of different staff. Tenders must adhere to strict submission deadlines, contract terms, specifications and even the presentation of the tender itself, and usually only suppliers experienced in winning and fulfilling this type of highly controlled supply ever win the business. It is not unknown for very successful companies to actually help the customer formulate the specifications of s solicitation, which explains why it is so difficult to price the business away from them.

Territory - the geographical area of responsibility of a sales person or a team or a sales organization. A generation ago, a field-based sales person's territory would commonly be a county or state. Now in this globalized age, where so much selling is done online and remotely by telephone rather than by expensive face-to-face selling, field-based sales people's territories are much bigger, and can be entire countries or continental regions.

Territory planning - the process of planning optimum and most cost-effective coverage (particularly for making appointments or personal calling) of a sales territory by the available sales resources, given prospect numbers, density, buying patterns, etc., even if one territory by one sales person; for one person this used to be called journey planning, and was often based on a four or six day cycle, so as to avoid always missing prospects who might never be available on one particular day of the week.

Trial close - the technique, by which a sales person tests the prospect's readiness to buy, traditionally employed in response to a buying signal, e.g. a prospect says "Do you have them in stock?", to which the sales person would traditionally reply, "Would you want one if they are?" Use with extreme care, for fear of looking unprofessional. If you see a buying signal there is no need to jump on it - just answer it politely, and before ask why the question is important, which will be far more constructive.

Unique/uniqueness - a differentiation that is discernible for a company, product, service, or solution that no competitor is appearing to offer it. Differentiation based on uniqueness is a much-overlooked aspect of selling. The vast majority of sales organizations focus their efforts on selling 'me too' products and services, where inevitably discussions tend to concentrate on price differences, whereas the most enlightened and progressive sales organizations strive to develop unique qualities in the propositions, which dramatically reduces competitive pressures.

Valid business reason – A term of art frequently used by Miller Heiman in their courses used to describe the incentive behind having a conversation with a prospective buyer that will resonate with the ways to identify and rectify their business problem. If you call someone with valued advice the results is that might listen more to you than someone who calls just to chat or set up a "howdy" call visit.

Value proposition – an accepted yet overused term of art essentially trying to succinctly state why a prospective client would consider your solution over someone else's. Quite often, the value proposition is made up from marketing words or industry jargon and has no real value unless it is seen that way by those involved in the buying decision-making.

Variable - an aspect of the sale or of a deal that can be changed in order to better meet the needs of the seller and/or the buyer. Typical variables are price, quantity, lead-time, payment terms, technical factors, styling factors, spare parts, back up and breakdown service, routine maintenance, installation, delivery, warranty. Variables may be real or perceived, and often the perceived ones are the most significant in any negotiation. Variables could be the prime contributors to the so-called value proposition if the buyer perceives them as having worth.